The Organic
Salad Garden

Joy Larkcom

Photographs by Roger Phillips

FRANCES LINCOLN

To our dear grandson Irie,
the first of a new generation
of gardeners

Frances Lincoln Limited
4 Torriano Mews
Torriano Avenue
London NW5 2RZ

The Organic Salad Garden
Copyright © Frances Lincoln Limited 2001
Text copyright © Joy Larkcom 2001

First Frances Lincoln edition: 2001
First paperback edition: 2003

British Library Cataloguing in Publication Data
A catalogue record for this book is available from the British Library

Design and typesetting by Caroline Hillier

ISBN 0 7112 1716 5 (hardback)
ISBN 0 7112 2204 5 (paperback)
Printed in China by Kwong Fat Offset Printing Co. Ltd

PAGE 1 Spring 'saladini': CLOCKWISE FROM THE
CHOPSTICKS salad burnet, pak choi flower, land cress,
pansies, *Bellis perennis*, chickweed, curly-leaved endive,
sprouted mung beans and lentils, broad-leaved endive,
winter purslane, 'Shanghai' pak choi, corn salad, self-
blanching celery, 'Ragged Jack' kale, 'Red Verona'
chicory, Japanese mustard 'Miike Giant', 'Treviso'
chicory, 'Green-in-the-Snow' mustard, mizuna greens,
hairy bitter cress, garden cress, angelica and rocket
PAGE 2 CLOCKWISE FROM TOP LEFT Land cress, fennel,
garden cress, gold-leaved purslane, dandelion, mizuna
greens, Red Salad Bowl lettuce, Chinese cabbage, red
chicory
PAGE 3 CLOCKWISE FROM TOP LEFT Salad burnet,
'Alaska' nasturtium, red orache, loose-leaved Chinese
cabbage, angelica, thyme, ornamental kale, red-veined
dock
RIGHT Mixed red and green cut-and-come-again
seedlings

Contents

Introduction

It is almost impossible to believe, from the viewpoint of the twenty-first century, how my garden and gardening ideas have changed since I first started growing vegetables seriously in the 1970s. Then my garden was a very plain plot (an allotment in fact), whereas today our kitchen garden includes several picturesque little 'potagers' – each carefully designed to have shape, colour and form all year round. Way back then the salad plants we grew could be counted on the fingers of one hand – lettuce, tomatoes, cucumbers, radish ... Today, during the course of two or three seasons, we grow well over 150 salad plants.

Finding these plants and learning how to grow them has been a long, and wonderful, voyage of discovery. Its first 'leg' was what we fondly called our 'Grand Vegetable Tour'. In August 1976, my husband Don Pollard and I, with our children Brendan and Kirsten, who were then seven and five years old, left Montrose Farm for a year to travel around Europe in a caravan. Our main purpose was to learn about traditional and modern methods of vegetable growing, and to collect the seed of local varieties of vegetables, which, as a handful of far-sighted people had begun to appreciate, were an invaluable genetic heritage that was vanishing fast.

Moving in a southward arc, we travelled from Holland to Hungary, through Belgium, France, Spain, Portugal, Italy and Yugoslavia. We gleaned information from seedsmen, seed catalogues and the backs of seed packets; from research stations and markets; from market gardeners, peasants, cooks, botanists and housewives. We managed to collect seed of quite a number of old local varieties (over 100 samples were safely housed in the seed bank later established at Wellesbourne in the UK), and we learnt a great deal about cultivation methods. But we were totally unprepared for the many new salad plants we found, especially plants that could be grown in the colder months of the year. In Holland, Belgium, France and Italy we found beautiful varieties of lettuce, chicory and endive that were previously unknown to us; in Belgium we 'discovered' sparkling iceplant (*Mesembryanthemum crystallinum*) and winter purslane or claytonia (*Montia perfoliata*), that pretty escapee from the American continent; and in Italy, in early spring, we saw people parking their cars on motorways to scour the fields for young leaves of wild plants – our first inkling of that vast neglected heritage of wild plants that can be used raw. Coupled with these new plants were new ideas on how to grow salad plants, above all the 'cut-and-come-again' concept (see p. 127). This extends from cutting broadcast patches of seedlings up to five times, to cutting mature heads of chicory, endive and lettuce and leaving the stumps to resprout for further pickings.

We returned home eager to try out these new plants and ideas. Shortly afterwards I was asked to participate in an exhibition on the history of English gardening at the V&A Museum, and this led me to old English gardening books, a hitherto unknown world to me. I discovered John Evelyn's *Acetaria: a Discourse of Sallets*, written in 1699, and his *Directions for the Gardiner at Says Court*, compiled a few years earlier; I also discovered Batty Langley's *New Principles of Gardening* (1728) and other seventeenth- and eighteenth-century classics. One day in the British Museum I tracked down a frail, handwritten, fifteenth-century cookery book, with one of the earliest-known lists of 'herbes for a salade'. These books were a revelation, for here were lists, written hundreds of years ago, of the sort of salad plants we had found still in cultivation on the Continent, along with instructions for growing seedling crops, for forcing and blanching salad plants for winter use, for gathering plants from the wild, and even for using flowers, flower buds and shoot tips in salads, either fresh or pickled for winter.

At about the same time, suspecting another untapped treasure trove of useful salad plants, I began to try out some of the Chinese and Japanese vegetables that were becoming available through enterprising seed catalogues. This proved to be the start of a ten-year odyssey, taking me to China, Taiwan, Japan and later to the USA and Canada, unravelling the mysteries of Asian vegetables. The fast-growing leafy greens, above all, came to fill a key role in our own salad making.

On our return from our European travels, we turned our garden into a small, experimental, market garden run on organic principles. We supplied unusual vegetables to wholefood and health shops, our speciality being bags of mixed fresh salads, which we called 'saladini' (see p. 140). Even though our winter temperatures were often as low as –10°C/14°F, we found that it was quite possible, with the aid of unheated polythene tunnels (now universally known as polytunnels), to grow fresh salads all year round. We usually managed to produce at least twenty different types of plant for each bag.

Growing salads for sale and researching oriental vegetables ran in parallel for several years. All the while I was becoming increasingly aware of how on the one hand many people had only tiny areas in which to grow vegetables, but on the other there was a reluctance to grow vegetables in the typical small front garden, as they were deemed 'ugly' or at best 'inappropriate'. Yet what was more beautiful than the 'Purple Giant' mustard, feathery fennel, deeply curled red 'Lollo' lettuce or the glossy, serrated leaves of mizuna greens? What could be more productive and vibrant-looking than a small patch of pak choi, dill or golden purslane? Vegetable plots, I was convinced, can feed the soul as well as the body.

The happy marriage of beauty and productivity lies at the heart of the modern 'potager'. Although 'potager' is no more than the ordinary French word for a kitchen garden (the place where vegetables are grown for *potage* or soup) it has been hijacked to mean any vegetable plot which has been designed, making it a place of intrinsic beauty. So a potager may be enclosed by a hedge, fence, wall or trained fruit; there may be arches and seats to add a structural element; the beds may be of varying shapes and sizes and grouped to form patterns; and thought will have been given to the paths between the beds and edging materials. Most important of all, the vegetables will be chosen and grown to enhance their natural beauty, as vegetables offer a palette with which a living painting can be created. I began to use that palette.

By the 1980s we had reorganized our kitchen garden and laid it out in parallel narrow beds – a practical, efficient, centuries-old system, enabling the gardener to develop a high state of fertility in the beds. My first step in 'painting with vegetables' was to make 'patchwork quilts' within the beds. Initially I simply interplanted red and green lettuces; then I sowed cut-and-come-again lettuce in parallel drills in small patches. I would have, say, green Salad Bowl lettuce in the first patch, sown in one direction, and red Salad Bowl in the next, the rows at right angles to the first patch. I got such a kick out of watching the seedlings emerge – neat little bands at first,

Creating effects with patches, intercropping, and edible flowers: in the left-hand bed, from the front, pot marigolds, alfalfa, red Salad Bowl seedlings, Texel greens, edible chrysanthemum, in the right-hand bed 'Tom Thumb' lettuce intercropping onions.

within a week or so merging into a solid colourful, patchwork.

Not long afterwards I made my first Little Potager, an area no more than 6.3 by 4.5m/7 by 5 yds. It was later enclosed in an undulating woven willow fence. Then followed a Winter Potager, primarily for edible plants which retain leaf, stem or flower colour in winter; these include leeks, hardy Chinese mustards, purple-flowering pak choi, hardy chicories, Swiss chard, kales, corn salad, 'Parcel' celery and winter pansies. Partially edged with low, stepover apples, the Winter Potager is surrounded on three sides by a trellis of vines, clematis and honeysuckle. With luck it remains colourful and decorative even in mid-winter. The full story is told in my book *Creative Vegetable Gardening*, but what is relevant here is the decorative potential of so many salad plants.

Here are some of the ways I use salad plants to create visual effects. To get height, a key element in potagers, I train tomatoes up attractive spiral steel supports, sometimes intermingling them with ornamental climbers like *Ipomea lobata* (previously *Mina lobata*) or canary creeper. Red orache and the purple-hued giant spinach

'Magentaspreen' are plants that reach theatrical heights, both being useful additions to salads in their early stages. I always leave a few clumps of chicory to run to seed in their second season: they too grow over 2m/6ft high, producing fresh flushes of sky-blue (edible) flowers every morning over many weeks. The giant winter radishes will do the same, making glorious pink- or white-flowered clumps in their second spring, and a seemingly endless crop of delectable, edible seed pods. To make the most impact with colourful plants, I almost always plant in groups at equidistant spacing rather than in traditional rows. Favourites are 'Bull's Blood' beetroot, with its scarlet leaves, red cabbage, ornamental cabbages and kales, and the many bright red lettuces now available. For textured effects I value the ground-hugging iceplant, glossy-leaved purslanes, dill and fennel. And every year I succumb to the temptation to make patterns with the many salad plants grown as cut-and-come-again seedlings. I sow them in circles, waves, triangles, zigzags – whatever takes my fancy, often outlining the patterns with leeks. Exceptionally pretty, in the ground and in salads, are the purplish-leaved 'Red Russian' kale, the crêpe-like Tuscan kale, along with cresses, purslanes, chicories and oriental greens. Lastly, I make full use of the many edible flowers and flowering herbs to infiltrate scent and pure colour into the garden: nasturtiums, pot marigolds, thymes, day lilies ... It is an endless list. A favourite edging plant is the 'Gem' series of tagetes: neat and bright all summer long and, to my mind, the flowers adding a real, fruity flavour to salads.

Not everyone, of course, wants to make a potager, but there is plenty of scope for slipping a few of the more decorative salad plants into flower beds and borders or growing them in containers on patios

The patterns in this bed are outlined with a zigzag of multi-sown leeks. The right-hand triangles are planted with gold-leaved purslane, the left with mixed red lettuce.

RIGHT Lettuces of different types and colours can be used to create delightful effects: CLOCKWISE FROM LEFT green butterhead, red Salad Bowl, red Lollo, green crisphead.

BELOW A circular patch of sweet corn edged with colourful *Tagetes* 'Orange Gem'.

OPPOSITE In early summer in the 'salad garden' in the potager at Bingerden House in the Netherlands, beds of Lollo and Salad Bowl lettuce are planted with mathematical precision, edged with upright onions and leeks.

and balconies. This revised edition of *The Salad Garden* includes suggestions for making the most of a plant's ornamental qualities.

Recent years have seen an upsurge in people growing their own vegetables, fuelled by food scares and widespread anxiety about genetically modified crops. Many are doing so organically, and I have titled this new edition *The Organic Salad Garden* to mark our commitment to organic gardening. For over twenty-five years our garden has been run on organic lines, without using chemical fertilizers, weedkillers or pesticides other than the handful of non-persistent chemicals approved by the organic standards authorities. Bar the endless war against slugs, we have encountered no major problems in growing organically and believe our plants are more robust, better-flavoured, and remain fresh longer as a result.

Perhaps at this point I should define a salad plant. I think of it as any plant that tastes good raw, or is good eaten cooked and cold. That embraces an enormous number of plants, and I suspect there are still more to be discovered.

When this book was first published in 1984, many of the plants it covered were virtually unknown outside a limited area. Now they can be found in supermarkets, street markets and restaurants, and, crucial for us gardeners, the seed is available mainly through mail-order seed catalogues but increasingly in garden centres. Sadly, there are also commercial pressures to limit the number of old varieties in circulation. The legal restrictions imposed by the European Union and the vested interests of multi-national seed companies threaten some traditional vegetable varieties. I urge gardeners to support organizations such as the Henry Doubleday Research Association in the UK, which runs a heritage seed library, and similar organizations elsewhere, to prevent the erosion of our genetic heritage.

Notwithstanding these pressures, there is still today an enormous choice of varieties (or cultivars as they should be called) of the most popular salad plants. New varieties are constantly being introduced, sometimes to disappear a couple of seasons later. It is almost impossible to keep up to date. On the whole, I recommend only those varieties that I have grown or seen myself, and hope will remain available. But there are many other excellent varieties. Follow the gardening press to keep abreast of good new ones.

I have tried to make this book as comprehensive as possible, accommodating both established salad crops and the minor, less well-known ones. Space, however, is limited, and it was impossible to cover all the mainstream crops in depth. Whole books, after all, have been written on tomato growing. The emphasis here is on growing vegetables for use as salads. Where growing for other purposes is substantially different and is not covered here, please refer to general books on vegetables in Further Reading, pp. 162–3.

The first part of the book, Salad Plants (pp. 12–90), describes individual salad plants and their cultivation, grouped broadly according to the main parts used in salad (leaves, roots and so on) and within these groups in order of their importance. All practical techniques referred to in this section are described in full in Salad Growing (pp. 92–136). In both these sections I refer to 'seasons' (not calendar months), which are explained in the note on p. 160. Salad Making (pp. 138–158) looks at different approaches to salad making, and includes favourite recipes for the plants described in the book.

I would encourage all gardeners to approach salad growing in a spirit of adventure and enquiry. Every garden is unique, and there are few rights and wrongs in gardening. Be prepared to experiment; don't be bound by rules! Do, however, keep detailed records. Your own notes on sowing times, varieties grown, quantities sown, methods used and harvesting times will eventually become far and away the best guide to producing salads for your family.

Finally, a word on the photographs in *The Organic Salad Garden*. They were taken especially for the original edition by Roger Phillips. Most of the plants illustrated were grown in my garden in one season. This is how, at the time, I described that season and its aftermath: '… an unusually odd season it was. We had more than twice the average rainfall in April, followed by an exceptionally cold May, and a very long drought in summer, which included the highest July temperature ever recorded here. So, as can happen in any garden, we had our failures, and a few specimens were not as good as we would have liked.' I was delighted when Roger agreed to do the supplementary photography for this new edition, but once again, eighteen years later, we have experienced a year when weather records were being broken. Only now everyone is labelling it 'global warming'. Who knows what lies ahead? But rest assured, whether it gets warmer, colder, drier, wetter or windier, there will always be something you can grow from the vast storehouse of salad plants.

JOY LARKCOM May 2001

salad plants

leafy salad plants

Lettuce *Lactuca sativa*

Lettuce is rightly one of the most widely grown salad plants. Not only is the quality and flavour of fresh home-grown lettuce far superior to anything you can buy, but the colourful varieties now available are exceptionally decorative in the garden.

Even in small gardens there is always space for a few lettuces. The pretty loose-leaf 'Salad Bowl' types make excellent edges to vegetable and flower beds; small hearting types, such as 'Tom Thumb' and 'Little Gem', are ideal for intercropping; patches of seedling lettuce and 'leaf lettuce' (see p. 16) require minimum space.

Lettuce is essentially a cool-climate crop, growing best at temperatures of 10–20°C/50–68°F. With the exception of the Asiatic stem lettuce (see p. 14), it does not do well in very hot climates. In most temperate climates you can grow it all year round, provided you sow appropriate varieties each season. Some protection is usually advisable for the winter crop, while in colder regions artificial heating is essential to ensure a continuous winter supply.

Where greenhouse space is limited in winter, it may be better to devote it to endives and chicories. Compared to lettuce, they are far more tolerant of the low light levels and damp weather typical of northern-latitude winters and probably far more nutritious.

TYPES OF LETTUCE

Lettuces can be divided roughly into hearting and non-hearting types, with a few intermediate, semi-hearting varieties. The principal hearting types are the tall cos or 'romaine' lettuce, and the flat 'cabbage' type, subdivided into 'butterhead' and 'crisphead' lettuce. Non-hearting types include the loose-leaf 'Salad Bowl' varieties and stem lettuce. While lettuces are predominantly green, there are now red and bronze forms in virtually every type of lettuce. For varieties, see p. 17.

Cos These are large, upright lettuces with long, thick, crisp, distinctly flavoured leaves forming a somewhat loose heart. They are slower-maturing than other types, but stand hot and dry conditions well without running to seed, besides tolerating low temperatures. Several varieties are frost hardy and can be overwintered, and some are suitable for sowing thickly as leaf lettuce (see p. 16). Cos lettuces keep well after cutting. 'Semi-cos' lettuces are a smaller type, exemplified by 'Little Gem', a compact variety notable for its sweet, crisp leaves – and arguably the best flavoured of all lettuces.

Butterhead This is the softer type of cabbage lettuce, typified by a flat round head of gently rounded leaves with a buttery texture and mild flavour. They tend to wilt quickly after picking. Butterheads generally grow faster than crispheads, but are more likely to bolt prematurely in hot weather. While mainly grown in the summer months, they are reasonably well adapted to the short days of late summer and autumn, and many winter varieties are in this group.

Crisphead This group of cabbage lettuce is characterized by crisp-textured, often frilled leaves. The term 'Iceberg' has been adopted for large crispheads sold with the outer leaves trimmed off, leaving just the crisp white heart. Crispheads generally take about ten days longer than butterheads to mature but stand well in hot weather without bolting – especially the American Iceberg varieties. Crispheads keep reasonably well after picking. Many are considered flavourless, but an exception is the group loosely known as 'Batavian'. Of European origin, they often have reddish-tinged leaves and tend to be relatively hardy.

Loose-leaf Lettuces in this group form only rudimentary hearts, but produce a loose head of leaves that can be picked individually as required. The heads normally resprout if cut about 2.5cm/1in above ground. The group are also known as 'gathering' or 'cutting' lettuces, or Salad Bowl types, after the variety of that name. The leaves are often deeply indented (the 'oak-leaved' varieties closely resemble oak

TYPES OF LETTUCE

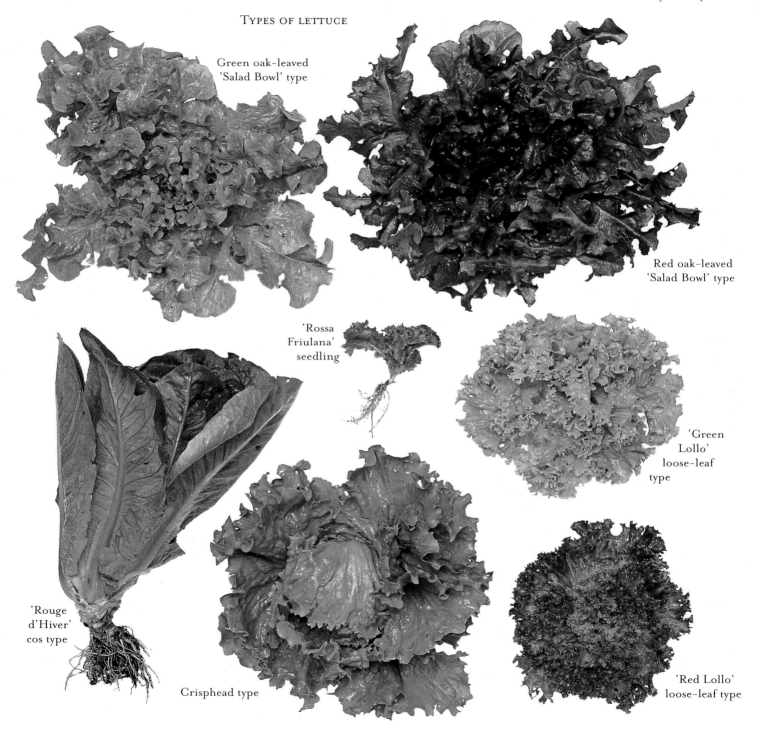

Green oak-leaved
'Salad Bowl' type

Red oak-leaved
'Salad Bowl' type

'Rossa
Friulana'
seedling

'Green
Lollo'
loose-leaf
type

'Rouge
d'Hiver'
cos type

Crisphead type

'Red Lollo'
loose-leaf type

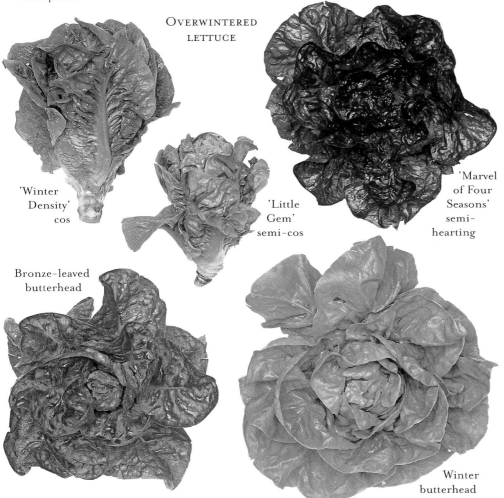

OVERWINTERED LETTUCE

'Winter Density' cos

'Little Gem' semi-cos

'Marvel of Four Seasons' semi-hearting

Bronze-leaved butterhead

Winter butterhead

LEFT Photographed in late spring, these lettuces were sown in early autumn, and planted in an unheated polytunnel in late autumn and late winter for the year's earliest supplies.

ABOVE This Asiatic lettuce is grown primarily for its edible stem. It requires fertile soil and plenty of moisture.

leaves) while others, notably the beautiful red and green 'Lollo' varieties, which originated in Italy, are deeply curled. Loose-leaf lettuces are generally slower to bolt than hearting lettuce, which, coupled with their ability to regenerate, gives them a long season of usefulness. The central leaves of reddish-tinged varieties tend to become darker-coloured with successive cuts. Loose-leaf types are suitable for cut-and-come-again seedling crops. Most are reasonably hardy, and seem less prone to mildew than other types. Leaves are generally soft, are easily damaged by hail and wilt soon after picking. They are amongst the prettiest lettuces for potager use; the red-leaved varieties make dainty pinnacles if left to run to seed.

Stem lettuce This Asiatic lettuce, also known as 'asparagus lettuce' or 'celtuce', is grown primarily for its stem, which can be 2.5–7.5cm/1–3in thick and at least 30cm/12in long. Its leaves are coarse and palatable only when young, unless cooked. Cultivate it like summer lettuce, spacing plants 30cm/12in apart each way. It is tolerant of both low and high temperatures, but needs fertile soil and plenty of moisture to develop well. The stem is sliced and used raw in salads, but can also be cooked. It has a distinct lettuce flavour. Mature, firm-stemmed plants can be uprooted in autumn and transplanted into cold frames, with the leaves trimmed back. They may keep in good condition for a month or more.

SOIL AND SITE

Lettuces require an open situation, but in the height of summer and in hot climates can be grown in light shade. They can be intercropped between taller plants, provided they have adequate space and light. They do well in containers in fertile, moisture-retentive soil or compost.

CULTIVATION

Lettuce can be sown *in situ*, in an outdoor seedbed for transplanting or in seed trays or modules for transplanting.

Sow *in situ* for seedling cut-and-come-again crops and leaf lettuce (see p. 16); in very hot weather, when transplanted seedlings wilt badly after planting, unless raised in modules; and for some overwintered sowings. Its disadvantage is that germination and early growth are erratic if soil and weather conditions deteriorate, and, seedling and leaf lettuce crops apart, for good results thinning is essential. Start thinning as early as possible – and use the thinnings in salads. Final spacing depends on the variety: small varieties like 'Little Gem' 13–15cm/5–6in apart; cabbage lettuces 23–30cm/9–12in apart; cos and 'Iceberg' types about 35cm/14in apart.

Sow in an outdoor seedbed only where there are no facilities for raising plants indoors, or no ground is available for direct sowing. On the whole sowing in modules or *in situ*, rather than in a seedbed, produces better plants as there is no transplanting setback.

Sowing indoors, preferably in modules, produces good-quality plants and gives planting flexibility. Transplant young plants outside when conditions are suitable, or under the cover of cloches, frames, greenhouses or polytunnels.

Lettuces are best transplanted at the four-to-five-leaf stage. Plant most types shallowly with the lowest leaves just above soil level, though cos lettuces can be planted a little deeper. I recommend planting at equidistant spacing, rather than in rows.

Lettuce germinates at surprisingly low temperatures – it even germinates on ice – but some of the butterheads, and my favourite 'Little Gem', have 'high-temperature dormancy', which means that they germinate poorly at soil temperatures above 25°C/77°F. These temperatures frequently occur in late spring and summer. You can take various measures to overcome the problem, of which the main options are:

• Use crisphead varieties, which germinate at soil temperatures of up to 29°C/85°F.

• Sow between two and four in the afternoon. The most critical germination phase then coincides with cooler night temperatures.

• Put seeds somewhere cold to germinate, such as in a cold room, in a cellar or in the shade. Or cover seed trays with moist newspaper to keep the temperature down until germination.

• If sowing outdoors, water the seedbed beforehand to cool the soil; or cover it with white reflective film after sowing and remove it as soon as the seeds germinate.

WATERING

Common lettuce problems, such as bitterness, bolting and disease, are exacerbated by slow growth, often caused by water shortage. In the absence of rain, water summer crops at the rate of up to 18 litres per sq. m/4 gallons per sq. yd per week. If watering regularly is difficult, concentrate on one really heavy watering about seven to ten days before harvesting. Water autumn-planted lettuce well when planting, but subsequently water sparingly during the winter months as damp leaves invite disease. Lettuce responds well to being mulched with organic material or polythene film.

SOWING PROGRAMME

For a continuous supply of lettuce, make several sowings during the year, using appropriate varieties for each season (see p. 17). **Summer supplies** For the earliest outdoor summer lettuce, sow under cover in early spring, transplanting outside as soon as soil conditions are suitable. Continue sowing in spring and early summer by any of the methods described above, when summer temperatures are high.

A problem in maintaining a steady summer supply of hearting lettuce is that growth rates vary during the season, from six and a half weeks to as much as thirteen weeks. Relevant factors include the variety, speed of germination, and soil and air temperature. In hot weather some varieties run to seed soon after maturing. In other words, regular sowing at ten- to fourteen-day intervals, as is often advocated, does not guarantee a steady supply. Later sowings may overtake earlier sowings, leading to gluts and gaps. The best way to iron out fluctuations is to make the 'next' sowing when the seedlings from the last sowing have just emerged. The Salad Bowl types of lettuce stand well for several months. One or two sowings normally ensure a supply throughout the summer.

Autumn supplies Sow from mid- to late summer, using any of the methods on p. 15. In areas where autumn is normally wet, grow mildew-resistant varieties. If the weather deteriorates in autumn, cover outdoor lettuces with cloches or low polytunnels to keep them in good condition. These sowings can also be transplanted into frames, polytunnels or greenhouses if space is available.

Winter supplies Sow winter-hearting varieties in seed trays or modules in late summer and early autumn, transplanting into frames, greenhouses or polytunnels in late autumn. Successful cropping depends to some extent on the weather: in poor winters plants may not mature until spring. They will, of course, crop earlier if grown in gently heated conditions with a minimum night temperature of 2°C/36°F and day temperature of 4.5°C/40°F. Winter and early spring lettuce are very vulnerable to fungal diseases such as grey mould and downy mildew (see p. 17). Avoid overcrowding and keep them well ventilated.

Spring supplies The earliest spring lettuce comes from crops grown in unheated greenhouses and polytunnels during winter. Use only varieties specifically bred for this period. Sow in autumn in seed trays or modules (each variety has a recommended sowing time), transplanting under cover. In slightly heated greenhouses, continue sowing in mid-winter/early spring for follow-on crops under cover.

The earliest outdoor spring lettuce comes from hardy varieties (capable of surviving several degrees of frost) that have been overwintered in the open. Sow *in situ* outdoors in late summer/early autumn, thinning initially to about 8cm/3in apart, and to the final spacing the following spring. Plants will be of better quality, and more likely to survive in good condition, if protected from the elements under cloches or low polytunnels or in frames.

Alternatively, you can sow the same hardy varieties or plant them under cover in late summer/early autumn, and thin in the same way. You can also sow them in seed trays or modules in late autumn, overwinter them as seedlings under cover, and plant in spring in the open or under cover.

There is always an element of chance with overwintered lettuce because of the vagaries of winter weather. It is worth the gamble.

SEEDLING CROPS

Several varieties of lettuce are suitable for use at the seedling or baby leaf stage. In the past, seedling lettuce was commonly sown in heated frames in winter, providing out-of-season salading. The technique is still useful for early sowings under cover, as seedlings will be ready far sooner than hearting lettuce sown at the same time. You can make sowings throughout the growing season, a patch often providing two or occasionally three cuttings over several months. Seedling lettuce lends itself to intercropping and making decorative patterns (see p. 8). Besides the traditional 'cutting' lettuce varieties, it is worth experimenting with others, perhaps utilizing left-over seed. Only a few varieties prove bitter at the seedling stage.

LEAF LETTUCE

This concept, based on the old seedling lettuce techniques, was developed in the 1970s at what is now Horticulture Research International at Wellesbourne in the UK. The aim was to produce a crop of single leaves, to save caterers from having to tear apart the heart of a lettuce. The researchers discovered that if certain varieties of cos lettuce are sown closely, they grow upright without forming hearts, and regrow after the first cut, allowing a second crop within three to seven weeks. The method is easily adapted for use in the salad garden. A family of four could be kept in lettuce all summer by cultivating approximately 5 sq. m/6 sq. yd, and making ten sowings, each of about 80 sq. cm/1 sq. yd, cutting each crop twice.

The soil must be fertile and weed-free. Prepare the seedbed carefully to encourage good germination. Either broadcast the seed, thinning later to about 5cm/2in apart, or sow thinly in rows about 13cm/5in apart, thinning to about 3cm/1½in apart. Plants must have plenty of moisture throughout growth.

Starting in spring, make the first seven sowings at weekly intervals. Make the first cuts in each case about seven weeks later, and a second cut a further six to seven weeks after that, during the summer. Make the last three sowings at weekly intervals in summer. These mature more rapidly, allowing the first cut after about three weeks (just overlapping with the tail end of the early sowings) and the second cut four weeks or so after the first. This gives continual cropping into autumn. Cut the leaves when 8–13cm/3–5in high, about 2cm/¾in above ground level.

VARIETIES

For summer supplies Early sowings: most cos, semi-cos and Salad Bowl varieties; selected butterheads, for example 'Clarion', 'Hilde II', 'Tom Thumb', 'Unrivalled'; successive sowings: all cos, loose-leaf and crisphead varieties, and all butterhead varieties except those bred specifically for short winter days.

For autumn supplies 'Little Gem' and Salad Bowl types; fast-growing cabbageheads, for example 'Minetto' (crisphead), 'Tom Thumb' (butterhead); mildew-resistant varieties, for example 'Avondefiance', 'Plenty' (butterheads); 'Challenge' (crisphead); 'Frisby' (loose-leaf – Batavian x 'Little Gem').

For winter supplies (in unheated greenhouses) 'Kelly' (crisphead), 'Kwiek', 'Oscar' (butterheads).

For spring supplies (overwintering outdoors or under cover) Cos: 'Little Gem', 'Lobjoit's Green', 'Rouge d'Hiver', 'Winter Density'; butterheads: 'Arctic King', 'Imperial Winter', 'Valdor'; loose-leaf and semi-hearting: 'Catalogna', 'Marvel of Four Seasons'; 'Parella' (small red Italian variety).

For seedling lettuce Salad Bowl varieties, smooth and curly-leaved cutting lettuce; reddish-leaved 'Rossa Friulana'; most cos and semi-cos varieties.

For leaf lettuce 'Lobjoit's Green', 'Paris White Cos', 'Valmaine'.

My shortlist for flavour: all cos and semi-cos, including 'Bubbles', 'Little Gem', 'Pinokkio', 'Sherwood'; Batavian: 'Kendo', 'Nevada', 'Regina Ghiacci'/'Queen of the Ice', 'Pierre Benite', 'Rouge Grenobloise'; red iceberg: 'Sioux', 'Tiger'.

My shortlist for decorative quality: red and red-tinged loose-leaf types: 'Cerize', 'Cocarde', 'Freckles', 'Ibis', 'Impuls', 'Lollo Rosso,' 'Mascara', 'Revolution', 'Salad Bowl'; green loose-leaf types : 'Bergamo', 'Catalogna', 'Frillice', 'Frisby', 'Green Lollo', 'Salad Bowl'.

PESTS

Unless otherwise stated, for protective measures and control, see p. 125.

Birds Seedlings and young plants are most vulnerable, though mature plants are attacked from time to time.

Slugs Slugs can cause serious damage at every stage, especially in wet weather and on heavy soils.

Soil pests Wireworm, cutworm and leatherjackets all destroy plants, and are most damaging in spring.

Root aphids Colonies of yellowish brown aphids attack the roots, secreting a waxy powder. Plants grow poorly, wilt and may die. There are no organic controls: practise rotation and grow varieties with a measure of resistance, for example 'Avondefiance', 'Musette', 'Dynamite'.

Leaf aphids (greenfly) Attacks are most likely outdoors in hot weather and under cover in spring.

DISEASES

There are no organic remedies for diseases, so prevention is all-important. Watch in current seed catalogues for new varieties with disease resistance or some degree of tolerance. (Older resistant varieties tend to disappear, as the resistance eventually breaks down.)

Damping off diseases Seedlings either fail to emerge or keel over and die shortly afterwards. Avoid sowing in cold or wet conditions; sow thinly to avoid overcrowding; keep indoor crops well ventilated.

Downy mildew (*Bremia lactuca*) Probably the most serious lettuce disease, occurring in damp weather, mainly from autumn to early spring. Pale angular patches appear on older leaves and white spores on the underside. Leaves eventually turn brown and die. Avoid overcrowding; keep foliage dry by watering the soil rather than the plants; avoid watering in the evening; keep greenhouses well ventilated. Cut off infected leaves with a sharp knife. Burn them and debris from infected plants, which harbour disease spores. Use resistant varieties. Transplanted crops are less susceptible to mildew than direct-sown crops.

Grey mould (*Botrytis cinerea*) A rotting disease which commonly manifests itself at the base of the stem, causing plants to rot off. It is most serious in cold damp conditions. Avoid overcrowding and deep planting; take preventive measures as above for downy mildew. Currently there are no varieties with effective resistance.

Mosaic virus A seed-borne disease causing stunted growth and yellowish mottling on the leaves, which become pale. Burn infected plants; try to control aphids, which spread the disease; use seed with guaranteed low levels of mosaic infection (less than I per cent); grow resistant varieties.

Chicory *Cichorium intybus*

The chicories are a wonderfully diverse group of plants with a long history of cultivation for human, animal and medicinal use. The classical Roman writers often referred to the use of chicory as both a cooked and salad vegetable, and Italy is still the hub of the chicory world. The Italians grow an enormous range of chicories, some scarcely known further afield. 'Radicchio', a popular Italian name for chicory, has become widely identified with the red-hearted chicory. These red chicories have been embraced by the restaurant trade and have become a key ingredient in supermarket salad packs.

For the gardener, chicories have many merits. They are naturally robust, are mostly easily grown and have few pests, though the red chicories are prone to rotting diseases in autumn. Their main season is from late summer to spring, when salad material is scarcest, and they can often be sown or planted after summer crops are cleared, utilizing ground that would otherwise be idle in winter, both in the open and under cover.

TYPES OF CHICORY

There are several distinct kinds of chicory. While the majority are grown for their leaves, some are cultivated for their roots and shoots.

The most striking of the leaf types are the red-leaved Italian

'Versuvio' F1, an improved Treviso type of red chicory

chicories. Of the green-leaved chicories, the most widely grown is the 'Sugar Loaf' type, used at the seedling stage, or when the crisp 'loaf-like' head has developed. Among other forms of leaf chicory are the rosette-shaped, extraordinarily hardy 'Grumolo' chicory, and various wild, narrow-leaved chicories, not unlike dandelion. The 'Catalogna' chicories, grown mainly for their spring shoots, are another distinct group.

Best known of the root chicories is 'Witloof' (or 'Belgian') chicory. The roots are forced in the dark to produce white, bud-like 'chicons'. Other root chicories are used raw in salads, much like winter radishes, while a few varieties were traditionally dried and ground as a coffee substitute. The beautiful pale blue chicory flowers can be used in salads, fresh or pickled.

Chicories have a characteristic flavour, with a slightly bitter edge – addictive to those who acquire the taste, but less popular with the sweet-toothed. The bitterness can be modified by shredding the leaves, by mixing them with milder plants (see p. 141) and, where appropriate, by blanching the growing plants. Chicories can also be cooked, typically by braising, acquiring an intriguing flavour in the process. Bitterness varies with the variety and the stage of growth. Seedling leaves are less bitter than mature leaves, the inner leaves of Sugar Loaf chicories less bitter than the outer, and the red chicories become sweeter in cold weather. Washing leaves gently in warm water removes some of the bitterness.

CULTIVATION

Chicories are deep-rooting, unfussy plants. They adapt to a wide range of soils, from light sands to heavy clay, and even to wet, dry and exposed situations. They tolerate light shade. Although most are naturally perennial, for salad purposes it is best to treat them as annuals, resowing every year. Plants left to flower in spring will sometimes seed themselves but, because they cross-pollinate, resulting seedlings may not be true to type. In recent years plant breeders have improved the traditional varieties of red chicory beyond recognition. Unfortunately the high cost of this seed means that retail seedsmen supply only a limited choice. Mixtures of hardy chicories, sometimes sold as 'Misuglio', make colourful seedling patches (see photograph on p. 22). Treat them initially as cut-and-come-again seedling patches, then allow a few plants to mature.

RED-LEAVED CHICORIES

The outstanding feature of the so-called red chicories is their colour, which ranges from deep red and pinks to variegated leaves with flashes of red, yellow and cream on a green background. The old varieties were predominantly green in the early stages, but, chameleon-like, became redder and deeper-coloured with the onset of cold autumn nights. At the same time the leaves turned inwards, developing a nugget of sweeter, crisp, attractive leaves. The degree of hearting and colouring was always a lottery. Improved modern varieties develop earlier, more consistently, and are deeper-coloured. Varieties differ in their hardiness, from those that tolerate light frost, to 'Treviso', a unique loose-headed variety of upright leaves which, in our garden, has survived temperatures of –15°C/ 5°F.

Cultivation In my experience the best hearting chicories are obtained by sowing in modules and transplanting. Red chicory can also be sown outdoors in rows, or in the traditional method of broadcasting, and plants thinned in stages to about 25cm/10in apart. In practice broadcast patches seem to 'thin themselves' by a kind of survival of the fittest. Varieties of the 'Treviso' type respond well to broadcasting.

Germination, particularly outdoors, can be erratic in hot weather, so take appropriate measures (see p. 105). Chicory is sometimes trimmed back on transplanting to 8–10cm/3–4in above ground to stimulate growth – especially in hot weather. Space plants 25–35cm/10–14in apart, depending on variety.

For summer supplies Sow from mid- to late spring using suitable early varieties, or plants may bolt prematurely. Protect plants with perforated film or fleece in the early stages.

For autumn/early winter supplies Sow from early to mid-summer. The hardier varieties will survive mild winters outdoors.

For winter/early spring supplies under cover Sow mid- to late summer. Transplant under cover, or cover the plants *in situ*, in late summer/early autumn. Do not overcrowd this useful crop.

For cut-and-come-again seedlings Sow patches from late spring to mid-summer, extending the season with slightly earlier and slightly later sowings under cover.

Harvesting With successive sowings you can have hearted chicories from late summer until the following spring. Either pick individual leaves as required, or cut the heads about 2.5cm/1in or so above ground level, leaving the lowest leaves intact. The stumps normally produce further flushes of leaf over many weeks.

With cut-and-come-again seedling patches, start cutting when leaves are 5–8cm/2–3in high. Some will be tender at this stage; others may be bitter, depending on variety and the weather. You can later thin the seedlings, allowing a few to grow to maturity.

Winter protection The challenge with hearted chicories is to keep plants in good condition from late autumn into winter. In humid conditions they have a tendency to rot, usually starting with the outer leaves of the hearts. (Remove them carefully and you may find perfectly healthy hearts beneath.) Outdoor crops often keep well if protected with a light covering of straw, bracken or dead leaves – although there is a risk of attracting mice and even rats in severe winters. Glass cloches or low polytunnels can give additional protection, though polytunnels may encourage high humidity. We have harvested beautiful plants from under the snow: it can be a good insulator.

In unheated greenhouses and polytunnels, make sure there is good ventilation, and remove rotting leaves to limit the spread of infection. Keep plants reasonably well watered, or they may suffer from tipburn at the leaf edges.

Forcing and blanching Certain varieties of red chicory, such as 'Red Verona' and 'Treviso', can be lifted and forced in the dark like Witloof chicory (see p. 22). They can also be blanched *in situ* by covering with an upturned pot with light excluded. Cut back hearted varieties such as 'Red Verona' to within 2.5cm/1in of the stump, so that it is new growth that is blanched. You can force 'Treviso' this way, or alternatively blanch it more quickly by simply tying the leaves together before covering the plant. Blanched red chicories are exceptionally beautiful, the whitened leaves overlaid with pink hues.

Varieties Improved varieties: 'Cesare' (for early sowings), 'Firebird' F1, 'Indigo' F1, 'Firestorm' F1, 'Leonardo' F1; traditional varieties: 'Palla Rossa Bella', 'Rossa Verona' (Verona type); 'Castelfranco', 'Sottomarina' (variegated); Treviso types: 'Treviso', 'Carla' F1, 'Versuvio' F1.

GREEN-LEAVED CHICORIES

Sugar Loaf chicory

A mature Sugar Loaf chicory forms a large, light green, tightly folded conical head, not unlike cos lettuce in appearance. The inner leaves are partially blanched by the outer leaves, and are pale, crisp, distinctly flavoured and sweeter than most chicories – though the 'sweetness' is only relative. They are naturally vigorous, responding well to cut-and-come-again treatment at every stage: seedlings, semi-mature and mature. Most varieties tolerate only light frost in the open, but if grown under cover in winter and kept trimmed back, are likely to survive winter well, giving regular pickings and resprouting vigorously in spring. They require fertile, moisture-retentive soil, but seem to have better drought resistance than comparable salad plants, such as lettuce, possibly because of their long roots.

For a hearted crop Sow by any of the methods used for red-leaved chicory (p. 19). You can obtain good results by sowing in modules and transplanting, or by sowing *in situ*. Space or thin plants to 15–30cm/6–12in apart, the closer spacing for the older, less vigorous varieties.

For summer supplies Sow in spring/early summer. (A few varieties are unsuited to early sowing: be guided by information on the seed packet.)

For autumn supplies Sow in early/mid-summer; transplant later sowings under cover for winter crops, or cover *in situ*.

For winter or early spring supplies Sow in late summer and transplant under cover. This crop is a gamble as tight heads may not form until the following spring. However, loose leaves can generally be cut during the winter (see above). Like the red chicories, Sugar Loaf heads are prone to rot in damp winter weather. Keep plants well ventilated and remove rotting leaves, but leave the stumps: even 'hopeless cases' may regenerate in spring. Traditionally, Sugar Loaf plants were uprooted in early winter and stored for several weeks, in closely packed heaps covered with straw in cellars or frames.

Cut-and-come-again seedlings Some older varieties of Sugar Loaf chicory are primarily used for cut-and-come-again crops. Sow from late winter/early spring through to early autumn, making the earliest and latest sowings under cover. These protected sowings are exceptionally good value. The first sowing under cover can be made as soon as soil temperatures rise above 5°C/41°F in spring. The late autumn seedling sowings under cover survive lower temperatures than mature plants, and start into renewed growth very early in the year.

Make the main sowings in succession throughout the summer for a continuous supply of fresh young leaves. They are best cut when 5–7.5cm/2–3in high; older leaves may be coarse. Growth is rapid, sometimes allowing a second cut within fifteen days of the first. A patch can remain productive over many weeks, provided the soil is fertile and there is plenty of moisture. Supplementary feeding with a liquid fertilizer will help sustain growth towards the end of the season. Cut-and-come-again seedlings can eventually be thinned to about 15cm/6in apart and left to develop small heads.

Varieties Traditional varieties, mainly recommended for cut-and-come-again seedlings: 'Bianca di Milano', 'Bionda di Triestino'; heading varieties: 'Sugar Loaf'; 'Poncho', 'Snowflake' (both Sugar Loaf selections), 'Jupiter' F1, 'Pluto' F1.

Grumolo chicory

This rugged little chicory from the Italian Piedmont survives the roughest winter weather to produce a ground-hugging rosette of smooth, rounded, jade-green leaves in spring. The leaves are upright during the summer months, but acquire a rosette form in mid-winter. They appear to die back in the depth of winter, but reappear remarkably early – green rosebuds at ground level! They tolerate poor soil, weedy conditions and low temperatures. They are naturally rather bitter, but you can blend them into mixed salads – they earn a place on the shape and colour of their leaves alone. The more mature leaves are coarser, but can be shredded or used cooked. Light and dark green forms are available.

Cultivation While Grumolo chicory can be sown from spring to autumn, the most useful sowings are in mid-summer, for autumn-to-spring supplies. Grumolo chicory lends itself to being broadcast thinly in patches but can be sown thinly in rows 15cm/6in apart. In hot climates mid-summer sowings can be made in light shade. During the summer cut the young leaves when 5–30cm/2–13in high, but in autumn leave them to form rosettes. Patches will not normally need thinning unless they have been sown too thickly, in which case

RED AND GREEN CHICORIES

Traditional
red-leaved
chicory
showing
root

Blanched
loose-headed
red chicory 'Red
Treviso'

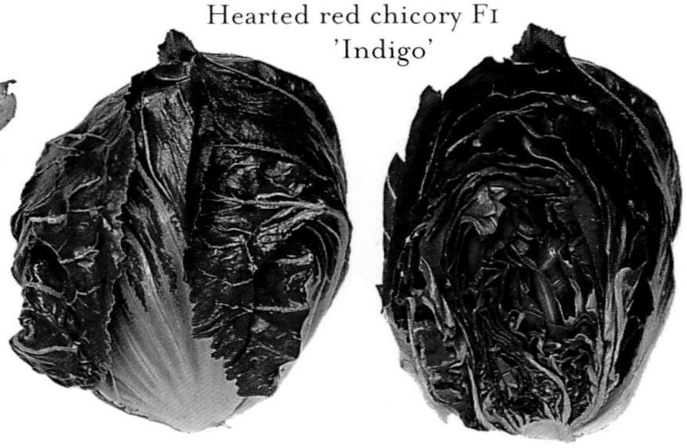

Hearted red chicory F1
'Indigo'

Grumolo
chicory

Hearted red
chicory 'Red Verona'

Sugar loaf
seedling

Traditional
variegated red
chicory 'Sottomarina'

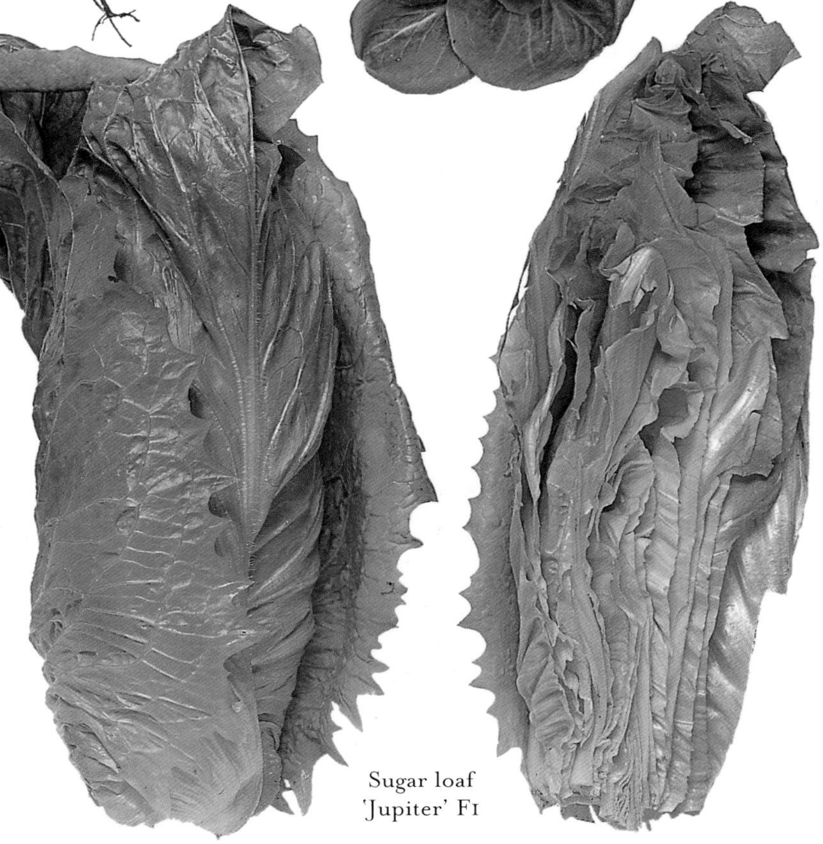

Sugar loaf
'Jupiter' F1

thin to about 7.5cm/3in apart. In spring, or when the chicory is freshly sown, it may be necessary to protect from birds. Cloche protection in early spring will bring plants on earlier and make the leaves more tender. Cut the rosettes in spring, leaving the plants to resprout. The subsequent growth is never as prettily shaped and tends to become coarse, but may fill a gap in spring salad supplies. Leave a few plants to run to seed – they form spectacular clumps 2m/6½ft high, covered in pale blue flowers that tend to fade at noon. Pick these in the morning for use in salads. You can grow Grumolo chicory as a perennial by sowing a patch in an out-of-the-way place and letting it perpetuate itself.

Spadona chicory

This equally hardy chicory of narrow-bladed leaves never forms a rosette. Cultivate and use it as Grumolo chicory above. I was told that Italians feed it to chickens and rabbits during the summer, then leave the plants to resprout for winter and spring salads. It is fairly bitter but extremely hardy.

Catalogna chicory

Also known as 'asparagus chicory', this tall chicory from south Italy has long narrow leaves, which can be smooth-edged or serrated with green or cream stalks. The 'puntarelle' types are grown primarily for the chunky buds (*puntarelle*) and flowering stems that develop in spring; they are bitter raw, but delicious cooked and cold in salads.

This patch of mixed chicories was sown in mid-summer and photographed the following spring after a mild winter.

The young leaves can be used in salads. Other types (such as *Catalogna frastigliata*) are grown for the leaves, picked either small, or as a bunch when 20–40cm/8–16in tall. 'Red Rib' and 'Italico' are forms with attractive dark red veins. They are naturally very bitter and for this reason are sometimes blanched.

The Catalogna chicories are reasonably heat tolerant but stand only light frost. They are undemanding about soil. Sow leaf types *in situ* in summer, as cut-and-come-again seedlings or thinning to 15cm/6in apart. Sow puntarelle types *in situ*; or sow them in modules and transplant, spacing plants about 20cm/8in apart. In temperate climates they can be planted under cover in late summer, and will form shoots the following spring. Catalogna chicories make beautiful flowering clumps in their second season.

Wild chicory

Capucin's beard or *barbe de Capucin* is the popular name for the jagged-leaved wild chicories. The young leaves can be eaten green (generally shredded), but blanching mature plants develops their unique flavour. Like many bitter and blanched plants, wild chicory is excellent *aux lardons* (see p. 141). Sow from late spring to early summer *in situ*, thinning plants to about 15cm/6in apart. Blanch *in situ* or transplant under cover (see p. 132). The top of the root is edible and well flavoured.

ROOT CHICORIES

Witloof chicory

Also known as Belgian chicory, this chicory was allegedly 'discovered' when a Belgian farmer threw some wild chicory roots into a warm dark stable. The whitened shoots which developed laid the foundations for the modern Witloof industry. Witloof chicory is easy to grow, tolerating a wide range of conditions. Avoid freshly manured ground, as it can result in lush plants and fanged roots. Improved modern varieties produce excellent, plump chicons.
Cultivation Sow in early summer, in drills 30cm/12in apart, or in modules for transplanting. Thin or space plants to about 23cm/9in apart. No further attention is required, other than keeping plants weed-free and watering in very dry weather.
Forcing Roots can be forced *in situ* or transplanted indoors. The

latter is more convenient, but roots forced outside are said to be better flavoured. For forcing *in situ*, see p. 131. To force indoors, dig up the roots in late autumn/early winter, and leave them exposed to light frost or low temperatures for a week or so. In theory fanged or very thin roots should be rejected (they should be at least 4cm/1½in thick at the neck), but in practice even poor roots produce chicons of a sort. Cut back the foliage to 2.5cm/1in above the neck, and trim the roots to about 20cm/8in. For a continuous supply, force a few at a time, storing surplus roots in layers in boxes of moist sand, kept in a frostproof shed or cellar.

The simplest way to force roots is to pot several roots close together in a 23–30cm/9–12in flower pot, filled with soil or old potting compost. (This is to support the roots, not supply nutrients, as nourishment comes from the roots themselves.) Water gently, and cover the pot with an inverted pot of the same size with the drainage hole blocked to exclude light. (See illustration on p. 133.) Alternatively put the pot in total darkness. Keep the pot at a temperature of 10°C/50°F or a little higher. Inspect it from time to time, water if the soil has dried out and remove any rotting leaves. The chicons will normally be ready in about three weeks. Chicory can, of course, be forced in any darkened container large enough to take the roots.

Witloof chicory can also be transplanted into frames and greenhouses, using various means to create darkness (see p. 132).

Once the chicons are ready, use them soon or they deteriorate. Cut them 2.5cm/1in above the root, and keep them wrapped in aluminium foil or in a refrigerator, as they become green and bitter on exposure to light. The root can be left in the dark to resprout: it will normally produce more leaf, but not a dense chicon.
Varieties 'Apollo', 'Zoom' F1.

Other root chicories

Some chicories have large edible roots, white and surprisingly tender – a useful winter standby. They are used raw, chopped or grated in salad, or cooked and eaten cold. Sow in spring or early summer by broadcasting, or sowing in rows or modules for transplanting, spacing plants eventually about 10cm/4in apart. The roots are moderately hardy and can be lifted during winter as required.
Varieties 'Magdeburg', 'Geneva', 'Soncino'.

ROOT CHICORIES

Wild chicory

Witloof chicory
root before forcing

Forced
Witloof
chicon

'Soncino'
root chicory

Endive *Cichorium endivia*

The endives are a versatile, attractive group of plants in the chicory family: indeed, in the non-English-speaking world they are known as 'chicory'. They are a cool-season crop, growing best at temperatures of 10–20°C/50–68°F and tend to become bitter at higher temperatures. Don't grow them in mid-summer where this is likely to be the case. All varieties survive light frost. Endives are more resistant to pests and disease than lettuce and, provided appropriate varieties are used, less likely to bolt in hot weather. They are also better adapted to the low light levels and dampness of autumn and winter. Their flavour is fresh and slightly piquant, but plants can be blanched before use, which makes the leaves milder, crisper and an attractive creamy white colour. Many of the newer varieties are virtually self-blanching and naturally sweeter. Endive has become a popular ingredient in supermarket pre-packed salads.

TYPES OF ENDIVE

Curly-leaved (frisée, staghorn, cut-leaved) These have a low-growing habit, and fairly narrow, curled, fringed or indented leaves, making a pretty head. They are more heat tolerant than broad-leaved endives, but more prone to rotting in damp and cold weather, making them the best varieties for summer use. They are among my potager favourites – neat and pretty: I often use them to outline vegetable patterns. They are also excellent as cut-and-come-again seedlings.

Broad-leaved (Batavian, escarole, scarole) These are larger plants, with broader, smoother, somewhat furled leaves, which can be upright or low-growing and compact. They can withstand temperatures as low as –9°C/15°F, so are generally the best value for winter-to-spring crops. Mature plants respond well to cut-and-come-again treatment, making them among the most productive salads in winter under cover.

Modern plant breeding is producing intermediate varieties, with some of the characteristics of each type.

CULTIVATION

Endives like an open situation and fertile, moisture-retentive soil, with plenty of well-rotted organic matter worked in beforehand. Very acid soils should be limed.

Either sow *in situ* and subsequently thin out or transplant, or sow in modules for transplanting. Transplanted endive is said to grow faster and be less likely to become bitter. Seed germinates best at 20–22°C/68–72°F. Germination may be poor at higher soil temperatures, with slow-germinating plants being prone to premature bolting. (For sowing in hot conditions, see Lettuce, p. 15.) Depending on variety, space plants 25cm–35cm/10–14in apart. On average endives take about thirteen weeks to mature. Use thinnings in salads or transplant to maintain continuity.

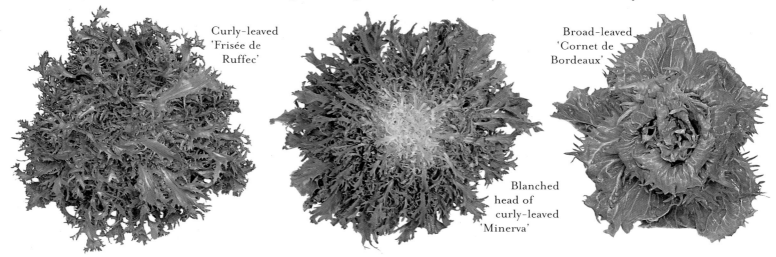

Curly-leaved 'Frisée de Ruffec'

Blanched head of curly-leaved 'Minerva'

Broad-leaved 'Cornet de Bordeaux'

SOWING PROGRAMME

Early summer supplies Sow under cover very early in spring, transplanting outdoors as soon as soil conditions allow. Protect with cloches or crop covers. These early sowings may bolt prematurely if temperatures fall below 5°C/41°F for several days.

Main summer supplies Sow in mid- to late spring.

Autumn supplies outdoors Sow in early to mid-summer. Use hardier varieties for the late sowings; in mild areas they may stand well into winter. Protect with cloches or crop covers if necessary.

Autumn and winter supplies under cover Sow in mid-summer to early autumn, transplanting under cover in autumn. With cut-and-come-again treatment, of the broad-leaved types in particular, it may be possible to make several cuts during winter.

Late spring supplies Sow hardy broad-leaved varieties in modules under cover in late autumn, overwintering them as seedlings and planting early in the year, under cover or outside.

Cut-and-come-again seedling crops Sow from late winter to early autumn. Make the earliest and latest sowings under cover, provided the soil temperature is above 15°C/59°F. Curly endive makes particularly appealing salad seedlings, though all types can be used. They lend themselves to intercropping and being sown in decorative patches.

BLANCHING

Whether or not you blanch endives before harvesting is largely a matter of taste. I find most of them quite palatable 'as they are', although there is something irresistible about the crisp white centre of a blanched curly-leaved endive. For blanching techniques, see p. 131. In the main, endives are blanched *in situ*, using covering methods for compact low-growing varieties and tying the heads of looser-leaved varieties. Curly-leaved endives benefit most from blanching in hot weather, when they tend to be more bitter. A simple old-fashioned blanching method is to cover one endive with an uprooted one. Simply pull up one plant, then place it, with the head down and root in the air, on to the head of a growing plant. Mutual blanching results!

VARIETIES

Curled For spring and summer supplies: 'Frisela', 'Ione', 'Sally'; for autumn and winter supplies: 'Minerva' (Wallonne type), 'Naomi', 'Pancalière', 'Ruffec'.

Broad-leaved For supplies for any season: 'Golda', 'Elysée', 'Grosse Bouclée 2', 'Jeti'. Hardiest: 'Cornet de Bordeaux', 'Géant Maraîchère' race 'Margot' and race 'Torino', 'Ronde Verte à Coeur Plein' ('Fullheart').

Cabbage *Brassica oleracea* Capitata Group

Cabbage is among the most widely grown of cool-climate crops, and for aficionados there is a cabbage for every season. In spring there are loose-headed 'spring greens' and perky, mainly pointed hearted cabbages; in summer and autumn there are large green and red cabbages; while in winter there are hardy savoys and red-tinged 'January King' types, and the option of stored 'Dutch Winter White' cabbage. Any cabbage can be used as a raw salad or coleslaw, especially if finely shredded, but in my view the light green, sweeter spring and summer cabbages, the thin-leaved Dutch Winter Whites, the tasty savoys and the colourful red cabbages are the best for salads, simply because they are the most palatable raw. (For ornamental cabbages and kales, see p. 29.)

SOIL AND SITE

Cabbages require fertile, well-drained, slightly acid soil, though if clubroot is endemic, it should be limed to bring the pH to marginally alkaline. Cabbages have high nitrogen requirements, and are a good crop to follow a nitrogen-fixing green manure. They are among the many brassicas (in the *Cruciferae* family) that should be rotated, ideally over a three-or-four-year cycle, to avoid the build-up of clubroot and brassica cyst eelworm.

SOWING AND PLANTING

The most reliable way of raising cabbages is to sow in modules for transplanting, though traditionally they were sown in seedbeds and transplanted. Plant in their permanent positions when quite small, at the three-or-four-leaf stage, planting firmly with the lower leaves just above the soil. Always plant into firm ground, never into freshly manured soil. It is often sufficient just to clear or rake the ground prior to planting, without digging. Otherwise fork the soil several weeks in advance, leaving it to settle before planting. In very light soil or windy, exposed gardens, plant in shallow furrows about 10cm/4in deep, filling in the soil as the plants grow. Secondary roots develop on the buried stem, increasing the plant's stability. Large plants may need staking during the winter months.

Space cabbages from 30–45cm/12–18in apart, depending on the type and the size of head required. As a general rule, the wider the spacing, the larger the head will be. As cabbages are slow-growing and relatively widely spaced, they lend themselves to intercropping.

Cabbages need plenty of moisture throughout their growth. In the absence of rain, water weekly at the rate of 9–14 litres per sq. m/2–3 gallons per sq. yd. Failing this, aim to give them at least one very heavy watering two or three weeks before harvesting. If growth seems slow mid-season, apply a liquid feed.

SOWING PROGRAMME

For appropriate varieties, see p. 28.

For spring and early summer supplies In areas where winter temperatures rarely fall below about –6°C/20°F, sow in late summer, by any method, transplanting seedlings into their permanent positions in early autumn. Space plants 30cm/12in apart for headed cabbages. For unhearted spring greens, space them initially 10cm/4in apart in rows 30cm/12in apart; harvest the majority young, leaving one plant in three to heart up. Pull soil around the stems in winter as added protection, and cover the plants with cloches or fleece in very cold weather. Once the soil has warmed up in spring, growth can be stimulated with an organic feed. To follow this early crop, sow in seedtrays or modules in autumn, overwintering the seedlings under cover. Plant as early in spring as soil conditions allow.

For summer and autumn supplies Make the first sowings in gentle heat, at about 13°C/55°F in late winter/early spring, planting out after hardening off as soon as soil conditions allow. (In my area of low rainfall, I find late winter sowings far better than spring sowings for the main red cabbage crop in summer. Seedlings are overwintered in a cold frame and planted out as early as soil conditions allow in spring.) Continue sowing in late spring, initially under cover then in the open. Space summer cabbage 35–45cm/14–18in apart, depending on the size of head required. Older varieties of summer cabbages tended to bolt rapidly when mature but improved varieties, such as F1 hybrids 'Minicole' and 'Stonehead', stand in good condition for up to three months. Plant autumn cabbage by mid-summer; space them 50cm/20in apart.

'Mini' cabbage These are tiny cabbages with no wasted outer leaves, produced by growing plants very close together. They are exceptionally tender in salads. Only certain varieties are suitable. Sow from early to late spring, *in situ* or in modules, thinning or planting to 12cm/5in apart. Harvest heads about twenty weeks after sowing.

For winter storage supplies These are mainly Dutch Winter White cabbages, though you can also store late varieties of red cabbage. Sow in mid-spring, planting in early summer 50cm/20in apart. Use heads fresh in early winter, but lift them before heavy frost, pulling them up by the roots or cutting with 5–7cm/2–3in of stalk attached to use as a handle. Store them hung in a frost-free shed or cellar, or in cold frames, raised off the ground on wooden slats and covered with straw. Ventilate the frames on warm days. Cabbages can also be stored in heaps on a cellar floor, on a bed of straw with straw between the heads. Inspect stored heads regularly, and gently roll off any rotting outer leaves. They will often keep for three or more months.

For fresh winter supplies These are the hardiest cabbages, surviving outdoors where temperatures normally remain above about –10°C/14°F. The well-flavoured, crêpe-leaved savoys are the backbone of the hardy cabbages; more recently introduced cabbages are crossed with Winter White types. Watch out for pink-tinged varieties like 'Colorsa', which make a beautifully flavoured and coloured winter salad. Sow in late spring, planting by mid-summer 50cm/20in apart each way. Some will stand until the following spring, helping to fill the 'vegetable gap'.

CUT-AND-COME-AGAIN CABBAGE

Cabbages will often resprout after the main head is cut, producing a very useful crop of smaller secondary heads later in the season.

TYPES OF CABBAGE

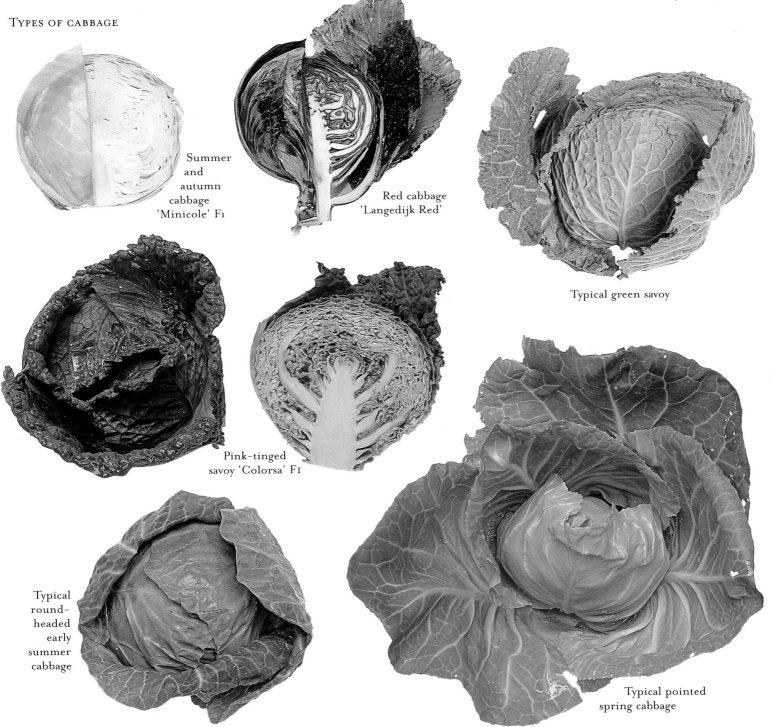

Summer and autumn cabbage 'Minicole' F1

Red cabbage 'Langedijk Red'

Typical green savoy

Pink-tinged savoy 'Colorsa' F1

Typical round-headed early summer cabbage

Typical pointed spring cabbage

VARIETIES

I have chosen these primarily for suitability for salads.

Spring supplies 'Avoncrest', 'Duncan' FI, 'Spring Hero'.

Early summer supplies As above; 'Ruby Ball' FI (red).

Summer supplies 'Hispi' FI, 'Minicole' FI, 'Spivoy' FI (summer savoy), 'Stonehead' FI, 'Winningstadt'.

Autumn supplies 'Rapier' FI, 'Minicole' FI, 'Stonehead' FI, 'Ruby Ball' FI (red) 'Primero' FI (red).

Mini cabbage 'Elisa' FI, 'Puma' FI, 'Protovoy' FI (savoy), 'Primero' FI (red).

Winter storage Dutch Winter White 'Hidena' FI, 'Langedijker 4', 'Polinius' FI.

Winter hardy 'January King Hardy Late Stock 3'; savoy x Dutch White hybrids: 'Celtic' FI, 'Tundra' FI; savoys: 'Colorsa' FI, 'Rigoletto' FI, 'Cappricio' FI.

PESTS

Unless otherwise stated, for protective measures and control, see p. 125.

Birds Attack seedlings and mature plants, especially in winter.

Slugs and snails Potentially serious at any stage, but most damaging on seedlings and young plants in wet weather.

Cabbage root fly Often a serious pest. Small white maggots attack the roots, causing plants to wilt and die. When planting, take measures to prevent the adult flies from laying eggs near by.

Flea beetle Tiny blue-black beetles nibble holes in seedling leaves of all brassicas; *in situ* sowings are the most vulnerable.

Caterpillars Attacks are most damaging in late summer.

Aphids Grey mealy aphids appear on the undersides of leaves in late summer and can be very destructive. Colonies of whitefly, which flutter up from plants in summer, are normally less serious. As aphids overwinter in brassica stumps, and emerge in late spring, old plants should be pulled out and burnt after cropping.

DISEASES

Clubroot This serious soil-borne disease manifests itself as solid swollen galls on roots of the brassica family. Plants eventually wilt and die. Practical measures to reduce clubroot are improving drainage and liming acid soils to a neutral or slightly alkaline level,

and rotation. Remember that swedes, turnips and radishes are also brassicas. In badly infected soils grow only fast-growing brassicas such as Texel greens and oriental cut-and-come-again seedlings. Or give plants a head start on the disease by sowing in modules and potting into 10cm/4in pots before planting out. Watch out for new remedies and resistant varieties.

Damping off diseases Seedlings are vulnerable when sown in adverse conditions.

Kale (Borecole) *Brassica oleracea* Acephala Group

I used to think kales were too harsh for anything but the most sparing use in salads. I've changed my mind, for several reasons. First, I realized how tender some of the thinner-leaved kales can be, such as 'Hungry Gap', 'Pentland Brig' and 'Red Russian'. (The latter has very pretty, blue-green leaves brushed with purple.) Then I discovered two exceptionally beautiful crisp-leaved kales: the old Italian Tuscan kale, also known as *cavolo nero*, black kale, palm cabbage and dinosaur kale, with its flavoursome, narrow, crêped blue leaves, and the newer 'Redbor' and 'Red Garna' varieties of curly kale, as hardy as the old forms but with striking, deeply curled bronze-red leaves. And I realized how productive and appealing these, and the traditional curly kales, are when grown as cut-and-come-again seedlings. Indeed, baby-leaved 'Redbor' and 'Red Russian' are popular ingredients in prepacked salads.

Seedling kales can be sown throughout the growing season, but come into their own in the colder months when salading is most scarce. Two or three cuts of small leaves can generally be made from one sowing. Mix them with other salad leaves, or use them on their own, accentuating their flavours with a strong dressing such as the Glorious Garnish dressing on p. 152.

Cultivation These rugged kales often succeed where other brassicas fail. They need well-drained, reasonably fertile soil, but are otherwise undemanding. They have some tolerance to clubroot. For mature plants, cultivate as for summer cabbage, sowing in late spring and early summer (see p. 26). Varieties mentioned below are as hardy as savoy cabbages. Mature leaves and the shoots that develop in spring are used as cooked vegetables from autumn to spring, but small leaves could be picked for salads.

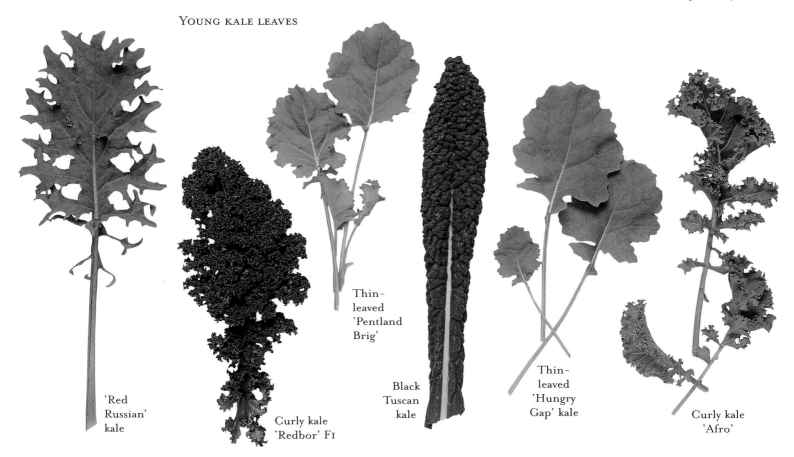

YOUNG KALE LEAVES

'Red Russian' kale

Curly kale 'Redbor' FI

Thin-leaved 'Pentland Brig'

Black Tuscan kale

Thin-leaved 'Hungry Gap' kale

Curly kale 'Afro'

For cut-and-come-again seedling crops, start sowing under cover in late winter; continue sowing outdoors from mid-spring to late summer (or later in mild areas). Make the last sowings under cover in early autumn. Kales are relatively slow-growing, but, depending on the variety and time of year, the first cutting of small leaves can be made any time from about six weeks after sowing.

Varieties These varieties can be grown as large plants, but are also recommended for cut-and-come-again seedlings. Others may be suitable, but I have not tried them. Black kale; curly kale, green: dwarf green curled 'Afro'; 'Shobor' FI, 'Starbor' FI; curly kale, red: 'Redbor' FI, 'Garna Red' FI; thin-leaved 'Hungry Gap', 'Pentland Brig', 'Red Russian' and 'Ragged Jack'. ('Ragged Jack' is similar to 'Red Russian' in appearance and texture, but may be less hardy.)

Ornamental cabbages and kales

These loose-headed cabbages and kales are notable for their wonderful colouring: the blue-green leaves are tinged with varying combinations of red, white, cream, purple and yellow. The leaves are also decorative shapes – deeply serrated, frilled or waved – sometimes packed into rosette heads in rings of contrasting colours. They are ideal plants for the decorative potager. They are at their best late in the year, as the colours deepen when night temperatures fall to about 10°C/50°F. There are dwarf, intermediate and tall forms, ranging from 30 to 60cm/12 to 24in tall. Seed catalogues rarely distinguish between cabbages and kales, but those with flat heads and relatively smooth leaves are generally cabbages, while the deeply serrated, coarser-leaved types are kales. The significant difference is that the kales are hardier. While all tolerate light frosts, in my experience the hardiest kales withstand temperatures of about –10°C/14°F, which would destroy the cabbages.

Ornamental cabbages and kales are mainly used in salads as a decorative garnish. Small leaves can be eaten whole and larger leaves shredded. Blanching briefly in hot water makes them more tender.

Soil and site Soil must be well drained and moisture-retentive, but these ornamental forms tolerate poorer soil than most brassicas. In rich soil they may become lush and fail to colour well. They like an open situation, but can be protected, or grown under cover, in winter in cold climates. Dwarf types can be grown as winter houseplants in cool conservatories.

For top-quality plants, sow in modules or seed trays, eventually potting into 8–10cm/3½–4in pots before planting out. Make the main sowings in late spring or early summer; modern varieties take only three months to mature. Space plants 30–40cm/12–16in apart, depending on variety, planting firmly at the five-to-seven-leaf stage, with the lower leaves just above soil level. For a late crop under cover, pot on into 15cm/6in pots and plant in early autumn. For winter container plants, pot dwarf varieties into 15cm/6in pots; or plant two or three closely into a 35cm/14in pot in good potting compost.

For pests, see Cabbages, p. 28. Caterpillars tend to be the worst pest (for control, see p. 126).

Harvesting Unless using a whole head for decoration, pick individual leaves just before use, as they wilt rapidly. Plants resprout over many months, sometimes lasting two seasons, with small secondary leaves developing on the stems. To perpetuate good varieties, cuttings can be made from young shoots.

Varieties Reliable F1 hybrids: round-leaved 'Osaka' series, 'Pink Beauty', 'White Christmas'; frilled types: 'Chidori' and 'Wave' series; serrated types (the hardiest): 'Feather' and 'Peacock' series.

'White Peacock' ornamental kale

The ornamental cabbages and kales are wonderfully colourful, both in the garden and, mainly as a garnish, in salad dishes.

'White Christmas' ornamental cabbage

'Red Feather' ornamental kale

'Red Chidori' ornamental kale

'Pink Beauty' ornamental cabbage

Oriental brassicas

A whole range of exciting oriental greens have gradually become available to gardeners in the West. Their subtle flavours when raw, crisp texture, lively colours and nutritional qualities make them valuable additions to the salad garden. Many are in their prime in autumn and early winter and, being fast growing, lend themselves to cut-and-come-again techniques.

A major hurdle with oriental brassicas is their confusing names. Not only are plants known by several names, but the same names are used for different plants. Then, to overcome the difficulties in pronouncing the original names, misleading Westernized names have been adopted. 'Pak choi', for example, is often called 'celery mustard' – yet it is neither celery nor mustard. I try to use the most sensible, or currently acceptable, name for each plant.

After writing the first edition of *The Salad Garden* in the 1980s, I spent several years experimenting with oriental vegetables, in particular the brassicas, trying to sort out the different types (see my book *Oriental Vegetables*). They are all superb cooked vegetables, but the most suitable for salads can be divided into the three groups below – all excellent with Chinese salad dressings (see pp. 149–50).

Mild-flavoured brassicas This includes Chinese cabbage, most types of pak choi, the komatsuna group and interspecific hybrids such as 'Senposai'.

The mustards The mustard group ranges from the mildly piquant mizuna and mibuna greens, to truly hot-flavoured mustards such as 'Green in the Snow', pickling mustards and red-leaved mustards.

The flowering brassicas Like Western broccoli, these are grown mainly for the young flowering shoots. They include edible rapes, flowering forms of pak choi and choy sum, such as purple-stemmed 'Hon Tsai Tai', and Chinese broccoli (also known as Chinese kale).

General cultivation

The oriental brassicas are in the main cool-season crops, ideally suited to summer and early winter cultivation in temperate climates, though there are varieties for warmer and tropical climates. They generally make excellent winter crops under cover. Some of the mustards are very hardy.

Oriental brassicas must be grown in fertile soil that is rich in organic matter, with plenty of moisture throughout growth. It is just not worth growing them in poor dry soils. Ideally soil should be neutral or slightly alkaline, as clubroot can be a problem (see p. 28). Soil fertility apart, a key factor in growing oriental brassicas is overcoming a tendency to bolt prematurely. This is caused by various interlocking factors, such as day length and low temperatures in the early stages of growth, and can be exacerbated by transplanting. The problem scarcely arises with cut-and-come-again seedlings, as they are harvested young. However, when growing plants to maturity, the safest bet is to delay sowing until early summer – that is, after the longest day – and to protect plants if a sharp temperature drop is expected. Some varieties are more bolt-resistant than others. Late sowing means that oriental greens, which are fast-growing, can follow early harvests of potatoes, peas, beans or salads, making full use of garden space.

On the whole, oriental brassicas do not transplant well, so sow them either *in situ* or in modules. They tend to have shallow roots, so, unlike other brassicas, need to be watered frequently, but moderately, especially when nearing maturity. Mulching, with organic materials or plastic films, seems to be beneficial for these greens. Unless the soil is exceptionally fertile, growth can be boosted with liquid feeds during the growing season. Oriental brassicas are subject to the same pests and diseases as Western brassicas (see p. 28). Caterpillars and slugs cause the most trouble (for protection, see p. 126). Growing under fine nets is highly recommended.

Mild-flavoured brassicas

These are notable for their rapid growth, which makes them excellent subjects for cut-and-come-again treatment, as seedlings and at semi-mature and mature stages.

Chinese cabbage *Brassica rapa* Pekinensis group

Popularly known as Chinese leaves, the hearted types of Chinese cabbage (known as Napa cabbage in the USA) form a barrel-shaped, rounded or tall cylindrical head of closely folded leaves, usually

CHINESE CABBAGE AND PAK CHOI

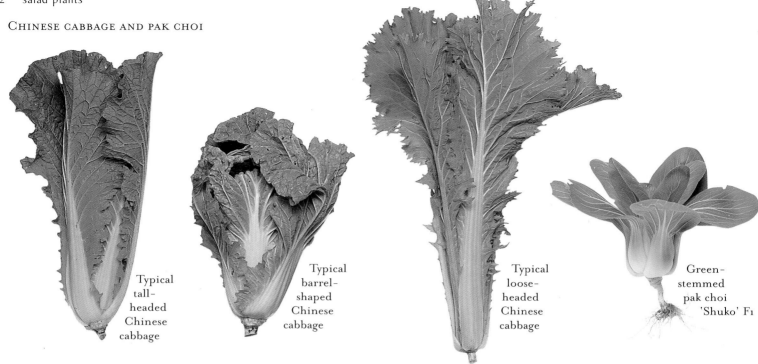

Typical tall-headed Chinese cabbage

Typical barrel-shaped Chinese cabbage

Typical loose-headed Chinese cabbage

Green-stemmed pak choi 'Shuko' F1

creamy to light green in colour, with a crinkled texture, prominent white veining and white midribs broadening out at the base. The tall cylindrical types are generally later and slower-maturing.

'Loose- or semi-headed' types are a distinct group that do not form hearts, used mainly as cut-and-come-again crops at the seedling and semi-mature stages. Varieties dubbed 'fluffy tops' have beautiful butter-coloured centres of crêpe-like leaves, ideal for salad use. All Chinese cabbages are crisp-textured with a delicate flavour.

They grow best at temperatures of 13–20°C/55–68°F. They tolerate light frost in the open, but with cut-and-come-again treatment plants remain productive under cover in the winter months. They have survived –10°C/14°F in my polytunnel. They are amongst the fastest growing of all leafy vegetables. In good conditions mature heads can be cut ten weeks after sowing, loose-headed types two to three weeks sooner, and seedlings four to five weeks after sowing. Chinese cabbage is a very thirsty crop: a single plant may need as much as 22 litres/5 gallons of water during its growing period. Harvested Chinese cabbage heads will keep for several weeks in a fridge, frost-free cellar or shed.

For the main late summer and autumn supplies Sow early to late summer. Space plants about 30cm/12in apart.

For an earlier summer crop Try sowing in late spring in a propagator, using bolt-resistant varieties; maintain a minimum temperature of 18°C/64°F for the first three weeks after germination. Protect plants with cloches or crop covers after planting.

For an autumn/early winter crop Sow in late summer, transplanting under cover in early autumn. The plants may not have time to develop full heads. Plant either at standard spacing or about 13cm/5in apart – in which case cut the immature leaves when 8–10cm/3–4in high. Do not overcrowd autumn plants, as the leaves tend to rot in damp weather. Cut hearted plants 2.5cm/1in above the base and allow them to resprout during the winter. In spring let remaining plants run to seed: the colourful flowering shoots make a tender salad and are colourful too.

For cut-and-come-again seedling supplies Use only loose-headed varieties, as hearting types often have rough hairy leaves at the seedling stage. Make the first sowings under cover in spring. Follow with outdoor sowings as soon as the soil is workable, giving protection if necessary. Continue outdoor sowings until late summer, and make final sowings under cover in early autumn.

Cut seedlings as soon as they reach a usable size, leaving the stems to resprout unless they have started to bolt.

Varieties Barrel types with reasonable bolting resistance: 'Tip Top' FI, 'Nagaoka 50 Days' FI, 'Kasumi' FI; tall cylindrical types: 'Jade Pagoda' FI, 'Green Tower' FI; loose-headed: 'Minato Santo'/'Santo'; 'Ruffles'/'Eskimo' (fluffy-top type).

Pak choi (Celery mustard) *Brassica rapa* Chinensis Group

The typical pak choi has smooth, shiny, somewhat rounded leaves, pale or dark green in colour. The pronounced midribs merge into stems that swell out at the base into a characteristic, almost bulb-like butt. They are normally white-stemmed, but some varieties are a beautiful light green. The many types range from small stocky varieties 8–10cm/3–4in high, to medium 15cm/6in-high varieties, to tall forms up to 45cm/18in high. (See also Rosette pak choi below.) Varieties differ in their tolerance to heat and cold, but most only stand light frost. Like Chinese cabbage, they are excellent winter crops under cover (see p. 32). All parts, from seedling leaves to the flowering stems, are edible raw or cooked. Pak choi has a delightful fresh flavour and succulent texture.

Pak choi is closely related to Chinese cabbage and grown in the same way (see p. 32). For the headed crop, use slow-bolting varieties for the earliest sowings. Space small and squat varieties 13–15cm/5–6in apart, medium-sized varieties 18–23cm/7–9in apart and large types up to 45cm/18in apart. Small heads are sometimes ready within six weeks of sowing. Leaves can be picked individually or the whole head cut, leaving the stump to resprout.

Cut-and-come-again seedling crops can be very productive. Depending on the season, the first cut of small leaves may be made within three weeks of sowing; it is sometimes possible to make two or three successive cuts.

Varieties White-stemmed: 'Joi Choi' FI (large); 'Canton Dwarf' (for tiny, closely spaced heads); small green-stemmed: 'Chingensai', 'Choko' FI (slow bolting, for summer), 'Mei Choi' FI, 'Riko' FI, 'Shuko' FI.

Rosette pak choi (Ta tsoi/Tah tsai and similarly spelt names) *Brassica rapa* var. *rosularis*

This unique form has crinkled, rounded, blue-green leaves, which, although upright initially, in cool weather develop into a flat, extraordinarily symmetrical rosette head. It is hardier than other pak chois, and in well-drained soil may survive –10°C/14°F. This makes it a favourite in my winter potager. Its pronounced flavour is highly rated by the Chinese; the leaves are very decorative in salads.

Grow it as single plants or cut-and-come-again seedlings. It is slower-growing and somewhat less vigorous than other pak chois and prone to bolting from early sowings, so it is best to sow it from mid- to late summer. Like Chinese cabbage and pak choi, it can be transplanted under cover for an excellent-quality winter crop. Adjust spacing according to the size of the plant required: 15cm/6in apart for small, unrosetted heads; 30–40cm/12–16in apart, depending on variety, for large plants. Pick individual leaves as required, or cut across the head, encouraging it to resprout.

Varieties Improved varieties 'Ryokusai' FI, 'Yukina Savoy'.

Komatsuna (Mustard spinach) *Brassica rapa* Perviridis Group

This diverse group of robust greens originated by crossing various brassicas. Most have large, glossy leaves. They tolerate a wide range of climates, some being very hardy. They are less prone to bolting, pests and diseases than many oriental brassicas and, being vigorous, respond well to cut-and-come-again treatment at any stage. Large

Mature rosette pak choi 'Yukina Savoy'

mature leaves can be used shredded in salads, but leaves from small plants and cut-and-come-again seedling leaves are more suitable. Depending on variety, the flavour has hints of cabbage, spinach and mustard. They are said to be very nutritious.

For general cultivation, see Chinese cabbage, p. 32. Sow outdoors from early to late summer, spacing plants 10cm/4in apart for harvesting young, or 30–35cm/12–14in apart, depending on variety, for large plants. For cut-and-come-again seedlings, start sowing in mid- to late winter under cover for a very early crop; sow outdoors from early spring to late summer, making a final sowing under cover in early autumn for a high-quality winter crop.

Varieties 'Green Boy' F1, 'Tendergreen', 'Torason' F1.

Interspecific hybrids

The variety 'Senposai' is an 'interspecific' hybrid between komatsuna and cabbage, with a marked cabbage flavour, bred in Japan and widely used for seed sprouting. I have found it a useful cut-and-come-again seedling crop for late summer in the open and winter under cover. Other hybrids may be developed in future.

THE MUSTARDS

Mizuna (Kyona, Potherb mustard)
Brassica rapa var. *nipposinica*

This beautiful Japanese brassica has glossy, serrated, dark green leaves, often 25cm/10in long. Mature plants can form bushy clumps well over 30cm/12in wide. It is an excellent plant for edging or infilling decorative potagers, and for various forms of intercropping. Mizuna tolerates high and low temperatures: if kept cropped it will survive about –10°C/14°F in the open. With its natural vigour and healthiness it responds exceptionally well to cut-and-come-again techniques at every stage, and can remain productive over many months. The leaves have a mild mustard flavour. Mature and seedling leaves can be used in salads, the latter being daintier and more decorative. Cultivate mizuna as komatsuna above. Sowings in hot weather are susceptible to flea beetle attacks. Less serrated, hardier hybrid varieties such as 'Tokyo Beau' and 'Tokyo Belle' have been introduced and are worth growing when available.

Mibuna greens *Brassica rapa* var. *nipposinica*

Mizuna's twin, mibuna, has narrow strap-like leaves 30–45cm/12–18in long, which are less glossy and probably milder-flavoured than mizuna but add an interesting dimension to salads. Mature plants form handsome architectural clumps. It is less productive than mizuna and less hardy – surviving temperatures of about –6°C/21°F in the open. It is a cool-season crop and best value in the late summer/early winter period, in the open or under cover. For cultivation, see Mizuna, above. Currently 'Green Spray' F1 is the only named variety. The flowering shoots of both mibuna and mizuna can be used in salads.

Hot-flavoured mustards *Brassica juncea*

This rugged group of hardy vegetables has rather rough leaves displaying varying degrees of fieriness. They add zing to a salad, but use them sparingly, shredding mature leaves to moderate them. Flavours seem to intensify as the plants run to seed. The flowering stems are edible too – again, approach them cautiously. I recently discovered, through serendipitous nibbling, that both the ordinary and flowering stems of the pickling mustards have a delectable, almost sweet flavour – superb in salads. It may be necessary to peel the outer skin before use.

The mustards are slower-growing than most oriental brassicas. They are mainly sown in mid-summer, *in situ* or in modules; space plants 25–40cm/10–16in apart, depending on variety and the size required. They can be planted under cover in late summer or early autumn for a more tender crop. They can be grown as cut-and-come-again seedlings, though regrowth is not very vigorous; early sowings are very liable to bolt. The following are among the most suitable types and varieties for salads.

Purple-leaved mustards

These are reasonably hardy, with magnificent red-tinged leaves acquiring deeper colours as temperatures lower. They add piquancy and colour to salads. I have seen them grown as seedling crops in summer in the Napa Valley in California, and the leaves cut for salads about 2.5cm/1in diameter.

Varieties 'Osaka Purple' (probably the most refined), 'Red Giant', 'Miike Giant'.

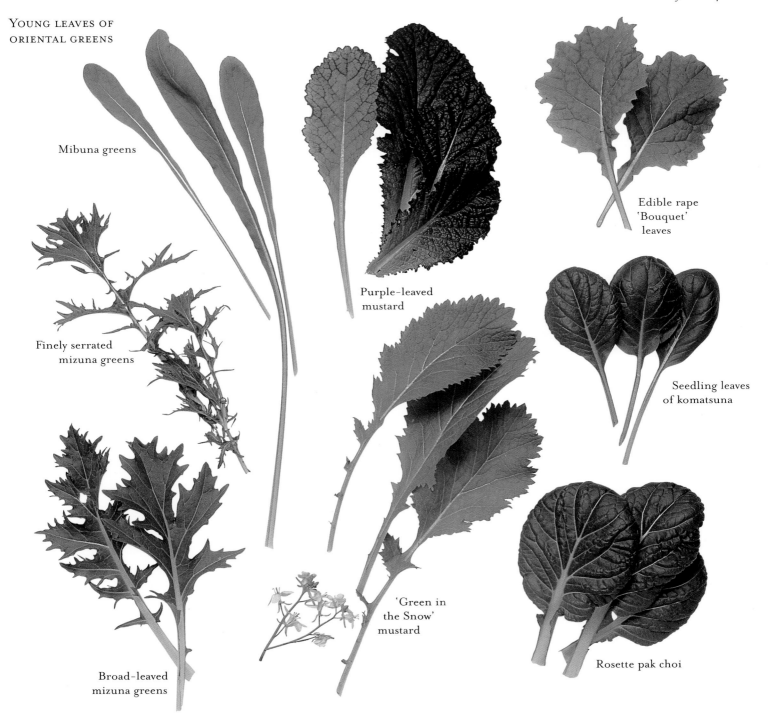

YOUNG LEAVES OF
ORIENTAL GREENS

Mibuna greens

Finely serrated
mizuna greens

Broad-leaved
mizuna greens

Purple-leaved
mustard

'Green in
the Snow'
mustard

Edible rape
'Bouquet'
leaves

Seedling leaves
of komatsuna

Rosette pak choi

'Green in the Snow' (Serifong, Xue li hong and assorted spellings!)

The Chinese name of this serrated-leaved mustard means 'Red in the Snow', indicating how hardy it is. (The leaves are, in fact, green.) It can develop into a large plant, but for salads is best grown as cut-and-come-again seedlings, or spaced 15–20cm/6–8in apart for small plants cut young before the leaves become too hot.

Pickling mustards

There are several Chinese varieties, sometimes with strangely contorted incurved heads and swollen leaf stems and stalks, grown essentially for pickling. It is difficult to grow them to mature perfection, but the leaves and stems have exceptional flavours when used raw in salads. They are not particularly hardy.

Varieties 'Amsoi', 'Wrapped Heart' and 'Big Heart' are typical – but be prepared to experiment with any that become available.

THE FLOWERING BRASSICAS

The flowering shoots of most oriental brassicas can be used raw in salads. Most are pleasantly sweet-flavoured, though mustards have a characteristic hot flavour. Pick shoots from mature plants when in bud. They generally produce a succession of shoots. The following are types grown primarily for flowering stems.

Choy sum (Hon tsai tai)
Brassica rapa var. *parachinensis*

This is sometimes classified as pak choi. There are green- and purple-stemmed forms. Grow as edible rape 'Bouquet' opposite. The old varieties of green types tended to be 'skimpy'. Use bulkier FI hybrids such as 'Autumn Poem' FI where available. The attractive purple-hued 'Hon Tsai Tai' is quite hardy, surviving –5°C/23°F outdoors. Space them up to 38cm/15in apart for large plants.

The purple-stemmed 'Hon Tsai Tai'

The stage at which to pick pak choi flowering shoot

Edible rape 'Bouquet'

Green-stemmed hybrid choy sum

Various oriental brassicas are grown for their tender, colourful flowering shoots

Chinese broccoli

Edible oil seed rape *Brassica rapa* var. *oleifera* and *utilis*

The purpose-bred variety 'Bouquet' F1 has chunky succulent stems with yellow flower buds, and pretty crêpe-textured leaves. It tolerates light frost and does well under cover in winter. Sow from early to late summer, *in situ* or in modules for transplanting, spacing plants 13–20cm/5–8in apart. Cut the shoots when 10cm/4in long.

Chinese broccoli (Chinese kale, Gai laan)
Brassica oleracea var. *algoglabra*

This distinct, thick-stemmed, white-flowered brassica tolerates several degrees of frost. Although it can be grown for much of the growing season, it does best from mid- to late summer sowings. Space plants 10–15cm/4–6in apart for harvesting whole when flowering shoots appear, or 25–38cm/10–15in for large plants, where individual shoots are picked over a longer period. 'Green Lance' F1 is a popular variety.

ORIENTAL SALADINI

Oriental saladini was originally a mixture I created in 1991 with the seed company Suffolk Herbs to introduce Westerners to the wonderful diversity of oriental greens. The mixture included loose-headed Chinese cabbage, pak choi, komatsuna, mibuna, mizuna and purple mustard. The various 'spicy green' mixtures on the market can be used in the same way. Its main use is for cut-and-come-again seedlings for salads or stir-fries, though you can prick out or transplant individual plants and grow them on to maturity. Sow as for Chinese cabbage cut-and-come-again seedling crops, p. 32. Spring and early summer sowings may allow only one cut before the plants start to bolt: the most productive sowings are from mid-summer onwards. Make the last sowings under cover in early to mid-autumn for use in winter and early spring. Patches often seem to 'thin themselves out' after several cuttings, leaving just a few large plants. Oriental saladini can be sown in containers or spent compost bags.

Leaf beet *Beta vulgaris* var. *cicla*

Leaf beets include Swiss chard (or seakale beet) and perpetual spinach (or spinach beet). Both are coarser than spinach and less distinctly flavoured, but seedlings can be used raw in salads.

Perpetual spinach or spinach beet

More like spinach than Swiss chard, this is very adaptable and a source of salad leaves all year round. Cultivate as Swiss chard below.

Swiss chard

These vigorous biennial plants have large, thick, glossy leaves and prominent leaf ribs and stalks, in some varieties luminescent yellow, orange, pink, purple or red. They are superb 'potager' plants. Mature chards require cooking, but retain some colour after cooking so can be mixed into salads cold. Chard is more heat-, cold-, drought- and disease-tolerant than spinach. It is slower-growing but can be grown for much of the year, cropping over many months. For cut-and-come-again seedlings, sow from spring to late summer outdoors – though very early outdoor sowings may bolt prematurely. For winter and

Seedling leaves of 'Bright Lights' chard

spring supplies, sow in early autumn and early spring under cover. The coloured-stemmed seedlings are the most appealing in salads. 'Red', 'Ruby' or 'Rhubarb' are older varieties. The 'Bright Lights'/'Rainbow' mixtures have variously coloured stems. 'Feurio' and 'Charlotte' are improved red-stemmed varieties.

Spinach *Spinacea oleracea*

My conventional English upbringing never led me to suspect that spinach could be a salad vegetable. It took a visit to the USA, where it has long been used in salads, for me to realize its merits and it has been a favourite ever since. To satisfy today's huge demand for 'baby leaf' spinach in prepacked salads, plant breeders are continually introducing improved hybrid varieties, whose good disease resistance and upright habit make for healthy plants.

Spinach has a unique flavour – 'spinachy' is the only word to describe it. The most popular varieties are round-leaved, though some older varieties and Asiatic spinach are pointed. Texture varies from thin smooth-leaved types to those with thicker, puckered leaves, which are more robust, less easily bruised and bulkier, so predominate in the salad packs found in supermarkets.

Mature spinach can be used in salads, though leaves may need to be torn or shredded to make them a manageable size. On the whole it makes far more sense, in terms of space, time and an end product 'just right' for salads, to grow spinach as a cut-and-come-again seedling crop.

CULTIVATION

Spinach is an annual, cool-season crop, with a natural tendency to

Thick-leaved spinach grown as cut-and-come-again seedlings

run to seed in the lengthening days of late spring and early summer, and at high temperatures. It grows best in early spring and late summer. Mid-summer sowings of traditional varieties were often unproductive. The hardier varieties survive light to moderate frosts in the open, but will be of far better quality if grown under cover in winter. The secret of a year-round supply in temperate climates is to sow appropriate varieties for the season.

Spinach needs fertile, well-drained, moisture-retentive soil that is rich in organic matter. Summer crops can be grown in light shade, provided there is adequate moisture. It is advisable to rotate spinach around the garden, as the resting spores of downy mildew, a scourge of spinach with no organic remedy, remain in the soil.

On account of its tendency to run to seed rapidly, spinach is usually sown *in situ*, but it can be sown in modules and transplanted. For single plants sow in drills 27–30cm/11–12in apart, thinning to 15cm/6in apart. Depending on the season, these plants may respond well to cut-and-come-again treatment. For cut-and-come-again seedling crops, make successive sowings at roughly three-to-four-week intervals (but see the sowing programme below). Bear in mind that very early sowings, or sowings in hot spells, run the risk of premature bolting. You can normally make the first cuts within thirty or forty days of sowing: two or three subsequent cuts are often possible. Seedlings can be thinned to 7.5–10cm/3–4in apart and grown as small plants.

SOWING PROGRAMME

For summer supplies Sow from late spring to early summer, using slow-growing, long-day varieties with good bolting resistance such as 'Medania' F1, 'Tetona' F1 and 'Bloomsdale' (all thick-leaved). **For autumn, winter and early spring supplies** Sow from mid- to late summer outside, and early to mid-autumn under cover. The late sowings may stop growing in mid-winter, but will start again in early spring. You can also sow under cover in early spring if soil conditions are suitable. For all these sowings, use faster-growing short-day varieties such as 'Galaxy' F1 and 'Giant Winter' (both thick-leaved).

Mild-flavoured leaves

These are easily grown, undemanding salad plants, with relatively mild flavours. Look on them as supplying the 'gentle notes' in a salad, softening the 'discords' of sharp flavours (see p. 138). They are listed here alphabetically according to their Latin names.

Leaf amaranth (Calaloo, Chinese spinach)
Amaranthus spp.

These highly nutritious, spinach-like plants are normally cooked, but the young leaves are surprisingly tasty in salads. Amaranths need a temperature of 20–25°C/68–77°F to flourish outdoors, and will not stand any frost. For salads, sow *in situ* from spring to summer, under cover or outside, provided the soil is above 20°C/68°F and there is no danger of frost. Grow it either as cut-and-come-again seedlings or space plants 10–15cm/4–6in apart and harvest the young leaves. The blotched red- and green-leaved forms are very productive and the most colourful in salads, but the pale, so-called 'white-leaved' varieties have a tender, buttery flavour.

Orache (Mountain spinach) *Atriplex hortensis*

Orache is a handsome annual plant, growing up to 2m/6ft high. Green- and red-leaved forms are the most widely grown, sometimes available as mixtures. So-called 'red' strains range from muddy brown to pure scarlet, so if you have a nicely coloured one, save your own seed! Use only young orache leaves in salads; they have a faint spinach flavour and almost downy texture. Either pick leaves from young plants, or grow cut-and-come-again seedlings.

For plants, sow *in situ* in spring and early summer, thinning to 20cm/8in apart. Plants grow rapidly, so keep them bushy and tender by regularly picking the topmost tuft of leaves. Even so, they eventually 'get away' from you! Leave a few of the best to self-seed. Bountiful seedlings appear early the following year. Alternatively, to grow as cut-and-come-again seedlings, make continuous sowings from late spring under cover, followed by outdoor sowings until late summer, with a final sowing under cover in early autumn. Summer sowings may bolt prematurely, but late sowings under cover may remain in usable condition for much of the winter.

Texel (Texsel) greens *Brassica carinata*

This brassica was developed in the late twentieth century from an Ethiopian mustard. Its small glossy leaves have a distinct, clean flavour with a delightful hint of spinach in them. It is very nutritious and rich in vitamin C. It is reasonably hardy (plants have survived –7°C/25°F in my garden) and very fast-growing. For this reason it is often grown where clubroot disease is a problem: it can be harvested

Red-leaved amaranth

'White-leaved' amaranth

before becoming seriously infected. It is useful for intercropping. Texel is appreciated as cooked greens in the Indian community, the plants being harvested when 25–30cm/10–12in high. At this stage the smaller leaves and young stems can be eaten raw in salads. Palatable leaves can even be picked from the flower stems. However, small seedling leaves are, in my view, the best-flavoured. (Ironically, it is sometimes grown 1.5m/5ft high as game cover!)

Texel may bolt prematurely in hot and dry conditions, and it grows best, and is best value, in the cooler, autumn-to-spring period. It is usually sown *in situ*. Make early cut-and-come-again seedling sowings under cover in late winter/early spring; continue sowing outdoors in late spring and early summer; avoid mid-summer sowings, but start sowing again outdoors in late summer/early autumn, with final sowings under cover in mid-autumn. You can sometimes make the first cut of seedling leaves within two to three weeks of sowing, with a second cut a few weeks later; occasionally these leaves are bitter.

Research has shown that small plants produce the highest yields when sown in rows 30cm/12in apart, thinned to 2.5cm/1in apart, or in rows 15cm/6in, thinned to 5cm/2in apart. In clubroot-infested soils, you can make successive sowings if you pull up plants by the roots when harvesting, leaving a three-week gap before the next sowing. Texel is generally a healthy crop, but flea beetle (see p. 28) may attack in the early stages. Growing under fine-mesh horticultural nets is a solution.

'Magentaspreen' tree spinach

Salad rape *Brassica napus*

Salad rape is often used as a mustard substitute in 'mustard and cress' packs; it has a milder flavour with a hint of cabbage in it. It is a very useful garden cut-and-come-again seedling crop, being much slower to run to seed than mustard or cress. I have had spring-sown patches that remained productive for four months. Moreover it does not become unpleasantly hot when mature. It germinates at low temperatures and in my experience survives –10°C/14°F. Seed can be sprouted and grown in shallow containers.

In temperate climates, sow as cut-and-come-again seedlings outdoors throughout the growing season. For exceptionally useful winter-to-spring supplies, sow under cover in late autumn and early winter, and again in late winter and early spring. Cut-and-come-again seedlings may give three, even four successive cuts. If left uncut, salad rape grows to about 60cm/24in high. At this stage the small leaves on the stems are still tender enough to use in salads. It grows very fast, so if you want it with cress, sow it three days later. Salad rape has one failing: it is very attractive to slugs (for control, see p. 126). I have even considered sowing strips as slug decoys!

Tree spinach *Chenopodium giganteum* 'Magentaspreen'

This handsome relative of fat hen or lamb's quarters (*Chenopodium album*) grows rapidly to at least 1.8m/6ft high. The tips of many leaves and the leaf undersides are a beautiful magenta pink, as are the flowering spikes. The leaves have a floury texture and a flavour reminiscent of raw peas. Only use young leaves in salads. Either grow it as cut-and-come-again seedlings, sowing throughout the growing season; or sow it in spring and early summer, *in situ* or in modules, spacing plants about 25cm/10in apart – in which case pick the young leaves for salads. It self-seeds prolifically, with abundant seedlings appearing early the following spring – ready for use in salads. It can become invasive, but it is a genial, easily uprooted invader, deserving a place (at the back) of any potager border.

Alfalfa (Lucerne, Purple medick) *Medicago sativa*

Alfalfa is a hardy semi-evergreen perennial in the clover family, with attractive blue and violet flowers. Mature plants can grow up to

90cm/36in high, becoming quite bushy. It is deep-rooting, so withstands dry conditions well. As both foliage and flowers are decorative, it is sometimes grown as a low hedge, dividing the garden into sections. The clover-like young leaves, which have a distinct, pleasant flavour, are used in salads. The seeds can be sprouted, and it is also grown as a green manure.

Grow it either as a perennial or as cut-and-come-again seedlings (use seed sold for sprouting). For perennial plants, sow *in situ* in spring or late summer to autumn, thinning to 25cm/10in apart, or alternatively sow in modules and transplant. Pick the young shoots for salads. Cut the plants back hard after flowering to renew their vigour. After three or four years, it is best to replace them; otherwise they become very straggly. For cut-and-come-again seedlings, sow in spring and early summer, and again in late summer and early autumn. For an extra tender crop, make the earliest and latest sowings under cover. You can make pickings throughout the growing season, but the leaf texture becomes tougher as the plants mature.

Winter purslane (Claytonia) *Montia perfoliata* (previously *Claytonia perfoliata*)

A native of North America, where it is known as miner's lettuce and spring beauty, this dainty hardy annual is an invaluable spring salad plant. Its early leaves are heart-shaped, but the mature leaves, borne on longer stalks, are rounded and wrapped around the flower stem as if pierced by it. Leaves, young stems and the pretty white flowers are all edible. They are refreshingly succulent, if slightly bland, which may be why children seem to like them. Avoid the pink-flowered 'pink purslane' (*Montia sibirica*): its leaves have an acrid aftertaste.

Winter purslane flourishes in light, sandy soils but, provided drainage is good, adapts to most conditions, including quite poor, dry soils. It is reasonably hardy outdoors in well-drained soil, but its winter quality is vastly improved with protection. Grow it as a cut-and-come-again seedling crop or – probably the most productive method – as single plants.

It can be grown for much of the year, but it is best value, and grows best, in late autumn and early spring. Crops under cover stop growing in mid-winter, but burst into renewed growth early in the year. The seeds are tiny, so sow shallowly, *in situ* or in modules for transplanting, spacing plants about 15cm/6in apart. For summer supplies, sow in early to late spring. For autumn and early-winter-to-spring supplies, sow in summer, planting the later sowings under cover, unless you are sowing *in situ*. Pick leaves from mature plants as required, or cut the whole head an inch above ground: it will resprout vigorously before eventually running to seed in late spring. Cut-and-come-again crops give at least two cuts.

Once established, winter purslane self-seeds prolifically, carpeting the ground with seedlings in autumn and spring. They are shallow-rooted, but can be carefully transplanted, perhaps under cover in autumn. If it becomes invasive, dig it in as a green manure in spring.

Iceplant *Mesembryanthemum crystallinum*

Iceplant is an attractive, sprawling plant with thick, fleshy leaves and stems covered with tiny bladders that sparkle in the sun like crystals. It grows wild on South African and Mediterranean shores. In hot climates it is perennial, and is cultivated as a substitute for spinach in summer. I feel it is far better raw in salads – if only for its unusual appearance. Leaves and sliced stems have a crunchy succulence (not to everyone's taste!) and an intriguing, albeit variable, salty flavour. It grows best in fertile soil, but tolerates poorer, but well-drained, soil. Although it is a sun-lover, in mid-summer it can be grown undercropping sweet corn. It makes an attractive ground-cover plant in a potager, and, with its trailing habit, looks effective in pots or hanging baskets.

Iceplant is not frost hardy, so make the first sowings in modules or seed trays under cover and plant out, initially with protection if necessary, when all danger of frost is past. Space plants 30cm/12in apart, and protect against slugs in the early stages (see p. 126). In warm climates, sow *in situ* outdoors in late spring or early summer. You can take stem cuttings in early summer (they root quite quickly) to provide a follow-on crop, which you can plant under cover in late summer.

You can normally pick individual leaves or small 'branches' of leaves and stems a month or so after planting. Keep picking regularly, to prevent plants from running to seed and getting coarse, and to encourage further shoots. Surprisingly, mature plants tolerate light frost and, if given protection, continue growing well into autumn, though the quality is slightly impaired.

Summer purslane *Portulaca oleracea*

Forms of purslane (not to be confused with winter purslane, which is a different plant) grow wild throughout the temperate world and have been cultivated for centuries. It is a low-growing half-hardy plant with succulent rounded leaves and slender but juicy stems. There are green and yellow forms. The green are more vigorous, thinner-leaved and, some say, better-flavoured; the yellow or 'golden' form has thicker, shinier leaves, and is more sprawling, but is very decorative in salads. The leaves and stems are edible raw and have a refreshing, crunchy texture but a rather bland flavour. In the past all parts were pickled for winter use. It is a pretty plant and a favourite in the summer potager: I love to make striped patterns with alternating rows of the two colours. They are productive for many weeks in summer, looking good throughout.

Purslane does best on light, sandy soil but succeeds on heavier soils if they are well drained. It grows profusely in warm climates, but in cooler conditions choose a sheltered, sunny site or grow it under cover.

It can be grown as single plants or, probably the more productive method, as cut-and-come-again seedlings. As the seed is tiny, and the fragile young seedlings are prone to damping off diseases (see p. 125), you gain nothing by sowing before the soil has warmed up. For an early start, sow in a heated propagator in late spring, planting out after all danger of frost is past – under protection if necessary. Sow *in situ* outdoors from late spring (in warm areas) to mid-summer. Space plants 15cm/6in apart. For very useful early summer and late autumn cut-and-come-again seedling crops, sow under cover in mid-spring and late summer.

Cut-and-come-again seedlings are normally ready within four or five weeks of sowing, and may give two or three further cuts. You can make the first pickings from single plants about two months after sowing. Pick single leaves or stemmy shoots, always leaving two leaves at the base of the stem, where new shoots will develop. It is essential to pick regularly or plants run to seed, becoming coarse. Remove any seed heads that develop: they are knobbly and unpleasant to eat. Keep plants well watered in summer. The gold-leaved forms are said to remain brighter if watered in full sun. Plants naturally decline in autumn, but may get a new lease of life if you cover them with cloches or fleece.

Corn salad (Lamb's lettuce, Mâche)
Valerianella locusta

This small-leaved hardy annual and closely related species are found wild in much of the northern hemisphere. Rarely more than 10cm/4in high, its fragile appearance belies its robust nature. Its gentle flavour and soft texture make it invaluable in winter salads, although it can be grown most of the year. The flowers are inconspicuous but edible. It is undemanding, tolerates light shade in summer and is ideally suited to intercropping. A traditional European practice was to broadcast corn salad seed on the onion bed prior to lifting the onions. The larger-seeded type has pale green, relatively large, floppy leaves, while the smaller-seeded types, known as *verte* or 'green', are darker, compact plants with smaller, crisper, upright leaves. They are reputedly hardier, and mainly used for late sowings.

Corn salad can be grown as cut-and-come-again seedlings or as individual plants, the latter probably being more productive. As plants are so small, it is normally sown *in situ*, although you can sow it in modules or seed trays and transplant, spacing plants 10cm/4in apart. It must be sown on firm soil, and may germinate poorly in hot, dry conditions. If so, take appropriate measures (see p. 105).

For early and mid-summer supplies, start sowing under cover in late winter/early spring (the first cuttings will help fill the 'vegetable gap'), continuing outdoors in mid- and late spring. For the main autumn/early winter supplies, sow from mid-summer to early autumn outdoors, making a final sowing in early winter under cover for top-quality winter plants. Although corn salad is very hardy, surviving at least −10°C/14°F, outdoor plants are always more productive if protected with, say, cloches or fleece.

Corn salad grows slowly, taking about three months to develop to maturity. Seedlings are ready several weeks sooner. Pick single leaves from the plants, or cut across the head to allow resprouting, or pull them up by the roots, as is done commercially – otherwise leaves wilt rapidly. Cut seedlings as soon as they are a useful size. They will resprout at least once. A patch can more or less perpetuate itself if you leave a few plants to seed.

Varieties Traditional large-leaved: 'Dutch', 'English', 'Italian', 'Valgros'; 'Green' varieties: 'Coquille de Louviers', 'Verte de Cambrai', 'Verte d'Etampes'; the newer variety 'Dante' is said to be suitable for year-round production.

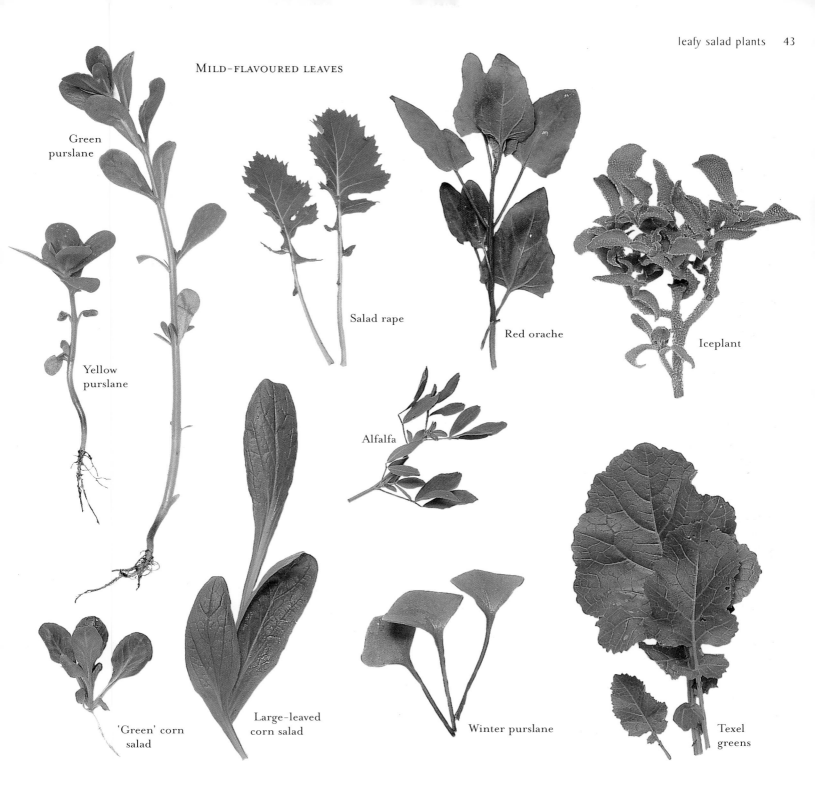

MILD-FLAVOURED LEAVES

Green purslane

Yellow purslane

Salad rape

Red orache

Iceplant

Alfalfa

'Green' corn salad

Large-leaved corn salad

Winter purslane

Texel greens

Strong-flavoured leaves

Not all the strong-flavoured plants in this group are to everybody's liking. But mixed into salads in small quantities, especially blended with mild-flavoured leaves, they can be the catalyst for wonderfully individual salads. The herb coriander (p. 80) could be included here. They are listed here in alphabetical order by their Latin names.

Land cress (American land cress, Upland cress) *Barbarea verna*

A very hardy, low-growing biennial, land cress has dark green, shiny, deeply cut leaves that remain green all winter. Its strong flavour is almost indistinguishable from watercress, and it is used in the same way, cooked or raw in salads. It grows best in moist humus-rich soils; in hot, dry soils it may run to seed prematurely. You can grow it in light shade in summer, and intercrop it between taller vegetables. It is at its best in the winter months, making a neat edging for winter beds. Although it is hardy to at least –10°C/14°F, the leaves will be far more tender to eat if you protect plants with, say, cloches. You can grow it as single plants, spaced 15cm/6in apart, or as cut-and-come-again seedlings. For sowing times and cultivation, see Corn salad, p. 42. The first leaves are normally ready for use within about eight weeks of sowing and cut-and-come-again seedlings several weeks sooner. Young plants are susceptible to flea beetle attack; for control, see p. 126. Land cress runs to seed in its second season. You can leave patches in out-of-the-way corners to perpetuate themselves. This sometimes seems the simplest way to grow it!

Chrysanthemum greens (Shungiku, Garland chrysanthemum, Chop suey greens) *Xanthophthalmum coronarium* (syn. *Chrysanthemum coronarium*)

This annual chrysanthemum, grown as an ornamental, has indented or rounded leaves, depending on variety, and pretty, creamy yellow flowers. The nutritious leaves are used widely in oriental cookery, but with their strong, aromatic flavour should be used only sparingly in salads when raw. The Japanese plunge them into boiling water for a few seconds, then into cold water, before mixing them into salads.

The flower petals are edible, but discard the centre, which is bitter. Mature plants can grow over 60cm/24in high; for salads it is best grown as small plants or cut-and-come-again seedlings.

It thrives in moist, cool conditions, and you can grow it in light shade in summer. Being tolerant of low winter light and moderately hardy, it is best value in the leaner months, from autumn to spring. The leaves stand well in winter, especially under cover.

For cut-and-come-again seedlings (it makes a pretty intercrop), start sowing under cover in early spring. Continue sowing outdoors as soon as the soil is workable. For an autumn-to-early-spring supply, sow in late summer outdoors and in early autumn under cover, protecting outdoor sowings if necessary. You can usually cut seedlings four or five weeks after sowing; further cuts may be possible, but uproot plants once the leaves become tough. You can also sow chrysanthemum greens in seed trays or modules, spacing plants 15cm/6in apart. These will be ready eight to ten weeks after sowing. Pick frequently to encourage further, tender growth, and remove flowering shoots. Bushy plants usually regenerate if cut back hard. Give them a liquid feed to stimulate growth. Plants left to flower may self-seed. Use improved named varieties where available.

Rocket (Mediterranean salad rocket, Arugula) *Eruca sativa* spp. *sativa*

Rocket is an annual of Mediterranean origin, prized for the delicious spiciness of its leaves. It is a small plant, with either indented or straight leaves. It can stand several degrees of frost, and grows best in cool weather, tending to run to seed rapidly in hot dry conditions, becoming unbearably pungent. In temperate climates, it is possible to have a year-round supply if you grow plants under cover in winter. It grows very fast, and is useful for intercropping. Seeds can be sprouted and you can grow seedling crops indoors on an inert base or in shallow containers. The off-white flowers are edible.

Rocket responds well to cut-and-come-again treatment at every stage. Grow it as cut-and-come-again seedlings or single plants, spaced 15cm/6in apart. It is normally sown *in situ*. Sow it outdoors from spring (as soon as the ground is workable) until autumn. Rocket

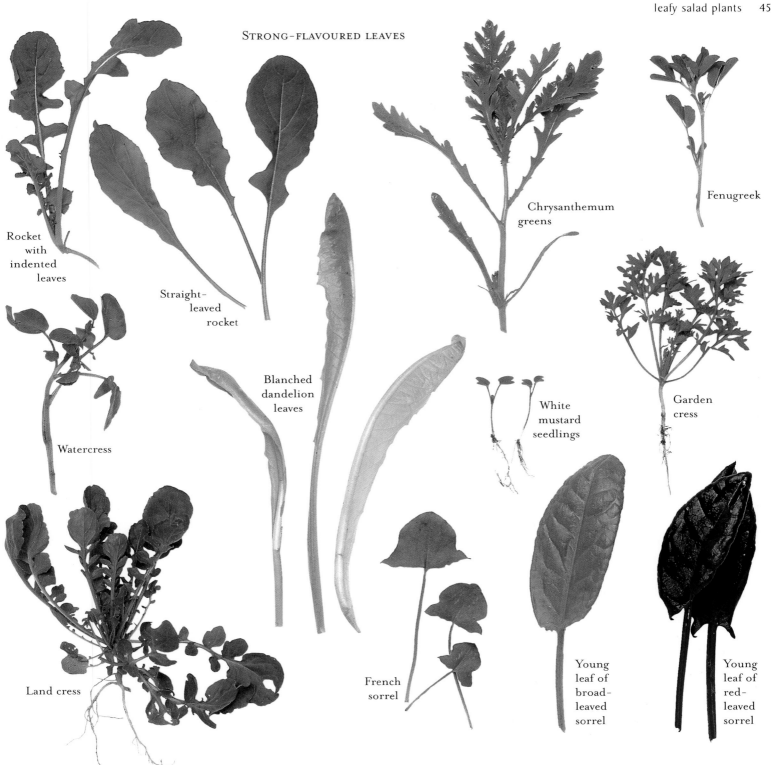

STRONG-FLAVOURED LEAVES

Rocket
with
indented
leaves

Straight-
leaved
rocket

Chrysanthemum
greens

Fenugreek

Watercress

Blanched
dandelion
leaves

White
mustard
seedlings

Garden
cress

Land cress

French
sorrel

Young
leaf of
broad-
leaved
sorrel

Young
leaf of
red-
leaved
sorrel

is one of the first and last crops I sow every year. In my polytunnel I sow in mid- to late winter for very early crops and early to mid-autumn for late crops. Make summer sowings in light shade, and keep them well watered. You can cut seedlings within three or four weeks of sowing, and make as many as four further cuts. It is easy to save seed, especially from plants seeding in early summer.

Wild rocket (Sylvetta) *Diplotaxis spp.*

This is normally perennial. Compared to ordinary rocket, it has smaller, deeply serrated, more pungent leaves. It is more prostrate, slower-growing and less prolific and has yellow flowers. Germination can be erratic.

Turkish rocket *Bunias orientalis*

True Turkish rocket is a hardy perennial with dandelion-like leaves, native in southern and eastern Europe where it is used as greens and in salads. Strains of salad rocket are sometimes misleadingly sold as 'Turkish rocket'.

Garden cress (Pepper cress) *Lepidium sativum*

For centuries hot-flavoured cress seedlings have been used in salads, partnered with mustard and, recently, salad rape. Cultivate it in shallow containers indoors or as cut-and-come-again seedlings in the garden. It does best on light soil with plenty of moisture during growth. A fast grower, it is invaluable for intercropping, making dense green patches in ornamental schemes. For sowing, see Salad rape p. 40. It has a shorter season of usefulness than rape, running

Wild rocket

to seed in hot weather unless grown in light shade.

Garden cress survives only light frost, but you can grow it under cover from mid-autumn to late winter, if you maintain temperatures of 10°C/50°F. At lower temperatures it will become dormant, but it will burst into growth again in spring. Spring sowings can be highly productive: a patch sown in my unheated greenhouse in spring yielded five cuts, boosted by one seaweed extract feed. Cut seedlings at any height from 4 to 15cm/1.5 to 6in. They are usually ready within three to four weeks of sowing. It is easy to save seed, especially from plants running to seed in spring.

Varieties The curly type is fastest-growing: 'Victoria' and 'Sprint' are improved varieties. Plain or large-leaved, and broad types may be bulkier and milder. 'Greek cress' is a distinct, well-flavoured variety.

Watercress *Nasturtium officinale*

This hardy aquatic perennial has shiny pungent leaves, which are rich in vitamins and minerals. It is a cool-season crop, growing best in spring and autumn in temperate climates. It is a native of fresh running streams in limestone areas and its ideal requirements are clean, flowing, alkaline water, a constant temperature of about 10°C/50°F and dappled shade: that is, bright light but not full sun – conditions not easily met in most gardens. If you have a stream, plant young, rooted pieces of watercress in the soil along the edges in spring, 15cm/6in apart. (Sprigs of watercress root quickly in a jar of water.) Pick lightly in the first season, pinching out tips and flowering shoots to encourage branching. You can usually cut established plants two or three times a season.

Small quantities of watercress can be grown in, say, 20cm/8in flower pots. Line the bottom of each pot with gravel or moss to prevent soil from being washed out, then fill it with rich garden or potting soil, to which some ground limestone has been added. Plant several young, rooted pieces in the pot, taken from established plants, or rooted as above. Stand the pot in a dish of cool, clean water, changing the water daily in hot weather, less frequently in cool weather. Put it somewhere sheltered in good light. Apply occasional liquid feeds and harvest as above.

Sorrel *Rumex* spp.

Sorrel is a hardy perennial, found naturalized in the wild all over the world. The leaves have a delicious, sharp, lemon flavour: in salads, it is superb partnered with rocket. It also makes excellent sauces and soups. Two species are grown for the kitchen. The most productive is *Rumex acetosa*, popularly known as common, garden or broad-leaved sorrel (and wrongly as French sorrel). This has fairly large, arrow-shaped leaves, up to about 25cm/10in long, and grows into clumps 30cm/12in wide. The true French or buckler-leaved sorrel (*Rumex scutatus*) has small shield-shaped leaves roughly 2.5cm/1in wide. A sprawling plant about 30cm/12in high, it makes excellent ground cover and is pretty as a container plant. It has good drought tolerance. But beware: its spreading roots and self-seeding habit can make it invasive. The tiny leaves have an exceptionally strong flavour, and remain green much longer in winter than common sorrel. There is an attractive silver-leaved form.

Sorrel does best in fertile, moist, slightly acid soil but tolerates a range of conditions, including light shade. It is a good plant for shaded urban gardens. It is normally grown as a perennial. You can renew plants every two or three years by division in the autumn, or leave a plant to run to seed and transplant the seedlings. You can raise plants by sowing in spring, by any method, finally spacing them 30cm/12 in apart. Pick leaves as required, and cut off any seed heads which develop. Sorrel naturally dies back in mid-winter, but you can extend the leafy phase by covering with cloches or low tunnels in autumn; similarly covering in spring will encourage earlier growth. For mid-winter pickings, plant young plants under cover in late summer.

Varieties 'Large de Belleville' (broad-leaved). In France there is an attractive red-leaved form, *R. acetosa* ssp. *vineatus*. This is apparently sterile, so it is propagated by dividing established plants.

White mustard *Sinapsis alba*

White mustard has long been partnered with cress in seedling packs; the hotter-flavoured black mustard (*Brassica nigra*) can also be used. Seeds of both types are used in making mustard. It has a peppery flavour and pretty leaves. Grow as salad rape, p. 40, but avoid mid-summer sowings, as it runs to seed fast in hot weather, becoming unpleasantly hot. Its useful life is shorter than rape, as once it is past the seedling stage, 5–7.5cm/2–3in high, the leaves can become tough and bristly. If you want it with cress, sow it three days later than cress. In areas of high rainfall, growth can be rampant.

Varieties 'Tilney' and 'Albatros' are improved varieties.

Dandelion *Taraxacum officinale*

Wild and improved forms of the perennial weed dandelion (see illustration on p. 89) have been grown for culinary use for centuries. All parts – flowers, leaves and roots – are edible. Use young leaves raw in salads, but older leaves are fairly tart unless blanched. The root tops have an excellent flavour and can be sliced raw into salads. Dandelion is most valuable in winter and spring; in temperate climates the leaves often remain green all winter.

Dandelion tolerates most conditions except waterlogged soil. Sow in spring and early summer, in seed trays or modules for transplanting, or *in situ*, spacing plants 35cm/14in apart. You can also thin out seedlings to 5cm/2in apart, so that a group can be blanched under one pot.

From late summer onwards, blanch a few plants at a time. The simplest method is to cover them *in situ*. Allegedly plants covered with leaves or soil have the finest flavour. Where winters are severe, lift plants from mid-autumn onwards and blanch in frames or cellars. They can also be cut back and forced like Witloof chicory (p. 23).

Varieties Where available, use the more prolific improved named varieties.

Fenugreek (Methi) *Trigonella foenum–graecum*

Fenugreek is a hardy, pretty, aromatic legume, grown for its spicy seeds, leaves, fodder and green manuring. Several stages are used in salads, each, I think, with subtly differing flavours. Sprouted seeds, eaten 1.3cm/½in long, are quite spicy; the smallest seedlings are faintly curry-flavoured; while larger seedlings, notably the leaf tips, have a pea flavour. Fenugreek tolerates a wide range of conditions, and survives temperatures as low as –16°C/3°F, which makes it a valuable winter salad under cover in cool climates. It requires plenty of moisture throughout growth. Grow it as a cut-and-come-again seedling crop, sowing every three weeks or so, as seedlings quickly become thick-stemmed and coarse. Sow in mid-autumn/early winter under cover for winter pickings, setting mouse traps if necessary; mice love fenugreek seeds! Cut seedlings when they reach 5–7.5cm/2–3in high – normally four or five weeks after sowing.

stems and stalks

Celery *Apium graveolens*

The celeries are marsh plants in origin, grown mainly for the distinct flavour and crisp texture of their stems. The stems of some types are blanched to make them paler, crisper and sweeter. The strong-flavoured leaves are used for seasoning and garnishing, both fresh and dried. The seeds are also used in flavouring. There are several closely related kinds, of varying hardiness.

GENERAL CULTIVATION

The celeries are all cool-season crops, requiring fertile, moisture-retentive soil that is rich in organic matter, and preferably neutral or slightly alkaline. Very acid soils are unsuitable. All types need generous watering and mulching to conserve moisture, and generally benefit from supplementary feeding.

Celery seed germinates at 10–15°C/50–59°F. The seed is small, so it is normally sown in seed trays or modules, in a heated propagator if necessary. It requires light to germinate, so sow on the surface or just covered lightly with sand. Keep the surface damp until germination. Prick out seedlings as soon as they are large enough to handle. Plant them at the five-to-six-leaf stage after hardening them off well. Seedlings may bolt prematurely if, after germinating, they are subjected to temperatures below 10°F/50°C for more than about twelve hours, so try and keep them at an even temperature. If cold threatens while they are hardening off, give them extra protection.

PESTS AND DISEASES

Unless otherwise stated, for protective measures and control, see p. 125.

Slugs Can be very damaging to young plants and mature stems.

Celery fly/leaf miner Tiny maggots tunnel into leaves, causing brown dried patches. Discard any blistered seedlings, remove mined leaves on mature plants by hand and burn infested foliage. Growing under fine nets helps prevent attacks.

Celery leaf spot Pinprick brown spots appear on leaves and stems. There are no organic remedies, but rotation, growing plants healthily and removing old plant debris all help prevent the disease.

Leaf celery (Cutting celery, Green celery)
Apium graveolens

This is the hardiest and least demanding type of celery, closely related to wild celery. It can survive –12°C/10°F, so can be a source of glossy green leaves all year round. It is a branching, bushy plant, 30–45cm/12–18in high, but in northern Europe it is also grown as fine-stemmed cut-and-come-again seedlings for use in salads and soup. It is naturally vigorous and responds to cut-and-come-again treatment at every stage. Varieties such as 'Fine Dutch' were developed for this purpose, but are no longer easily obtained. 'Parcel' is a distinct variety introduced to the West from Eastern Germany. It has crisp, shiny, deeply curled leaves with a strong celery flavour – a most decorative edging plant for a winter potager.

Cultivation For single plants, sow as described above throughout the growing season, indoors, or, when soil conditions are suitable, *in situ* outdoors. Space plants 23–30cm/9–12in apart. You can space them closer initially, then remove alternate plants and leave the remainder to grow larger. Make the first cuts within about four weeks of planting. Pot up a few plants in late summer and bring them under cover for winter. Leaf celery often perpetuates itself if one or two plants are left to seed in spring: seedlings pop up everywhere!

For cut-and-come-again seedlings, make successive sowings outdoors. You can make earlier and later sowings under cover. Cut seedlings as required when 10–12.5cm/4–5in high. You can obtain nice fine-stemmed clumps by multi-sowing up to eight seeds per module and planting the clumps 20cm/8in apart.

TYPES OF CELERY

Golden self-
blanching celery

Leaf
celery
'Parcel'

Self-
blanching
celery
'Pink Blush'

Celeriac

Green self-
blanching
celery

Standard
leaf celery

Self-blanching celery *Apium graveolens* var. *dulce*

These long-stemmed plants, about 45cm/18in high, are the most widely grown type of celery today. The standard type, once called 'Gold', have cream to yellow stems; planting them close will enhance their paleness and make them whiter, crisper and possibly sweeter. The 'American Green' varieties have green stems, are considered naturally better flavoured and do not need supplementary blanching. There are also beautiful varieties with a pink flush to the stem. Purists consider self-blanching celery less flavoured than traditional 'trench' celery (see below) but it is far easier to grow. It is not frost hardy, so is used mainly as a summer crop.

Cultivation Sow as described on p. 48 in spring in gentle heat in a propagator. Plant at even spacing in a block formation, to get the blanching effect. Do not plant too deeply. Space plants 15–27cm/6–11in apart: the wider apart they are, the heavier the plants and the thicker the stems will be. If you plant them close, you can cut intermediate plants when they are small, allowing the remainder to grow larger. For a late crop under cover, sow in late spring and plant under cover in late summer. This will crop until frost affects it.

Take precautions against slugs in the early stages (see p. 126). Keep plants well watered to prevent premature bolting and 'stringiness'. Feed weekly with a liquid feed from early summer onwards. If you are growing standard varieties, tuck straw between the plants in mid-summer to increase the blanching effect.

Start cutting before the outer stems become pithy. Standard varieties tend to stand longer in good condition; the 'green' varieties have a shorter period at their peak. You can dig up plants by the roots before the first frost and store them for several weeks in cellars or cool sheds. Traditionally plants were transplanted into frames or pits, 30cm/12in deep, and covered with dried leaves or straw.

Varieties Standard: 'Celebrity', 'Ivory Tower', 'Lathom Self-Blanching', 'Victoria' F1; green: 'Greensnap', 'Ventura'; pink: 'Pink Blush'.

Trench celery *Apium graveolens* var. *dulce*

This is the classic English celery. The long white or pink stems are crisp, superbly flavoured and handsome, but have to be blanched to attain their full flavour and texture – a labour-intensive procedure.

Trench celery is mainly grown today for exhibition purposes.

Cultivation In essence, raise plants as described on p. 48 and plant in a single row, spaced 30–45cm/12–18in apart. You can use various blanching methods. On heavy soils, plant at ground level. Blanch in stages by wrapping purpose-made collars, heavy lightproof paper or black film around the stems, fairly loosely to allow for expansion, leaving one third of the stem exposed each time. In light soils, plant in trenches at least 38cm/15in wide and 30cm/12in deep. Tie plants loosely to keep them upright, and blanch in stages by filling in the trench initially, then spading soil up around the stems, each time up to the level of the lowest leaves, until only the tops are exposed. Cut from early winter onwards. It will not stand much frost unless protected with straw or bracken. The red and pink varieties are slightly hardier and can be used later.

Varieties White: 'Giant White'; pink: 'Mammoth Pink'/'Giant Pink'.

Celeriac (Turnip-rooted celery)
Apium graveolens var. *rapaceum*

Celeriac is a bushy plant, grown for the knobbly 'bulb' that develops at ground level. It has a delicious mild celery flavour, is an excellent winter cooked vegetable, and is good in salads grated raw or cooked and cold. Its leaves are strongly flavoured but can be used sparingly. It is less prone to disease and much hardier than stem celery.

Cultivation Celeriac tolerates light shade, provided the soil is moist and fertile. The secret to growing large bulbs (essential, as much is lost in peeling) is a long, steady growing season. Raise plants as described on p. 48, sowing in gentle heat in mid-spring. Germination is often erratic: be patient! Plant in late spring or early summer 30–38cm/12–15in apart, with the base of the stem at soil level – no deeper. Celeriac normally benefits from feeding, every two weeks or so, with a liquid feed.

Plants stand at least –10°C/14°F, but tuck a thick layer of straw or bracken around them in late autumn for extra protection and to make lifting easier in frost. They can be lifted and stored, but their flavour and texture are better if they remain in the ground. A few leaves may stay green all winter, which are useful for flavouring and garnish.

Varieties 'Monarch', 'Regent', 'Snowhite'/'Snevhide' – among many good varieties.

Sea kale *Crambe maritima*

This handsome hardy perennial, a native of the seashore, is cultivated for its deliciously flavoured young leaf stalks, which are eaten raw after blanching.

CULTIVATION

Establish a sea kale bed in good, light, well-drained soil in a sunny position: lime acid soil to about pH7. Plants normally last at least seven years. Raise them by sowing fresh seed (seed loses its viability rapidly) in spring, *in situ*, in a seedbed or in modules for transplanting. Alternatively, buy young plants or rooted cuttings ('thongs') for planting in spring or autumn. Space plants 30–45cm/12–18in apart. They die right back in winter.

In its third season the plants are strong enough to force into early growth prior to planting. In late winter/early spring, cover the bare crowns with 7.5cm/3in of dry leaves and a traditional clay blanching pot, or any light-excluding pot or bucket at least 30cm/12in high (see p. 131). The shoots may take three months to develop. Cut them when they are about 20cm/8in long, then leave the plants uncovered to grow normally. Give them an annual dressing of manure or seaweed feed. You can also lift plants and force indoors at 16–21°C/60–70°F. They will be ready within weeks, but the plants will be weakened and must be discarded afterwards.

Kohl rabi *Brassica oleracea* Gongylodes Group

Kohl rabi is a beautiful but strange-looking vegetable, growing about 30cm/12in high (see illustration on p. 52). The edible part is the graceful bulb, 5–7.5cm/2–3in diameter, which develops in the stem, virtually suspended just clear of the ground. There are purple and green ('white') forms, the purple possibly sweeter but more inclined to be fibrous. Kohl rabi has a delicate turnip flavour. Normally cooked, it is also grated or sliced raw into salads; young leaves are also edible. It is fast-growing, withstands drought and heat well, and is less prone to pests and disease, clubroot included, than most brassicas. It is rich in protein, calcium and vitamin C. The old 'Vienna' varieties quickly became fibrous on maturity, but much-improved modern varieties stand well.

Kohl rabi grows best in light, sandy soil, with plenty of moisture, but tolerates heavier soil. It stands low temperatures, but grows fastest, and so is most tender, at 18–25°C/65–77°F, the optimum being 22°C/72°F. For salads, it should be grown fast, or grown as 'mini kohl rabi' (see below). Rotate it within the brassica group.

CULTIVATION

For the main crop, sow from spring to late summer *in situ* outdoors. Soil temperature should be at least 10°C/50°F, or early sowings may bolt prematurely. Thin in stages to 25–30cm/10–12in apart. Alternatively sow in modules and transplant. You can multi-sow with three or four seedlings per module, and plant as one. For an earlier summer crop, sow in mid-winter/early spring in gentle heat; for an early winter crop under cover, sow indoors in late summer/early autumn. For mini kohl rabi, sow *in situ* from late spring to late summer in drills 15cm/6in apart and thin to 2.5cm/1in apart. Use recommended varieties. Harvest at ping-pong-ball size, normally within eight weeks of sowing. Take precautions against flea beetle in the early stages (see p. 126).

In severe climates, lift kohl rabi in autumn and store in boxes of sand. Trim off the outer leaves but leave a small tuft on the crown to prevent the bulb from drying out.

VARIETIES

Purple 'Blusta', 'Delicacy Purple', 'Purple Danube' FI.
Green 'Quickstar' FI, 'Rapidstar' FI.
For mini kohl rabi 'Rolano' FI, 'Logo' (both green).

Florence fennel (Sweet fennel, Finocchio)
Foeniculum vulgare var. *dulce*

Florence fennel is a beautiful annual with feathery, shimmering green foliage, growing about 45cm/18in high. It is cultivated for its swollen leaf bases, which overlap to form a crisp-textured, aniseed-flavoured 'bulb' just above ground level. (For herb fennel, see p. 80.)

Fennel does best in fertile, light, sandy soil, well drained and rich in organic matter, but will grow in heavier soil. A Mediterranean marsh plant, it needs plenty of moisture throughout growth and a warm climate. Sudden drops in temperature or dry spells can trigger premature bolting without it forming a decent bulb. This tendency is exacerbated by transplanting and early sowing. Some new varieties have improved bolting resistance – but are not infallible.

CULTIVATION

Fennel should be grown fast. To minimize the risk of bolting, preferably sow in modules and delay sowing until mid-summer, unless you are using bolt-resistant varieties. Otherwise sow in seed trays, prick out the seedlings when they are very small, and transplant them at the four-to-five-leaf stage. Space plants 30–35cm/12–14in apart. For an early summer outdoor crop, sow in mid- to late spring using bolt-resistant varieties, at a soil temperature of at least 10°C/50°F. For a main summer crop, sow in early summer. For an autumn crop that can also be planted under cover, sow in late summer or even early autumn. Watch for slugs in the early stages (for control, see p. 126); keep plants watered and mulched. Occasional feeding with a seaweed-based fertilizer is beneficial.

In good growing conditions, fennel is ready eight to twelve weeks after sowing. When it reaches a usable size, cut bulbs just above ground level. Useful secondary shoots develop which are tasty and decorative in salads. Mature plants tolerate light frost, but plants that have previously been cut back survive lower temperatures.

Late plantings under cover may not develop large succulent bulbs, but the leaf bases can be sliced finely into salad, and the tender 'fern' often lasts well into winter.

VARIETIES

Standard 'Perfection', 'Sirio'.
Bolt resistant 'Rudy' F1, 'Victoria' F1, 'Zefa Tardo'.

VEGETABLES WITH
SWOLLEN STEMS

Purple
kohl rabi

Green
kohl rabi

Florence fennel

fruiting vegetables

Tomato *Lycopersicon esculentum*

The tomato is a tender South American plant, which was introduced into Europe in the sixteenth century as an ornamental greenhouse climber. It has deservedly become one of the most universally grown vegetables. Tomatoes are beautiful, rich in vitamins and versatile in use, both cooked and raw.

Types of tomato

Tomato fruits are wonderfully diverse in colour, shape and size. They can be red, pink, orange, yellow, red- and orange-striped, black, purple, green and even white. Size ranges from huge beefsteaks to the aptly named 'currant' tomatoes. They can be roughly classified on the basis of fruit shape and size, red and yellow forms being found in most types.

Standard Smooth, round, medium-sized fruits of variable flavour.

Beefsteak Very large, smooth, fleshy, multilocular fruits (that is, several 'compartments' evident when sliced horizontally); mostly well flavoured.

Marmande Large, flattish, irregular, often-ribbed shape, multilocular, fleshy, usually well flavoured, but some so-called 'improved' varieties though more evenly shaped are not necessarily as well flavoured as the old.

Oxheart Medium-sized to large, conical, fleshy; some are exceptionally well flavoured.

Plum-shaped Small to medium-sized, rectangular and firm; generally late maturing; variable flavour, mostly used cooked. (On account of their shape and firmness the 'Roma' varieties in this group were originally selected for the Italian canning industry.)

Cherry plum Small, firm, distinctly flavoured form of plum tomato for eating raw, typified by 'Santa'.

Pear-shaped Smooth, small to medium-sized, 'waisted', mostly unremarkable flavour and texture.

Cherry Small, round fruits under 2.5cm/1in diameter, mostly sweet or distinctly flavoured.

Currant Tiny fruits about 1cm/½in diameter; exceptionally rambling plants; hitherto not notably flavoured.

The growth habit of tomatoes affects how they are cultivated.

Tall, 'indeterminate' types The main shoot naturally grows up to 4m/12ft long in warm climates, with sideshoots developing into branches. These are grown as vertical 'cordons', which are trained up strings or tied to supports. Growth is kept within bounds by nipping out or 'stopping' the growing point and removing sideshoots. In a 'semi-determinate' sub-group, the main shoot naturally stops growing when about 1m/3ft high. Most Marmande types are in this latter group.

Bush or 'determinate' types In these types the sideshoots develop instead of the main shoot, forming a naturally self-stopping bushy plant of 60–120cm/2–4ft diameter that sprawls on the ground. They do not require stopping, sideshooting or supports. They are often early maturing, quite decorative when growing, and can be grown under cloches and films (see p. 56). Some varieties are suitable for containers.

Dwarf types These are exceptionally small and compact, often no more than 20cm/8in high. They require no pruning, and are ideal for containers and edgings.

Flavour

The quest for excellent flavour, which is rarely found in bought tomatoes, is a major incentive for growing your own. Nothing can compare with thick slices of a freshly picked 'Golden Boy' beefsteak on homemade bread, sprinkled with basil and black pepper. Flavour, essentially a balance between acidity and sweetness, is in practice determined by several interacting factors. It can vary from plant to plant, and fruit to fruit, depending on the season, maturity and even the time of day. My personal view is that overwatering and overfeeding commonly destroy flavour. Start with a potentially well-flavoured variety, and err on the side of 'starving' and 'underwatering' (see p. 116). You may not have the highest yields, but they will be the best tasting. Currently heirloom varieties are being reintroduced on the basis of their flavour. Some, undoubtedly, are exceptionally flavoured, but not all. In comparison with modern varieties, they tend to suffer from poor disease resistance and late maturity. Incidentally, green tomatoes, which must be picked while still green, are among the most highly rated for flavour.

CULTIVATION

The optimum temperature for tomatoes is 21–24°C/70–75°F. They grow poorly at temperatures below 10°C/50°F and above 32°C/90°F. They need high light intensity and most varieties require at least eight frost-free weeks from planting to maturity. Beefsteaks require somewhat higher temperatures in the early stages, pear-shaped tomatoes may not develop a true pear shape at low temperatures, and the slow-maturing 'Roma' varieties need a fairly long season. The method of cultivation depends on climate. If you are new to tomato growing, be guided by current practice in the locality. The main options, graduated from warm to cool climates, are:
• Outdoors, directly in the ground or in containers.
• Outdoors, initially protected by cloches or in frames which are removed when outgrown, using tall or bush types.
• Outdoors, under cloches or in frames, using bush types. Bush types can also be planted under perforated film or fleece which is removed later (see p. 56).
• Indoors, in unheated greenhouses or polytunnels. They can be grown in the ground unless soil sickness has developed (see p. 121) in which case they must be grown in containers or growing bags, by systems such as ring culture (see p. 121), or using plants grafted on disease-resistant rootstocks. Polytunnels are invaluable for tomato growing, as they are easily moved every three or four years, so avoiding the development of soil sickness.
• Indoors, in heated greenhouses. For culture in greenhouses, consult a gardening encyclopedia (see Further Reading, pp. 162–3).
   Some tomato varieties are bred solely for cultivation in greenhouses, but in practice most 'indoor' varieties can be grown outside and vice versa.

SOIL AND SITE

In temperate climates, grow outdoor tomatoes in a warm, sunny, sheltered position. Tomatoes are in the potato family and vulnerable to the same soil pests and diseases as plants in that family, so should be rotated accordingly. However, they are easily infected by potato blight (an increasingly serious disease in the British Isles) so avoid growing them near potatoes. Growing in polytunnels gives considerable protection against infection from the airborne blight spores. In greenhouses it is inadvisable to grow tomatoes in the same soil for more than three or four consecutive years.

   Tomatoes need fertile, well-drained soil, at a pH of 5.5–7. Ideally prepare the ground beforehand by making a trench 30cm/12in deep and 45cm/18in wide, working in generous quantities of well-rotted manure, compost and/or wilted comfrey leaves (whose high potash content benefits tomatoes).

PLANT RAISING

Sow in early to mid-spring, six to eight weeks before the last frost is expected. Seed germinates fastest at 20°C/68°F, though outdoor bush varieties germinate at slightly lower temperatures. Sow in a propagator, either in seed trays, pricking out into 5–8cm/2–3in pots at the three-leaf stage, or in modules. These can later be potted on into small pots. Seedlings can withstand lower temperatures, of about 16°C/60°F once germinated, but must be kept above 10°C/50°F. Keep them well ventilated, well spaced out and in good light. They are normally ready for planting in the ground or into containers six to eight weeks after sowing, when 15–20cm/6–8in high, with the first flower truss visible. When buying plants, choose sturdy plants in individual pots, with healthy, dark green foliage.

OUTDOOR CROPS

Harden off well before planting outside. If the soil temperature is below 10°C/50°F or there is any risk of frost, delay planting. Plant firmly with the lowest leaves just above soil level. Planting through white reflective mulch keeps plants clean and reflects heat up on the fruit – an asset in cool climates.

TOMATOES

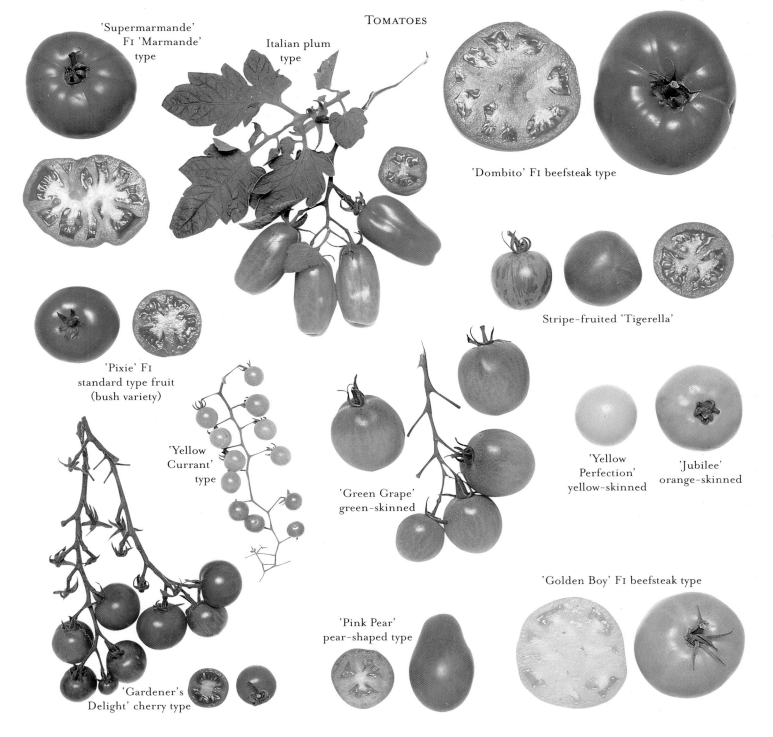

'Supermarmande'
F1 'Marmande'
type

Italian plum
type

'Dombito' F1 beefsteak type

Stripe-fruited 'Tigerella'

'Pixie' F1
standard type fruit
(bush variety)

'Yellow
Currant'
type

'Green Grape'
green-skinned

'Yellow
Perfection'
yellow-skinned

'Jubilee'
orange-skinned

'Gardener's
Delight' cherry type

'Pink Pear'
pear-shaped type

'Golden Boy' F1 beefsteak type

Remove sideshoots to concentrate the plant's energies (LEFT) and to 'stop' the plant remove the growing point two leaves above the topmost truss (ABOVE).

Tall types Plant 38–45cm/15–18in apart, in single rows or staggered in double rows. For supports, use strong individual canes, elegant metal spiral supports or posts at least 1.5m/5ft high; or erect 1.2–1.5/4–5ft posts at either end of the rows, running two or three parallel wires between them. Tie plants to the supports as they grow. In cool climates, protect plants in the early stages, for example with polythene film side panels. Remove sideshoots as they develop, and in mid- to late summer remove the growing point, so that remaining fruits mature (see photograph above). Depending on the locality, this will be after three to five trusses have set fruit. Except in very dry conditions, plants do not normally require watering until they are flowering and setting fruit. At this stage apply about 11 litres per sq. m/2 gallons per sq. yd weekly. If growth seems poor when the second truss is setting, feed weekly with a seaweed-based or specially formulated organic tomato feed, or liquid comfrey. In cool climates, towards the end of the season cut plants with unripened fruit free of the canes (without uprooting them), lie them horizontally on straw and cover with cloches to encourage further ripening. You can also uproot plants and hang them indoors for several weeks to continue ripening. Individual fruits ripen slowly wrapped in paper and kept in the dark indoors.

Bush and dwarf varieties Plant bush types 45–60cm/18–24in apart and dwarf types 25–30cm/10–12in apart. Closer spacing produces earlier crops, but wider spacing produces heavier yields and is advisable where there is a risk of blight. Water and feed as tall varieties above. Protect bush and dwarf varieties with cloches or grow in frames. (Low polytunnels are unsuitable, unless the film is

perforated, as humidity and temperatures rise too high.) For an earlier crop, plant under perforated polythene film or fleece, anchored in the soil and laid directly on the plants or over low hoops (see p. 123). Once the flowers press against the covering, slit it down the middle to allow insect pollination. To 'wean' the plants, make intermittent slits initially, then a week later cut the remaining gaps so that the film falls aside. Leave it there as a low windbreak. Water and feed as for tall outdoor plants (see above).

INDOOR CROPS

To grow crops in unheated greenhouses and polytunnels, prepare the ground and raise plants as above. Tall varieties make optimum use of this valuable space. Plant in single rows 45cm/18in apart, or at the same spacing in double rows with 90cm/36in between each pair of rows. I interplant with French marigolds (*Tagetes* spp.) as a deterrent against whitefly.

Plants need to be supported, with individual canes or some other system. One of the simplest is to suspend heavy-duty strings from a horizontal overhead wire or the greenhouse roof, looping the lower end around the lowest leaves of the tomato plant. Twist the plant carefully around the string as it grows.

To conserve moisture, either plant through polythene film or keep plants well mulched with up to 12cm/5in of organic material. (Wilted comfrey can be used.) Water well after planting, then lightly until the fruits start to set, when heavier watering is necessary. Plants need at least 9 litres/2 gallons per plant per week. One school of thought maintains that flavour is best if they are watered, at most, once a week, allowing the soil almost to dry out between waterings.

If fruit is slow to set in late spring/early summer, tap the canes or wires around midday to spread the pollen and encourage setting. Keep plants well ventilated. In hot weather, 'damp down' at midday – that is, sprinkle greenhouse and plants with water. The humidity helps fruit to set and deters pests.

Remove sideshoots as for outdoor tomatoes and stop plants in late summer (see photographs above), either when they reach the roof or when it seems that further fruit is unlikely to mature during the season. Vigorous plants may produce seven or eight trusses, continuing to ripen into early winter. Remove withered and yellowing leaves and dig up and burn any seriously diseased plants. For high yields, indoor tomatoes normally need weekly feeding, once the first truss has set, with a high potash feed (see Outdoor Tomatoes, p. 54).

TOMATOES IN CONTAINERS

Tomatoes are often grown in growing bags of potting compost, pots and hanging baskets. The larger the container, the better: 23cm/9in would be the minimum size of pot. Use good-quality potting compost. Careful watering is essential, so that the compost neither dries out nor becomes waterlogged. Once fruit starts to set, feed weekly as outdoor tomatoes, p. 56 (see also Containers, p. 124).

PESTS AND DISEASES

With outdoor tomatoes the main problems are poor weather and potato blight, which manifests itself as brown patches on leaves and ultimately fruits. There is no organic remedy.

Indoor tomatoes, which are being forced in unnatural conditions, are prone to various pests, diseases and disorders. You can avoid many of these by growing disease-resistant varieties, and growing plants well with good ventilation and avoiding overcrowding. Use biological control against whitefly (see p. 125).

VARIETIES

The choice today is vast and constantly changing. For specialist suppliers, see p. 163. The following are among my personal favourites, chosen for flavour, texture or some specific use or quality.

Standard Tall 'Alicante', 'Burpee Long Keeper', 'Counter' FI, 'Cristal' FI, 'Typhoon' FI; bush: 'Pixie' FI, 'Sleaford Abundance' FI.

Beefsteak 'Dombito' FI, 'Golden Boy' FI (gold).

Marmande 'Supermarmande' FI, 'Marmande'.

Plum-shaped 'Brigade' FI and 'Britain's Breakfast' (both excellent for freezing), 'Santa' FI, 'Sunbelle' (golden teardrop).

Cherry Tall 'Cherry Belle' FI, 'Gardener's Delight', 'Sungold' FI (yellow), 'Sweet 100' FI; bush 'Whippersnapper'.

Heirloom 'Brandywine', 'Green Grape', all 'Oxheart' varieties. 'Nepal'.

Cucumber *Cucumis sativus*

With their crisp texture and refreshing flavours, cucumbers are quintessential salad vegetables. In origin climbing and trailing tropical plants, for practical purposes they are divided into two main groups.

TYPES OF CUCUMBER

European greenhouse These have smooth, dark green skin and fine-quality flesh, and they are often over 30cm/12in long (though 'mini cucumbers' are mature when 10–15cm/4–6in long). The vigorous plants require high temperatures (roughly 18–30°C/64–86°F), and are normally grown in heated or unheated greenhouses. In older varieties (now mainly grown for showing), male flowers had to be removed as pollination made the fruits misshapen and bitter. Most modern varieties are 'all female', which virtually eliminates the problem. Unfortunately the seed is very expensive. In practice it is often as economic to buy young plants.

Outdoor 'ridge' The original 'ridge' types – so called as they were grown in Europe on ridges to improve drainage – were short and stubby, with rough, prickly skin, normally dark or light green, but occasionally white, yellow or cream. There are some compact bush forms. They are notably hardier and healthier than greenhouse cucumbers and tolerate much lower temperatures. Today's Japanese and 'burpless' hybrids are excellent improved varieties, often approaching greenhouse cucumbers in length and quality. Gherkins are a distinct group with thin or stubby fruits, notably prickly skinned, averaging 5cm/2in in length. Although grown for pickling, they can be used fresh in salads. Several more or less round-fruited, mainly heirloom types are juicy, well flavoured and decorative. They include the pale-skinned 'Crystal Apple', yellow-skinned, lemon-shaped 'lemon' cucumbers and the Italian 'melon cucumber' or 'carosello', which I believe has exceptional drought resistance.

All ridge varieties require insect pollination, and can be grown outside or under cover. They are the main types considered here. Ridge and all-female types should not be grown in proximity, or cross pollination will occur.

SOIL AND SITE

Cucumbers will not tolerate any frost. Outdoor plants require a warm site sheltered from wind, sunny but not liable to be baked dry. They tolerate light shade in mid-summer. Cucumbers do best where the roots can romp freely through reasonably fertile, humus-rich, moisture-retentive soil. Good drainage is essential. Very acid soils should be limed. Prepare the ground by making individual holes (or a trench) about 30cm/12in deep and 45cm/18in wide, working in well-rotted manure or garden compost. Cover with about 15cm/6in of soil, made into a small mound to improve drainage.

PLANT RAISING

Cucumbers require 100–140 frost-free days from sowing to maturity, so do not plant outside until all risk of frost is past. Where summers are cool or short, start them indoors in mid- to late spring, about four weeks before planting out. They need a minimum temperature of 18°C/65°F to germinate. As cucumbers transplant badly, sow in modules or in 5–8cm/2–3in pots. Sow seeds on their sides, singly or two to three per module or pot, removing all but the strongest one after germination. Try to avoid further watering until after germination, to prevent damping off diseases. Maintain a temperature of at least 15°C/60°F after germination. Seedlings grow fast. If you are growing cucumbers outdoors, plant them out at the three-to-four-leaf stage in early summer after hardening them off carefully. Take care not to bury the stem when planting, which invites neck rot. Protect plants if necessary in the early stages. Once the soil feels warm to the touch, seeds can be sown *in situ* outdoors, under jars or cloches if necessary. Space climbing plants 45cm/18in apart, and bush plants 90cm/36in apart.

SUPPORTS

Climbing cucumbers can be trained against any reasonably strong support suitable for climbing beans, against trellises, metal or cane tepees, or wire or nylon netting of about 23cm/9in mesh. Few varieties grow much over 180cm/6ft high. They are largely self-clinging, but may need tying in the early stages. Less vigorous varieties can sprawl on the ground – gherkins are usually grown this way – but plants are healthier, and less prone to slug damage, if trained off the ground even on low supports.

Nip out the growing point when plants reach the top of the supports. Modern hybrids bear fruit on the main stem, whereas older varieties tend to bear on lateral sideshoots. (In this case nip out the growing point above the first six or seven leaves, to encourage fruit-bearing sideshoots. Tie these sideshoots in if necessary. To control growth, nip them off later, two leaves beyond a fruit.) Once the plants are established, give them an organic mulch. Keep them well watered, but not waterlogged. If growth is not reasonably vigorous, apply an organic feed weekly from mid-summer onwards. Pick regularly to encourage further growth, picking the fruits young before the skins harden. If the cucumbers are too long for household use, cut the lower half and leave the top attached. The exposed end will callus over and can be cut later.

GROWING IN GREENHOUSES

To grow ridge cucumbers in a greenhouse or polytunnel, cultivate as above. They generally grow taller than outdoors, so may need higher supports. You can train them up strings (see Tomatoes, p. 56), but a strong structure such as rigid pig net or reinforced concrete mesh is more satisfactory.

Conditions in greenhouses and tunnels can increase the risk of pests and disease, so you need to strike a fine balance between humidity and ventilation. In hot weather, shading may be necessary. Damp down plants and soil regularly (see p. 120) to prevent the build-up of pests such as red spider mite. Mulch the whole floor area, paths included, with straw; this helps maintain humidity and keeps the roots cool. Water regularly, and once fruits are developing, combine watering with a liquid feed. If roots develop above ground, cover them with garden compost as an extra source of nutrients.

The all-female varieties are more temperamental than ridge types. They germinate best at about 21°C/70°F, and need minimum night temperatures of 16–24°C/60–75°F. Occasionally male flowers appear; remove these to prevent bitterness. (The female flowers are distinguished by the visible bump of the embryonic fruit which develops behind the petals.)

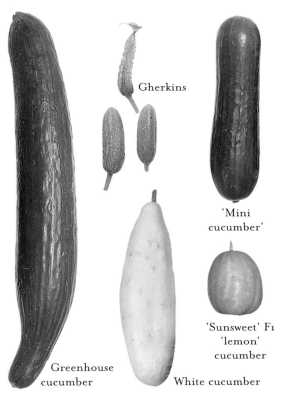

Gherkins

'Mini cucumber'

'Sunsweet' F1 'lemon' cucumber

Greenhouse cucumber

White cucumber

Examples of modern ridge cucumbers of the Japanese or 'burpless' type: BELOW 'Burpless Tasty Green' F1 and RIGHT 'Tasty King' F1. Their quality approaches that of the European greenhouses cucumbers, but they are far more robust and easily grown, indoors and outside.

GROWING IN CONTAINERS

Cucumbers are not 'naturals' for containers, as containers restrict their roots and the soil temperature tends to rise too high. With care they can be grown in growing bags or in pots of at least 25cm/10in diameter. Put them in a sheltered position.

PESTS AND DISEASES

Unless stated otherwise, for control and prevention, see p. 125.

Cucumbers flourish in suitable climates, but are prone to various disorders and diseases in less favourable conditions. Good husbandry is the key to success. Never, for example, take a chance on planting in cold soil. Destroy diseased foliage, and uproot and burn diseased plants. The most common problems are:

Slugs Young and trailing plants are the most vulnerable.

Aphids Colonies on the underside of leaves cause stunted and puckered growth.

Red spider mite Cucumbers grown under cover are very susceptible.

Cucumber mosaic virus This aphid-borne disease causes mottled, yellowed and distorted leaves; plants may become stunted and die. Remove and destroy infected plants and where possible control aphids. Varieties with a degree of resistance may become available in the future.

Powdery mildew White powdery patches occur on the leaves in hot weather, often spreading rapidly, and weakening and killing the plant. Good ventilation helps prevention. Currently some varieties have impressive resistance.

VARIETIES

Greenhouse, all-female with mildew resistance 'Carmen' F1; 'Passandra' F1 ('mini cucumber'), 'Tyria' F1.

Japanese and 'burpless' ridge type 'Burpless Tasty Green' F1, 'Kyoto', 'Slice King', 'Tasty King' F1, 'Tokyo Slicer'.

Standard ridge 'Bedfordshire Prize', 'Marketmore' (good mildew resistance), 'Sunsweet' F1 (lemon cucumber), 'White Wonder' (long white skin).

Sweet pepper (Capsicum) *Capsicum annuum* Grossum Group

Bell-shaped types

Bonnet-shaped types

Box-shaped types

Sweet peppers or capsicums are tender tropical annuals that produce very varied, beautiful fruits. Most of these are green when immature, becoming red, yellow, orange or even a deep purple-black when fully ripe. Fruit shape is also very variable. They can be square, box-shaped (almost rectangular), bell-shaped, squat (for example, the 'bonnet-' or 'tomato-shaped' pepper) and long. The long-fruited types can be broad-shouldered or narrow, some tapered varieties having twisted ends like goat horns. Fruits can be thin- or thick-walled, upright or pendulous. The plants are bushy in habit, with popular cultivars usually 30–45cm/12–18in high, though some are taller. (For chilli peppers, see p. 61.)

Sweet peppers are superb salad vegetables, contributing colour, flavour and crisp texture when raw. As they mature, their flavour undergoes subtle changes. Coloured ripe peppers are sweeter and richer-flavoured – and richer in vitamins. Flavours can also modulate to wonderful effect when peppers are cooked or blanched then cooled to use as salads.

CULTIVATION

Broadly speaking, sweet peppers require much the same conditions as tomatoes (see p. 54), though they prefer marginally higher temperatures. Depending on variety, most peppers reach a usable size slightly faster than tomatoes, but you should allow anything from three to six weeks for them to turn from the immature green stage to fully ripe. Like tomatoes, they need high light intensity to flourish. For the cultivation options in temperate climates, see Tomatoes, p. 54. Being dwarfer in habit than tomatoes, sweet peppers can be accommodated more easily under cloches and in frames or, in the early stages, under fleece. On the whole, modern thin-walled hybrids tolerate lower temperatures and lower light levels than the thick walled 'Bell Boy' types, so are recommended where summers are unreliable.

Peppers are in the potato and tomato family and susceptible to the same soil pests and diseases, so should be rotated accordingly. Fortunately, they seem to be less susceptible to potato blight and generally healthier than tomatoes. They also have lower fertility requirements. Digging in plenty of well-rotted manure before planting is normally sufficient: indeed, too much nitrogen can encourage leafiness at the expense of fruit production.

Peppers perform well in containers such as growing bags and pots, which should be 20–25cm/8–10in diameter, though dwarf varieties can be grown in smaller pots.

PLANT RAISING

For plant raising, see Tomatoes, p. 54. It is advisable to sow fresh seed, as viability drops off after a year or two. The aim with peppers is to produce sturdy, short-jointed plants. You can achieve this by potting on several times before planting out, initially into 7.5cm/3in pots, and subsequently into 10cm/4in pots. Seedlings are normally ready for planting about eight weeks after sowing, when they are about 10cm/4in high with the first flower truss showing. Harden them off well before planting outside, protecting them if necessary. Space standard varieties 38–45cm/15–18in apart and dwarf types 30cm/12in apart. You can interplant indoor plants with dwarf French marigolds to deter whitefly.

Peppers need to develop a strong branching framework. If growth seems weak, nip out the growing point when the plant is about 30cm/12in high to encourage sideshoots to develop. A small 'king' fruit may develop early, low on the main stem, inhibiting further development. Remove it at either the flower bud or young fruit stage. Once plants are setting fruits, nip back shoot tips to 20cm/8in or so to concentrate the plant's energy.

Branches can be brittle, and plants may need support if they are becoming top heavy. Tie them to upright bamboo canes, or support individual branches with small split canes. Earth up around the base of the stem for further support. Water sufficiently to keep the soil from drying out, but do not overwater. Heavier watering is required once fruits start to set. Mulching is beneficial. Keep plants under cover well ventilated, and maintain humidity by damping down regularly in hot weather (see p. 120). This also helps fruit to set. If fruits are developing well, supplementary feed is unnecessary. If not, apply a liquid feed as fruits start to set. At this point plants in containers should be fed every ten days or so with a seaweed-based fertilizer or tomato feed at half strength.

Start picking fruits young to encourage further cropping. Pick green fruits when the matt surface has become smooth and glossy. Where the season is long enough, you can leave fruits from mid-summer onwards to develop their full colour. Plants will not stand any frost. Towards the end of the season, uproot remaining plants and hang them in a sunny porch or greenhouse. They continue to colour up and may remain in reasonable condition for many weeks.

PESTS AND DISEASES

Poor weather is the main enemy of outdoor peppers. Under cover, red spider mite, whitefly and aphids are the most likely pests. For control measures, see p. 126.

VARIETIES

In warm climates, the choice is infinite. The following are reliable croppers in cooler climates: 'Ace' F1, 'Bell Boy' F1, 'Californian Wonder', 'Canape' F1, 'Gypsy' F1, 'Redskin' F1 (dwarf), 'Unicorn' F1.

Peppers interplanted with French marigolds to discourage whitefly

Chilli peppers *Capsicum frutescens* **and other spp.**

The chillies are notable for their fiery flavours, and are not much used in salads. Notable exceptions are the milder, fleshier 'Hungarian Wax' and 'Anaheim' types, such as 'Hot Mexico' and 'Antler'. These are superb cooked and cold. Cultivate as sweet peppers.

Mild fleshy chilli 'Antler'

the onion family

Bulb onions Allium cepa

The onions are a large family of biennials and perennials, with a characteristic flavour. Using appropriate types, it is feasible to have a year-round supply: all can be used in salads. They divide into bulb and 'green' types. Bulb onions (*Allium cepa*) are adapted to temperate climates, and are used fresh or stored, sliced, chopped or grated raw into salads. Most are creamy or white-fleshed, but the pink-skinned varieties have pretty pink-hued flesh. Flavour varies from mild to piquant, depending on variety, climate and growing conditions. Very small bulb onions are grown for pickling.

SOIL AND SITE

Bulb onions need an open site and fertile, thoroughly dug soil. Prepare it several months before sowing or planting, as growth will be too lush in freshly manured ground. Good drainage is essential. Lime acid soils to a pH of at least 6.5. In spite of the 'onion patch' tradition, try to rotate on a four- or at least three-year cycle to prevent the build-up of eelworm and soil-borne diseases.

CULTIVATION

Bulbs are the compact, swollen bases of the leaves. Bulb onions are very responsive to day length, and once a certain point is reached, about mid-June in the British Isles, no further leaves are initiated. In effect the bulb has reached its maximum potential: there is no 'catching up' if they were sown late. Success hinges on contriving the longest-possible growing season. It is essential to grow varieties suited to your climatic zone. 'Foreign' onions rarely succeed.

Sets or seed? Onions are grown from 'sets' – tiny, specially produced bulbs – or from seed. Each has its merits. Sets, being a more advanced stage of development, mature earlier, are easy to plant, can be planted in soil conditions unsuitable for sowing and escape onion fly attacks. Drawbacks are that planting dates are more critical, they are more prone to premature bolting and they are only available for certain varieties. Seeds are cheaper, available for all varieties, are more flexibile over sowing times, and premature bolting is less likely. They require more attention, and are more liable to onion fly attack. Where good-quality sets are available (as in the British Isles) their use simplifies onion growing!

Sowing programme To ensure a continuous supply in temperate climates, make two sowings or plantings. Sow in late winter/early spring, for (a) main summer supplies of fresh onions, ready from mid-summer onwards and (b) storage onions, ready to lift in late summer/early autumn. These normally keep until mid- to late spring the following year. Make a second sowing in late summer/early autumn, for the first fresh onions, which will mature in early to mid-summer the following year. Only hardy varieties capable of overwintering outdoors are suitable; currently most of these only keep for a few months after lifting.

Growing from sets Use appropriate sets for the planting season (for varieties, see p. 64). Plant firm, small to medium-sized sets, as large sets are more likely to bolt prematurely. Some varieties are 'heat treated' to destroy the flower embryo and prevent premature bolting: these must be planted later. Follow the supplier's instructions.

For the main summer and storage crops, plant standard sets *in situ* from late winter to mid-spring as soon as the soil is workable. Plant heat-treated sets later. If soil conditions are poor, start sets singly in 5cm/2in modules and plant out when conditions improve. Plant overwintering sets in early to mid-autumn.

Plant sets by pushing them gently into the soil, until only the tip is visible. For the highest yield of medium-sized onions, space them 15cm/6in apart; closer spacing gives smaller onions, wider spacing larger ones. If birds tweak the sets aside, uproot and replant carefully: pushing them back in damages developing roots. (For

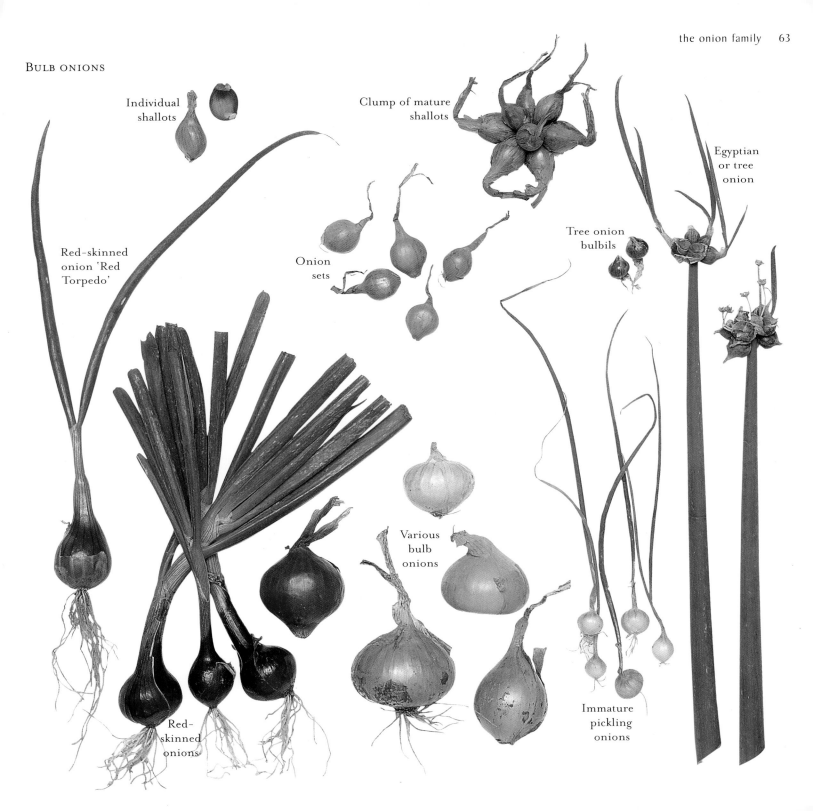

BULB ONIONS

Individual shallots

Clump of mature shallots

Egyptian or tree onion

Red-skinned onion 'Red Torpedo'

Onion sets

Tree onion bulbils

Various bulb onions

Red-skinned onions

Immature pickling onions

protection against birds, see p. 126.)

Growing from seed For that invaluable early start, sow indoors from late winter to early spring in seed trays or modules, at 10–16°C/50–61°F. If sowing in seed trays, prick out seedlings at the 'crook neck' stage, when they are still bent over, spacing them 5cm/2in apart. Onions can be multi-sown with up to six seeds per module. Once the seeds are germinated, maintain a temperature no higher than about 13°C/55°F before planting out, after hardening off. For maximum yields of medium-sized onions, space them 15cm/6in apart, or 4cm/1½in apart in rows 30cm/12in apart. As with sets, wider spacing produces larger onions and vice versa. Space multi-sown modules 25–30cm/10–12in apart each way.

Follow with *in situ* sowing outdoors as soon as the soil is warm. Prepare the ground ten days before sowing, effectively making a 'stale seedbed'. This allows the soil to settle, deterring onion fly, which is attracted by freshly disturbed soil. Onion seed is small, so rake the seedbed to a fine tilth. Sow thinly in rows 20–30cm/8–12in apart, thinning to the spacings above. Use thinnings as green salad onions. Sow hardy overwintering varieties in late summer to early autumn, according to the date recommended for the variety.

WEEDING AND WATERING

Keep onions weed-free, especially in the early stages, as the narrow upright leaves never form a weed-suppressing 'canopy'. An onion hoe is the ideal weeding tool. In dry weather, water carefully until plants are well established. Further watering is normally unnecessary.

HARVESTING AND STORAGE

For long-term storage, allow the foliage to die back and bend over naturally. Never forcefully bend it, as the resulting wounds lead to storage rots. Ease bulbs gently out of the ground. Dry them for about ten days, either outside off the ground on upturned boxes or racks, or, in wet weather, under cover, until the outer skins are papery. Store them hung in bunches or plaits, or loose in shallow boxes, in cool, well-ventilated, frost-free conditions.

For fresh and short-term storage, lift onions as required, once they are large enough to use. After the foliage has died back in late summer, the remaining onions must be lifted, or they deteriorate. Treat them as storage onions, using them up first.

PESTS AND DISEASES

Onion fly Groups of seedlings turn yellow and die as a result of attacks from tiny maggots. Onion fly is worst in hot dry conditions. Sow into a stale seedbed (see above), or grow under fine nets. Remove and burn damaged plants.

Mildews and rots There are no organic remedies for the diseases which attack in poor seasons. Handle storage onions gently, as rots start with cuts and bruises.

VARIETIES

(* = currently also available as sets)

Dual-purpose, fresh and storage *'Centurion', 'Marco' F1, *'Hyduro', 'Hygro' F1, 'Rijnsburger Robusta', 'Mammoth Red' (red), *'New Fen Globe', *'Red Baron' F1 (red), *'Setton', *'Sturon'.

Autumn sown 'Imai Early Yellow', 'Buffalo' F1.

Autumn-planted sets 'Electric' (red), 'Radar', 'Unwins First Early', 'Swift'.

Pickling onions *Allium cepa*

Varieties suitable for pickling never develop a papery outer skin. They grow best in fertile soil, but tolerate poorer conditions than bulb onions. Sow in spring in a sunny situation in wide drills or bands, spacing seeds about 1cm/½in apart, or in rows 30cm/12in apart, spacing seeds 6mm/¼in apart. The high density keeps the bulbs small; thinning is normally unnecessary. Seeds are usually sown about 1cm/½in deep, but in Holland they are sometimes sown 4–5cm/1½–2in deep, to make the bulbs whiter. Allow the foliage to die down, then harvest as bulb onions. If left in the ground longer they will resprout. They can be stored a while before pickling.

Typical varieties 'Paris Silver Skin' and 'Barletta' (white); 'Purplette' (red).

Egyptian onion (Tree onion) *Allium cepa* Proliferum Group

These curious onions produce clusters of tiny aerial bulbils, not unlike hazelnuts, which in turn sprout and develop further clusters, so the plant becomes two- or sometimes three-tiered. In due course the stems bend to the ground, where the bulbils root, the plant thus perpetuating itself. Egyptian onions are low yielding but extremely hardy: 'mid-air' bulbils can be picked in mid-winter.

Egyptian onions grow in most soils in a sunny spot, but prefer fertile, well-drained soil. Plant single bulbils or a cluster about 25cm/10in apart, in spring or autumn. The plants will keep going for several years, but may need thinning periodically.

Shallots *Allium cepa* Aggregatum Group

Typical shallots are flask-shaped bulbs, multiplying into a cluster at ground level. There are red-, brown- or yellow-skinned varieties – the reds being smallest but reputedly better-flavoured. Shallots have a distinct, clean onion flavour, with varying degrees of pungency. A major asset is their ability to keep sound, often until early or mid-summer the year after harvesting. This bridges the gap in late spring/early summer between stored and fresh onions. An exception is the long 'Jersey Long' type, which has outstanding flavour but does not keep well. Shallots tolerate much higher temperatures than bulb onions, while European varieties tolerate moderate frost. They are easily grown, sometimes from seed but usually from sets. Some stocks become virused: beware of cheap offers!

Cultivation For soil and situation, see Bulb Onions, p. 62. Plant single sets in late autumn in mild areas, otherwise in late winter/early spring. (Some varieties are only suited to spring planting.) The optimum size for planting is about 12mm/½in circumference; larger sets may bolt prematurely. Remove the loose, dry outer skin and plant as onion sets (p. 62), spaced 18cm/7in apart each way for the highest yield. If raising from seed, sow indoors in early spring as bulb onions (p. 64), planting 5cm/2in apart each way. Each seedling normally produces one bulb. Cultivate, harvest and store shallots as bulb onions (p. 62). Provided they are healthy, keep some for replanting the following season. They eventually become infected with virus, so buy fresh, clean stock every few years.

Varieties Yellow and brown: 'Golden Gourmet', 'Santé', 'Topper'; red: 'Piquant', 'Red Sun'; Long Jersey: 'Griselle', 'Jermor'.

Green onions

The main types of green onion are the European 'salad' or 'spring' onion (*Allium cepa*), grown for the young green leaves and tiny bulbs, and the larger more robust oriental bunching onion (*Allium fistulosum*), a form of 'Welsh' onion. These are adapted to both hotter and colder climates.

Spring onion (Salad or bunching onion, Scallion) *Allium cepa*

In these varieties of bulb onions the green leaves and white stems are harvested within two months of sowing. Some are straight-shanked, others form tiny bulbs. Their refreshing flavour and colour are invaluable in salads. Recent hybridizing with *Allium fistulosum* (bunching onion) is producing varieties with stronger, healthier leaves that remain green and erect far longer.

Cultivation For soil, cultivation, pests and diseases, see Bulb Onions, p. 62. For the main summer-to-autumn supply, sow from early spring to early summer outdoors, making the first sowings under cloches or protection if necessary. Sow in succession every two or three weeks. For very early spring supplies, sow hardier overwintering varieties in mid- and late summer. Where winters are mild and not too wet, sow in the open; otherwise sow under cover.

Sow either in single rows about 15cm/6in apart, or in roughly 10cm/4in wide drills, in both cases spacing seeds about 2.5cm/1in apart. When the young onions reach a usable size, pull as required.

Varieties (* = *A. fistulosum* hybrid) For summer and autumn crops: *'Parade', 'Ramrod', 'White Lisbon'; mainly autumn sowing: *'Guardsman'; 'Ramrod' 'Winter Hardy White', 'Winter White Bunching'.

Welsh and Oriental bunching onion
Allium fistulosum

Welsh onion is a hardy, perennial, evergreen onion, long cultivated in northern Europe. It can grow 50cm/20in tall, with fairly strong-flavoured, rather coarse, hollow green leaves, thickened at the base.

Oriental bunching onion 'Ishikura'. These sturdy green-leaved onions can be used in salads all year round.

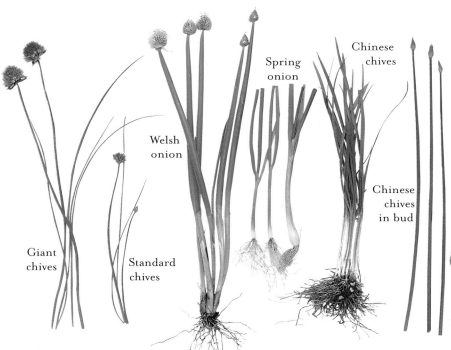

Welsh onion

Giant chives

Standard chives

Spring onion

Chinese chives

Chinese chives in bud

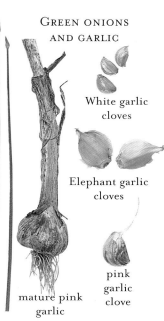

GREEN ONIONS AND GARLIC

White garlic cloves

Elephant garlic cloves

mature pink garlic

pink garlic clove

Propagate it by dividing established clumps every two or three years, replanting younger outer sections in a new site, 20cm/8in apart. Or sow seed *in situ* in spring or autumn, thinning to 20cm/8in apart.

In Asia, over many centuries, a diverse group of milder onions has been developed from the Welsh onion. There are different varieties for harvesting at every stage: seedlings, young leaves, leafy stems and the imposing leek-like white shafts of the single-stem types, 2.5cm/1in thick and 45cm/18in long. Some varieties have red-tinted stems. (For detailed cultivation, see my book *Oriental Vegetables*.)

Bunching onions grow best in light, fertile soil. Naturally healthy and vigorous, they tolerate a wide range of temperatures. Although perennial, they are best grown as annuals or biennials. For tender young salad leaves, sow *in situ* outdoors throughout the growing season, as for spring onions (p. 65), making early and late sowings under cover. They can also be multi-sown in modules, planted 7.5cm/3in apart. Pull for use at any stage from 5–15cm/2–6in tall, normally within five weeks of sowing. For larger plants with slightly thickened stems, thin to 4cm/1½in apart; pull these, or cut single leaves, when 30cm/12in high, usually within three months of sowing.

In temperate climates, hardier single-stem varieties, which survive moderate frost, can be grown for winter and early spring. The leaves may be coarse but can be sliced finely into salads. Sow from spring to early summer *in situ*, in rows 30cm/12in apart, thinning to 7.5cm/3in apart. Cut leaves as required. They often stand in good condition into spring and early summer, and are usable even after flower heads have formed.

Varieties For summer use: 'Kyoto Market', 'Laser', 'Long White Tokyo', 'Summer Isle', 'Savel'; for summer and overwintering: 'Ishikura', 'White Evergreen'.

Chives *Allium schoenoprasum*

Chives grow 23–30cm/9–12in high and both the slender leaves and tiny pink to purple flowers in the flower heads add a delicate onion flavour – and colour – to salads. 'Giant Chives' is a taller, handsome form. Chives tolerate light shade, but, as natives of damp meadows, do best in fertile, reasonably moist soil.

Cultivation Sow in spring in seed trays, or multi-sow about four seeds per module. Plant in clumps of about four seedlings, the clumps 23cm/9in apart. Lift and divide old clumps every three or four years in spring, replanting the younger, outer plants in clumps in a fresh site. Once they are established, cut foliage just above soil level.

Cut plants in sequence to allow them time to regenerate. Remove flower heads unless required for salads. In temperate climates, chives die back in mid-winter, but you can cloche or pot up a few and bring them indoors for early pickings.

Chinese chives (Garlic chives) *Allium tuberosum*

Chinese chives have light green, flat leaves which emerge early in spring. They have a unique, part garlic, part chives flavour. From summer onwards the clumps produce a mass of starry white flowers on 60cm/24in stems, fading into beautiful seedheads. Leaves, flowers buds and flowering stems are all edible. In China plants are covered after being cut with clay pots to produce a blanched crop of long, pale yellow, mild flavoured leaves. (For further reading, see my book *Oriental Vegetables*). Chinese chives are undemanding perennials, tolerating extremes of high and low temperatures.

Cultivation Chinese chives tolerate any well-drained, moderately fertile soil, and can be grown in containers. Sow fresh seed in seed trays or modules from spring to early summer, planting seedlings in their permanent position in late summer/early autumn when about 10cm/4in high. Plant in clumps of about six seedlings, the clumps 20cm/8in apart. They grow slowly. In the first season after planting, cut sparingly when the leaves are 15cm/6in high and remove any flowering stems. Feed in spring with manure or a liquid feed.

Chinese chives can also be propagated by lifting and dividing clumps, as for chives (p. 66). They are long-lived, and there is no need to divide them unless they are losing vigour. The leaves normally die back in mid-winter; bring plants into growth earlier by covering them with cloches in late winter.

Garlic *Allium sativum*

The unique flavour of garlic is indispensable in many salad dishes and dressings. Mature bulbs are used fresh or stored; immature bulbs sold as 'green' or 'wet' garlic are superbly flavoured. In China, garlic is also cultivated for the young green leaves and flowering stem. (For this and more on garlic, see my book *Oriental Vegetables*.) There are numerous garlic strains, the sickle-shaped cloves being white, pink or purplish and varying in pungency. Garlic stores from six to twelve months, depending on variety. It is crucial to plant healthy, disease-free stock suited to your climate.

Cultivation Garlic needs an open, sunny position, and grows best on moderately rich, light soil that is not freshly manured. Good drainage is essential. Bonfire ash can be incorporated when planting, as potash is beneficial. Lime acid soils. Garlic is hardy, surviving at least –10°C/14°F, and needs a long growing season. Although varieties differ in their requirements, most should be planted in late autumn. Otherwise plant in spring as soon as the soil is workable. Where winters are wet, start off cloves singly in modules, planting out in spring when conditions improve.

Plant plump, healthy cloves split from mature bulbs, ideally 1cm/½in in diameter. The bulbs develop below ground. On light soils, plant up to 10cm/4in deep; on heavy soils plant more shallowly, but cover the cloves with at least 2.5cm/1in of soil. Make sure the flat end is downwards: it is not always easy to tell. For optimum yield, space bulbs 18cm/7in apart. On wet ground, either plant on 10cm/4in-high ridges, or put coarse sand or potting compost beneath the cloves. Keep them weed-free and water in very dry weather early in the season.

Harvesting Unlike onions, garlic must be lifted when the foliage starts turning yellow, or the cloves resprout. Dig them up carefully (they bruise easily) and dry them hung or laid on trays in a breezy situation – under cover in wet weather. Baking in full sun is not necessary. Store for winter like onions (p. 64), ideally at 5–10°C/41–50°F.

Elephant garlic (*Allium ampeloprasum*)

Elephant garlic is a type of leek, which forms huge white, garlic-flavoured cloves. The flavour ranges from mild to fairly strong. Plant in autumn a month before frost is likely or in early spring, or start cloves in modules. Plant at least 2.5/1in deep and 30cm/12in apart. Harvest as garlic above.

rooting vegetables

Radishes *Raphanus sativus*

Radishes are a varied and versatile salad crop. The familiar sharp flavour of radish roots is muted to refreshing subtlety in sprouted seeds, and in the highly productive seedling crops. Perhaps the best-kept secret is the seed pods that develop after flowering. What a gastronomic treat, if picked young and green! In recent years the small radishes grown in the West have been joined by some of the large Asian radishes, for example the long white 'mooli' and the spectacular pink- or green-fleshed Chinese 'Beauty Heart' radishes. Most radishes are used raw in salads, but the larger types can be cooked like turnips, while 'leaf' radish (see p. 70) makes pleasant cooked greens. Some varieties are only available through heirloom seed libraries.

Summer radishes: CLOCKWISE FROM TOP LEFT 'Long White Icicle', 'French Breakfast 3 Sabina', 'French Golden', 'Salad Mixed', 'Scarlet Globe', 'Pink Beauty', 'Ilka', 'Prinz Rotin', 'Woods Frame', 'Sparkler 3', 'Easter Egg'

TYPES OF RADISH

Standard small radishes The popular small radishes are round, rarely more than 2.5cm/1in diameter, or long and tapered, usually up to 5cm/2in long, though some are much longer. All have white flesh but the skin can be white, red, pink, yellow, purple to black or in bicoloured combinations – making for colourful salads. They are used fresh throughout the growing season.

Asian radish This diverse group of large radishes includes the white- or occasionally green-skinned Japanese mooli or 'Daikon', which are typically 30cm/12in long, weighing 500g/1lb; some giants reach 27kg/60lb (see my book *Oriental Vegetables*). They are used fresh or stored, cooked or raw, mainly in summer and autumn. The various forms of the Beauty Heart types are round, oval or tapered, and pink- or green-fleshed. Rounded varieties are 5–10cm/2–4in in diameter; tapered green varieties up to 20cm/8in long. These decorative radishes are sweet and used raw in salads.

Storage and winter hardy radish These are roughly the size of Beauty Heart types, and display varying degrees of frost hardiness. Some of mine have survived –10°C/14°F outside. There are round and long forms, with black, pink, brown or violet skin. They can be lifted and stored for winter use. They tend to be on the coarse side.

SOIL AND SITE

Radishes grow best in well-drained, light, fertile soil with a neutral pH. Avoid freshly manured ground, which encourages lush leafy growth at the expense of the roots. They tolerate light shade in mid-summer. Adequate moisture throughout growth is essential. In hot, dry soils, growth is slow and there is a risk of radishes becoming pithy, woody, hollow and unpleasantly hot-flavoured. Rotate the larger slow-growing types as brassicas. All radishes are susceptible to flea beetle attacks at the seedling stage; for control, see p. 126.

CULTIVATION OF STANDARD SMALL RADISHES

These are normally ready three to four weeks after sowing, so are ideal for intercropping, sowing among carrots or above potatoes and marking rows of slow-germinating seeds.

For spring to autumn supplies Sow 'little and often' at roughly ten-day intervals. Make the first sowings under cover in late winter, followed by outdoor sowings in spring as soon as the soil is workable. Make the earliest sowings in a sheltered spot, protect with cloches or fleece if necessary and use quick-maturing 'forcing' varieties. Continue sowing outdoors until early autumn, making the last sowings under cover in mid-autumn.

Sow thinly *in situ*, broadcast, or in rows 15cm/6in apart, or in shallow wide drills. The commonest cause of failure is overcrowding: entangled lanky seedlings never develop properly. Aim to space seeds 2.5cm/1in apart, or thin early to that, or slightly wider, spacing. Sow at an even depth of about 12mm/½in – slightly deeper for long-rooted varieties. This prevents seeds nearest the surface from germinating first and swamping those sown deeper. In dry weather, water weekly at the rate of 11 litres per sq. m/2 gallons per sq. yd. Pull radishes as soon as they are ready. Most varieties bolt rapidly on maturity, though some have good bolting resistance.

Mid-winter crops Certain small-leaved, slow-growing varieties have been developed for winter culture in unheated greenhouses and polytunnels. Night temperatures should normally be above about 5°C/41°F. Sow from mid-autumn to late winter, thinning to 5cm/2in apart. Keep them well ventilated. They require little watering, except in sudden hot spells: leaves turning dark green indicate that watering is necessary. Give extra protection if colder weather is forecast. They will be ready in late winter/early spring.

CULTIVATION OF ASIAN TYPES

These large radishes respond to day length and low temperatures in the same way as oriental brassicas (see p. 31), so it is best to delay sowing until early to mid-summer. Bolt-resistant varieties of white mooli can be sown earlier, in late spring. Once ready, these types stand in good condition far longer than ordinary radishes. They are susceptible to the normal range of brassica pests and diseases (see p. 28). Growing under fine nets gives excellent protection against cabbage root fly, which is particularly damaging.

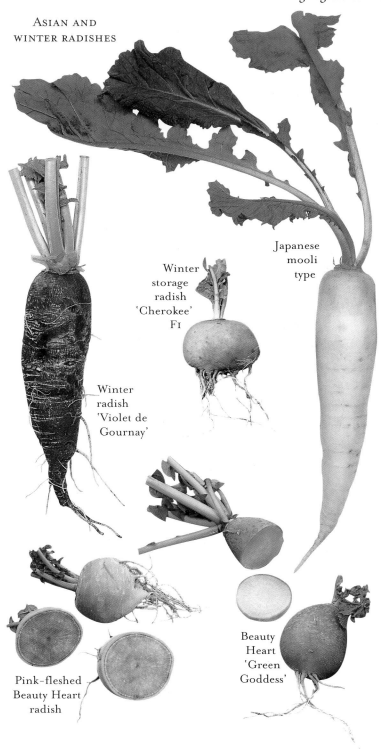

ASIAN AND WINTER RADISHES

Japanese mooli type

Winter storage radish 'Cherokee' F1

Winter radish 'Violet de Gournay'

Pink-fleshed Beauty Heart radish

Beauty Heart 'Green Goddess'

Standard mooli These take seven to eight weeks to mature. Sow *in situ* 1–2cm /½–¾in deep; or sow in sunken drills 4cm/1½in deep and pull soil around the stems as they develop for extra support. Plants grow quite large, so it is advisable to sow in rows at least 30cm/12in apart – spacing varies from 7.5–10cm/3–4in apart for smaller varieties to at least 30cm/12in apart for the largest; or you can sow mooli singly in modules and transplant. You can also pull them when immature, leaving the remaining plants to grow larger.

Beauty Heart types The pink-fleshed forms take ten to twelve weeks to mature. Do not sow until mid-summer, partly to avoid premature bolting, but equally because the deep internal colour develops only when night temperatures fall to about 10°C/50°F in autumn. Sow *in situ*, spacing plants 20cm/8in apart each way, or 12.5cm/5in apart in rows 30cm/12in apart. For more reliable results, sow in modules, singly or two seeds per module, and plant as one 30cm/12in apart, at the four-to-five-leaf stage. Where summers are short, plant under cover to extend the season. These types tolerate light frosts, but if there is likely to be heavy frost lift them and store in cool conditions indoors, as hardy winter radish below. Internal colour intensifies with maturity and continues to deepen in storage.

Grow green varieties the same way, but as they mature sooner they can be more closely spaced. They can be lifted sooner, as the pale green colour is constant.

Leaf radish Some fast-growing mooli varieties have been selected for cutting 20–25cm/8–10in high for cooked leaves. These varieties are excellent for cut-and-come-again seedlings, cut 5–7.5cm/2–3in high sometimes two to three weeks after sowing. They stand high and low temperatures, so you can sow them from late winter to mid-autumn, with the earliest and latest sowings under cover.

STORAGE AND HARDY WINTER RADISH

These radishes are a valuable source of radish in winter and spring. Sow from mid- to late summer as for Beauty Heart radish above. In temperate climates, you can leave them in the ground during winter; tuck straw around them to make lifting easier in frost. In more severe climates, or where slug damage is serious, lift the roots in late autumn, trim off the leaves and store in boxes of sand in cool conditions. They should keep sound until spring. Once cut, wrapped roots will keep in a refrigerator for several weeks.

Pickled radish seed pods

Flowering radish seed heads with edible pods just forming

RADISH PODS

The immature seed pods of radishes have an excellent flavour and crisp texture, and are used raw or pickled. Allow a few plants to run to seed for this purpose. The larger the radish, the more succulent the pods seem to be. A single hardy winter radish left in the soil over winter will yield a huge crop of pods the following spring. Pick pods regularly while they are young and crisp, to encourage production over several weeks. Alternatively grow varieties with exceptionally long pods, such as Bavarian 'Munchen Bier' and 'Rat's Tail'. Sow from spring to summer, thinning to 30cm/12in apart. Pollen beetle attacks can damage radish flowers and prevent pods from forming. Spray with derris, or grow plants under nets. I discovered recently that the leaf radish 'Jaba' produces excellent pods.

VARIETIES

Standard radish 'Crystal Ball', 'French Breakfast', 'Long White Icicle', 'Pink Beauty', 'Cherry Belle', 'Sparkler'.
Good bolting resistance 'Pontvil', 'Prince'/'Prinz Rotin'.
For winter under cover 'Helro', 'Marabelle', 'Robino', 'Saxa'.
Summer mooli (slow-bolting) 'April Cross' F1, 'Minowase Summer Cross' F1.
Beauty Heart (red) 'Mantanghong' F1.
Beauty Heart (green) 'Green Goddess', 'Misato Green'.
Storage and hardy winter 'Cherokee' F1, 'Black Spanish Round', 'Violet de Gournay'.
Leaf radish 'Bisai', 'Jaba'.

Carrot *Daucus carota*

My long-standing dislike of grated raw carrot makes it hard for me to be enthusiastic about them as salad vegetables, although I love them cooked. The outstanding exceptions are young carrots, exemplified by 'mini carrots' – small, finger-thick carrots harvested at most 7.5cm/3in long. These are sweet, tender and delicious raw, whether nibbled whole or sliced. A case can also be made for the unusually coloured carrots. (For cultivation of other types, consult a general gardening book; see Further Reading pp. 162–3.)

CULTIVATION OF MINI CARROTS

Carrots require deep, light, fertile, well-drained soil, with a pH between 6.5 and 7.5. Avoid heavy, compacted or clay soils, which prevent roots from swelling, and stony soils, which cause forking. Ideally dig in well-rotted compost or manure several months before sowing. Small carrots are excellent subjects for growing bags or large pots of potting compost. Carrots are cool-season crops, growing best at temperatures of 16–18°C/60–65°F. Seed germinates very slowly at temperatures below 10°C/50°F, so delay sowing until the soil has warmed up: lingering carrots are never succulent. Prepare a finely raked, weed-free seedbed, as carrot seedlings are easily smothered by weeds and awkward to weed.

Mini carrot production depends on growing appropriate varieties at dense spacing. Varieties used commercially are developed from the slender 'Amsterdam' types, and slightly broader 'Nantes' types, which are both cylindrical, stump-rooted carrots traditionally used for forcing and early crops. They are fast-growing and smooth-skinned with a small central core – all factors making for tenderness.

For a continuous supply, sow outdoors *in situ* from mid-spring to mid-summer, at two- to three-week intervals. Sow thinly in rows 15cm/6in apart, spacing seeds about 4cm/1½in apart so that thinning is unnecessary, or thinning early to that spacing. Alternatively sow in shallow drills 10–15cm/4–6in wide, with seedlings about 2cm/¾in apart. Water sufficiently to prevent the soil from drying out. The carrots will be ready for pulling eleven to thirteen weeks after sowing.

Make earlier and later sowings under cover; protect early outdoor sowings in frames, under cloches or by fleece. Unless the weather becomes very hot, small carrots can be grown under fleece to maturity. This also protects them from carrot fly.

Carrot fly can be a serious problem, though early sowings often escape attack. Either grow the carrots under fleece or fine nets, or surround them with 60cm/2ft-high barriers (of clear polythene film, for example) to deter the low-flying, egg-laying flies. They are

Novelty carrots: white 'Belgian White', red 'Purple Dragon', orange 'Comet', yellow 'Jaune Obtuse de Doubs'

attracted by the smell of bruised foliage, so thin in the evening, burying thinnings in the compost heap.

Varieties
Suitable for mini carrots 'Amini', 'Ideal', and most Amsterdam and Nantes types, such as 'Amsterdam Forcing 3-Minicor'.

Novelty carrots
Although we are conditioned to orange-fleshed carrots, heirloom European yellow and white carrots, often used as fodder crops, are surprisingly sweet-fleshed and well flavoured. Colourful purple-skinned carrots, sometimes pure purple inside, sometimes blended with orange, are being developed and becoming available. They could be the carrots of the future. Needless to say, all make colourful dishes. Currently available varieties are mainly recommended cooked (preferably by steaming) and cold, as some have strong 'off flavours', as they are termed in the trade, when raw.

I recently saw green-fleshed carrots in Tunisia, which were very palatable. If they become available, do try them.

Beetroot *Beta vulgaris*

Beetroot are available all year round – fresh during the growing season and stored in winter. They can be flat, round, tapered or cylindrical in shape, and while the textbook modern beet has evenly coloured deep red flesh, older varieties are also white- or yellow-fleshed, and in the case of the Italian heirloom 'Chioggia' characterized by target-like rings of pink and white. These are all considered well flavoured. Beet are normally cooked whole (otherwise the flesh bleeds) by baking in foil, steaming or boiling, and then used cold. Although not everyone's taste, beet can also be grated raw into salads. The young leaves are edible raw or lightly cooked, the scarlet-leaved varieties being highly decorative. Small beet, about 5cm/2in diameter, make delicious pickles. Baby or 'mini beet', roughly ping-pong-ball size, are probably the beetroot most worth growing for salad use: they develop fast, take least space and are arguably the best-flavoured. (For cultivation of standard and storage beet, consult a general gardening book; see Further Reading, pp. 162–3.) Sugar beet, incidentally, makes a very sweet-flavoured salad: a psychological drawback is its pale colour.

Leaves of 'Bull's Blood' beetroot

Beetroot: LEFT TO RIGHT 'Moneta', 'Burpee's Golden', 'Chioggia', 'Blankoma'

CULTIVATION OF MINI BEET

For growing temperatures, soil and cultivation see Carrots, p. 71, though beet grow successfully on heavier soil than carrots. Beet withstand moderate frost, but risk premature bolting if young plants are exposed for long to temperatures much below 10°C/50°F. Early spring sowings should only be made with bolt-resistant varieties. Seed germinates poorly at temperatures below 7°C/50°F. A chemical inhibitor in the seed sometimes prevents germination; if so, soak seed for half an hour in tepid water before sowing. Beet 'seed' is actually a seed cluster, so several seedlings germinate close together and require thinning. ('Monogerm' varieties are single-seeded, avoiding the problem.) Beet is normally sown *in situ* as it does not transplant well, unless sown in modules.

For mini beet, sow *in situ* from mid-spring to mid-summer. Sow at two-to-three-week intervals for a continuous supply from early to mid-summer until autumn. Sow seeds 2cm/¾in deep, in rows 15cm/6in apart, thinning seedlings to 2.5cm/1in apart. This will produce small, even, high-quality beets, ready for pulling on average twelve weeks after sowing. If larger beet are required, a few can be left to develop. The earliest outdoor sowings can be protected by sowing in frames or under cloches. Sowing under crop covers such as fleece, removed after four or five weeks, doubles the yields from early sowings.

VARIETIES

For mini beet 'Pronto'. If unavailable use standard round red varieties such as 'Action' F1, 'Red Ace' F1, 'Pablo' F1 or bolt-resistant varieties such as 'Bikores'.

Novelty beetroot

The striped, yellow, and white beets lend themselves to artistic display. Sow *in situ* from late spring to early summer, in rows 23cm/9in apart, thinning to 7.5–10cm/3–4in apart; or multi-sow in modules, about three seeds per module; if numerous seedlings germinate, thin to four or five per module before planting out 'as one' 20cm/8in apart. The highly coloured red-leaved 'Bull's Blood' beet is a mainstay of my potagers, retaining its leaf colour late into winter; it has excellent beets. Plant a few under cover in early autumn for quality leaves until spring.

Varieties 'Blankoma' (white); 'Burpee's Golden' (yellow); 'Chioggia' (striped), 'Bull's Blood' and 'McGregor's Favourite' (red-leaved).

Turnip *Brassica campestris* Rapifera Group

Most turnips are too strongly flavoured for salads, although turnip seedlings are mild-flavoured and suitable for cut-and-come-again seedlings or sprouting. (For general cultivation, consult a general gardening book; see Further Reading, pp. 162–3.) Small turnips harvested at ping-pong-ball size are pleasantly sweet, mild and crisp. They are mainly white Japanese varieties. Grow as mini beet above, sowing from mid-/late spring until late summer for early summer to mid-autumn use. They will be ready within seven weeks of sowing. Continue sowing in frost-free greenhouses until mid-autumn for a mid-winter harvest. Growing bags are ideal for this crop.

VARIETIES

Suitable varieties include 'Tokyo Cross' F1, 'Arcoat' and 'Oasis' F1.

Small white round turnip 'Tokyo Cross' F1

Potato *Solanum tuberosum*

'Pink Fir Apple'

'Kipfler'

'Nicola'

'Charlotte'

SALAD POTATOES

'Aura'

'Maris Peer'

'Anya'

Solanum ajanhuri

There has been a sea change in the attitude towards potatoes since the first edition of *The Salad Garden* in the 1980s. The potato revolution was spearheaded by the late Donald MacLean. Not only did he set about cleaning up the virused stock of old varieties, but he made the public aware of the innate diversity of potatoes – how each has something unique to offer in terms of cooking quality, pest or disease resistance, flavour or appearance. Gardeners are now far more discerning and knowledgeable: hundreds attend the annual 'potato days' held by HDRA, the national centre for organic gardening in the UK, and relish the opportunity to learn more and buy a few tubers of unusual varieties. Garden suppliers have responded by producing specialist potato catalogues, offering a very wide choice. The best of the old are being augmented by excellent new varieties.

Where garden space is limited, it may seem logical to forgo potato growing. They are used in fairly large quantities, are cheap to buy and occupy a lot of space for a long period – nearly five months for 'late main' types. Logic goes out of the window once you discover the superior flavour of carefully chosen varieties, freshly dug from your own garden. It is worth finding space for at least a few, more if possible. The less demanding early varieties can also be grown successfully in large tubs or barrels. For general cultivation of potatoes, consult a general gardening book; see Further Reading, pp. 162–3. Here I look at what makes a salad potato and suggest some appropriate varieties.

WHAT MAKES A SALAD VARIETY?

The texture of a potato largely determines how it is best cooked. At one end of the spectrum are potatoes high in dry matter: these become light and fluffy when cooked, and are best for baking, roasting and chips. At the other end are waxy potatoes, closer textured and low in dry matter. After cooking they remain intact without disintegrating, and keep firm if sliced or diced and mixed with dressings. These make the best salad potatoes. There are exceptions to every rule where potatoes are concerned, but waxy potatoes seem to have some of the best flavours, which are often brought out to the full when cooked and cold.

For practical purposes, potatoes are grouped according to the average number of days they take to mature, though the category chosen for a variety can be a little arbitrary. These are commonly used groupings: 'very early earlies' – 75 days; 'first earlies' – 90 days; 'second earlies' – 110 days; 'early maincrop' – 135 days; 'late

'Ratte', an excellent-quality salad potato, introduced in 1870

'Roseval', an attractive high-yielding salad potato from 1950

maincrop' – 150 days. What is significant is that the earlier, fast-maturing potatoes are initially lifted young as 'new' potatoes before the skins have set. (Within limits, the younger they are lifted, the better the flavour.) They are scrubbed whole before cooking. Simply because they are small, firm and immature, new potatoes often make good salad potatoes, although they will not necessarily have the outstanding flavour of acclaimed salad varieties. They must be eaten fresh: the 'new potato' quality is soon lost and declines as the season progresses. You can also plant early varieties mid-season, to get small 'new' potatoes later in the year. Maincrop potatoes are slower-maturing but grow larger, have much higher yields and can be lifted and stored in frost-free conditions for winter use.

Most salad varieties are in the earlier maturing groups, with the exception of the old, long, knobbly European varieties such as 'Pink Fir Apple' (which stores well), 'Ratte' and the species potato *Solanum ajanhuri*. Salad potatoes are mostly yellow-, creamy- or white-fleshed, but an interesting group of heirloom varieties have deep blue or purple flesh. Their quality is often reasonable and they are highly decorative. Potato performance and flavour can vary enormously with local climate and soil conditions. It is worth trying many varieties to see which perform well in your garden.

Varieties

The supply of potato varieties is constantly changing. These are currently available and highly recommended for salads. (GP) indicates those that are also general purpose in use. Colour refers to flesh colour.

Early groups 'Alex' (white), 'Anya' (cream, smaller, less branched 'Pink Fir' type), 'Belle de Fontenay' (yellow, esteemed old French variety), 'BF' (slightly earlier than 'Belle de Fontenay' parent), 'Charlotte' (creamy, high yield, GP), 'International Kidney'/'Jersey Royal' (yellow), 'Juliette' (cream, high yield), 'Lady Christl' (yellow, excellent flavour, GP), 'Linzer Delicatesse' (creamy yellow), 'Maris Peer' (creamy yellow), 'Nicola' (creamy yellow, high yield), 'Roseval' (yellow with pink tinge, carmine skin, high yield).

Maincrop 'Pink Fir Apple' and 'Rose Fin Apple' (yellow, knobbly, historic), 'Ratte' (light yellow, rampant grower, historic).

Waxy potatoes These are some of the varieties that, on account of their waxy texture and good flavour, are particularly suitable for salads – although unfortunately some of the more unusual salad varieties are not easy to obtain other than from specialist suppliers: 'Pink Fir Apple', 'Aura', 'Kipfler', 'Maris Peer', 'Red Craig's Royal' and the species potato *Solanum ajanhuri*.

Hardy roots

The hardy root crops are a neglected group of nutritious, often sweet-flavoured vegetables, which are most useful during the winter months when there is a scarcity of leafy green salads. Some can be grated or sliced raw into salads, but their flavour is often brought out when cooked and cooled. The more knobbly tubers can be difficult to peel. If so, scrub them, and steam for a few minutes – the skins then come off easily.

Most root crops do best in deep, light soil, with well-rotted manure or compost worked in several months before sowing. They are undemanding other than needing to be weeded in the early stages and watered to prevent the soil from drying out. Those included here normally survive temperatures of –10°C/14°F in the open. They can be lifted and stored in clamps (on a base of straw and covered with straw and/or soil) or in cool conditions under cover, but their flavour and quality often deteriorate. In most cases the leaves die down in winter, so mark the ends of the rows so you can find them in snow. Covering with straw makes lifting easier in frosty weather.

The following notes highlight their salad use. For cultivation, consult a general gardening book; see Further Reading, pp. 162–3.

Horseradish *Armoracia rusticana* This vigorous perennial, with leaves up to 60cm/24in long, has stout roots that are used to make a strongly flavoured relish. They can be grated raw into a salad to add a wonderful piquancy. When about 5cm/2in long, the young leaves have a very pleasant flavour and can be used in salads. It is often found in the wild (see illustration, p. 89).

Jerusalem artichoke *Helianthus tuberosus* These tall, hardy perennials produce very knobbly, branched underground tubers, upwards of a hen's egg in size. They are nutritious, with a distinctive sweet flavour, and excellent raw or cooked and cold. The problem lies in scrubbing them clean! The tall plants make good windbreaks and their rugged, fibrous root system helps break up heavy ground. The variety 'Fuseau' is smoother than most.

Parsnip *Pastinaca sativa* Parsnips have large, sweetly flavoured roots up to 25cm/10in long and 10cm/4in wide at the crown. They are excellent cooked and cold, but unsuitable for use raw in salads.

Hamburg parsley *Petroselinum crispum* var. *tuberosum* Hamburg parsley is a dual-purpose member of the parsley family. The large roots resemble parsnips and are used in the same way. The dark glossy foliage looks and tastes like broad-leaved parsley, but retains its colour at much lower temperatures, making it invaluable in winter. The young leaves can be used whole or chopped in salads, or for garnishing and seasoning. It is probably easier to grow than parsnip or parsley, and is tolerant of light shade.

Scorzonera (Viper's grass) *Scorzonera hispanica* Scorzonera is a perennial with black-skinned roots and yellow flowers. Roots and flower buds – both eaten cooked and cold – flowers and young shoots or 'chards' are all used in salads, and have an intriguing flavour. (See salsify below and flower illustration on p. 87.)

Chinese artichoke *Stachys affinis* These white, spiral-shaped knobbly tubers are rarely more than 4cm/1½in long and 2cm/¾in wide. They have a crisp texture, appealing translucent appearance and delightful nutty flavour raw. They need diligent scrubbing. Being small, the tubers shrivel fairly soon once lifted. (For further information, see my book *Oriental Vegetables*.)

Salsify (Oyster plant) *Tragopogon porrifolius* Salsify is a biennial, usually grown for its long, brown-skinned, tapering roots, which have a most delicate flavour when cooked and eaten cold. Less well known is the mysterious flavour of the plump flower buds and light purple petals, which develop in its second season, both used cooked and cold in salads (see p. 86.) In the past salsify was also cultivated for the young blanched leaves, or chards, which develop in spring and are tender enough to use raw in salads. For chards, cut back the withering stems just above ground level in autumn, and cover with about 15cm/6in of soil, straw or leaves. The chards push through in spring; cut them when 10–15cm/4–6in long.

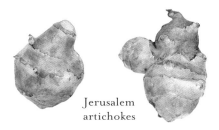

Jerusalem artichokes

Chinese artichokes

peas and beans

Peas and beans are among the most popular of vegetables, in the main used cooked. Indeed beans, that is French and runner beans (*Phaseolus* spp.), and broad beans (*Vicia faba*), must be cooked to destroy the toxins in raw beans. In salads, peas and beans are often used cooked and eaten cold. Peas and the pods of mangetout types are delicious raw. More unusual candidates for salads are the leafy tips of broad beans and the tips and tendrils of peas. All have a seductive flavour. For general cultivation of peas and beans, consult a general gardening book; see Further Reading, pp. 162–3. These brief notes highlight their potential use in salads.

Peas (Garden peas) *Pisum sativum*

Young shelling peas are pleasant raw, the sweet, wrinkled-seeded varieties being preferable to the round-seeded rather starchy, hardy peas used for early sowings. Most tempting raw are the 'mangetout' or sugar peas, grown for their edible, parchment-free pods, and mostly eaten when the peas inside are still minuscule. They are sweet and refreshingly crisp. Types range from giant, flat-podded sickle-shaped varieties to the 'Sugar Snap' types. Uniquely, these are round in cross section, with the round young peas 'welded' to the outer skin. For flavour and texture they are hard to beat. Peas can also be sprouted, for young shoots harvested about 5cm/2in high. (See also Seed sprouting, p. 133).

A delicacy in many parts of the world (notably China) are pea tendrils and 'pea shoots' – the top pairs of leaves at the tip of the stem. They are grown by sowing peas closely together and harvesting the shoots as they develop. More economical, and an excellent alternative, are the tendrils of 'semi-leafless' peas, ordinary varieties with leaves modified into wire-like tendrils. These enable neighbouring plants to twine together, so virtually becoming self-

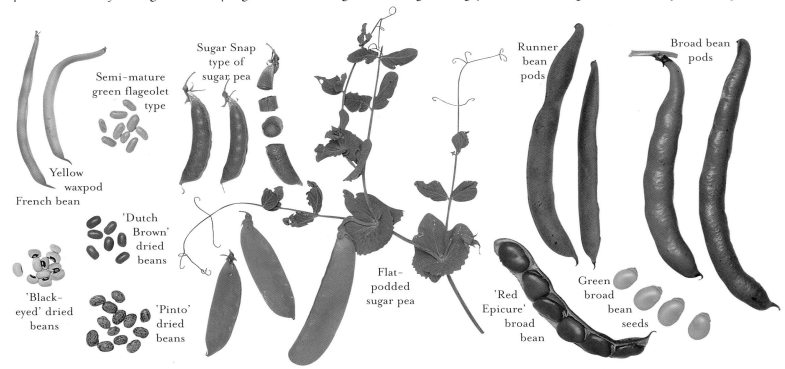

Yellow waxpod French bean

Semi-mature green flageolet type

Sugar Snap type of sugar pea

'Black-eyed' dried beans

'Dutch Brown' dried beans

'Pinto' dried beans

Flat-podded sugar pea

Runner bean pods

'Red Epicure' broad bean

Green broad bean seeds

Broad bean pods

supporting. Clumps look beautiful in a potager. Nip off the tendrils while they are still soft and pliable, and enjoy the most delicate pea flavour. The plants will still produce a crop of normal peas.

Varieties Those currently available include 'Markana' and 'Novella'

Runner beans *Phaseolus coccineus*

Originally introduced to Europe from America as climbing ornamentals, these robustly flavoured beans made the British Isles their home. The flattish pods can be well over 23cm/9in long, but are most tender picked at half that length. They are excellent cooked and eaten cold, but the beans inside are normally too coarse for salads, unless used very small. Most runner beans grow over 3m/10ft tall, but there are some dwarf varieties, less productive than climbers, but pretty enough to grow in flower beds.

French beans (Kidney beans) *Phaseolus vulgaris*

French beans are used at several stages: the immature pods as 'green beans' (though they can be other colours); the semi-mature bean seeds as 'flageolets'; and the mature, ripened beans dried as 'haricot' beans, usually stored for winter. All can be used in salads after being cooked, though some varieties are more suited to one use than another. Be guided by catalogue descriptions. Varieties grown for pods are green, purple-yellow or flecked; in my view the yellow 'waxpods' (the pods *are* waxy) and the purple-podded varieties have the best flavour. Pod shape varies from flat (in some climbing varieties) to the very fine, 'filet' or Kenya beans, which have a melting quality. When dried, French beans display a huge range of colour and patterning, which can be used to great effect in salads. Among my favourites are 'Borlotto', a red-flecked white bean, the khaki 'Dutch Brown', spotty 'Pinto' and 'Black-Eyed'. There are climbing and dwarf forms of French beans.

Broad beans *Vicia faba*

These large, very hardy beans have a unique flavour. For salads, either pick ordinary varieties young, before the seeds develop their own tough skin, or use the smaller-seeded, more delicate varieties grown primarily for freezing, such as 'Jade', 'Lingo', 'Stereo' and 'Talia'. The shorter-podded green- or white-seeded 'Windsor' broad beans, sown in spring, are more refined and better-flavoured than the hardier, autumn-sown 'longpod' types. All must be eaten cooked.

Another treat lies in the leafy tips of the plants. Picked young and tender once the pods are developing, they can be steamed as greens or used raw in salads, though sparingly, as they are strongly flavoured. The tops of fodder bean plants, which I grow for green manure, are equally tender.

Broad bean flowers are ornamental and flavoursome in salads; particularly beautiful are those of the heirloom 'Crimson Flowered' bean.

Edible tops of broad beans grown for green manure

Edible tendrils of the 'semi-leafless' pea 'Markana'

herbs

The deft use of herbs transforms a salad. Add a little chopped coriander or fenugreek to evoke the Orient; a few leaves of balm or lemon thyme for a hint of lemon; chervil or sweet cicely to create the subtle tones of aniseed. Or go for a more daring flavour with lovage, or a generous sprinkling of dill, or a little sage, tarragon or basil. Almost any culinary herb can find a role in salad making: experiment with what you have to hand. The only guiding principle should be that the stronger the herb, the more lightly it is used. The eminent twentieth-century gardening writer Eleanour Sinclair Rohde put this neatly: 'It is just the suspicion of flavouring all through the salad that is required, not a salad entirely dominated by herbs.' She would mix a teaspoon of as many as twenty finely chopped herbs to sprinkle into a salad. For suggestions on the use of herbs with different salad plants and dishes, see pp. 144–6.

Do not overlook the decorative qualities of herbs in salads. Many have variegated and coloured forms, and many have leaves of outstanding beauty – the delicate tracery of salad burnet, sweet cicely, dill, and the bronze and green fennels, for example. Add these, freshly picked, for a last-minute garnish.

It is a truism that fresh herbs are infinitely better-flavoured than dried or preserved herbs. In temperate climates most culinary herbs die back in winter, but chervil, caraway, coriander and parsley are some that can be grown under cover for use fresh in winter. Others can be potted up in late summer and brought indoors. Basil, thyme, mint, winter savory and marjoram can be persuaded to provide pickings from a winter windowsill.

Although many herbs can be preserved and are useful in cooking, only a handful, such as some mints, retain their true flavour. Several of the more succulent herbs, such as chives, parsley and basil, can be deep-frozen as sprigs or chopped into ice-cube trays filled with water. Thaw the cubes in a strainer when you need to use the herb. Otherwise herbs are usually preserved by drying. Pick them at their peak, just before flowering, and dry them slowly in a cool oven, or hung indoors, covered with muslin to prevent them from becoming dusty. When they are completely dry, store them in airtight jars.

Herbs are worth growing for their ornamental qualities. Walls, patios, dry areas and spare corners can be carpeted with thymes, lemon balm or creeping mint. Ordinary and Chinese chives, parsley, hyssop and savory make effective edging plants, while mature plants of fennel, angelica and lovage are handsome features in their own right. So many are colourful when in flower. All in all, a salad lover's garden should be brimming with herbs.

Here are brief descriptions and cultural information, for some of the most useful salad herbs, listed in alphabetical order by common name. For more detailed cultural information, see Further Reading, pp. 162–3.

Angelica *Angelica archangelica* A beautiful, vigorous biennial, growing up to 3m/10ft high when flowering, angelica is one of the first herbs to reappear in spring. The typical angelica flavour is found in the leaves, stems and seeds. All can be used in salads when young.

Angelica requires fairly rich, moist soil and needs plenty of space. Sow fresh seed *in situ* in autumn, thinning the following spring to at least 1m/3ft apart; very young seedlings can be transplanted. Angelica dies after flowering in its second season, but in suitable sites perpetuates itself with self-sown seedlings.

Basil *Ocinum* spp. The basils are wonderfully aromatic tender annuals, used in many salad dishes but above all associated with tomatoes. They are in the main clove-flavoured. There are many varieties. Lettuce-leaved (Neapolitan) is the largest, growing up to 45cm/18in high with huge leaves; common, sweet or Genovese basil has medium-sized leaves; bush basil is a smaller plant with smaller leaves again, while the various forms of 'Greek', fine-leaved or miniature basil have tiny, strongly flavoured leaves and are exceptionally compact and low-growing. There are red-leaved forms, and many varieties with distinct flavours including cinnamon, anise, lemon and lime – the last two being outstanding.

Basils cannot stand frost or cold conditions. In cool temperate climates, grow them in a very sheltered, warm, well-drained site or under cover. Sow indoors in late spring, planting outdoors or under cover about 13cm/5in apart, depending on variety. To prolong the season, make a second sowing in early to mid-summer of bush or compact basil, potted into 10–12.5cm/4–5in pots. Bring indoors in early autumn. They may provide fresh leaf for several months.

Chervil *Anthriscus cerefolium* Chervil is a fast-growing, hardy annual or biennial, about 25cm/10in high before seeding. The delicate leaves have a refreshing aniseed flavour, and can be chopped like parsley into many salad dishes. A great asset in temperate climates is that it remains green in winter.

Chervil is not fussy about soil. For summer supplies, sow *in situ* in spring in a slightly shaded situation, thinning to 10cm/4in apart. Keep the plants well watered. For autumn-to-early-spring supplies, sow *in situ* in late summer, either outside or under cover for good-quality winter plants; or sow in modules and transplant under cover. Chervil can be cut several times before it runs to seed; if left to flower, it usefully seeds itself.

Coriander (Cilantro, Chinese parsley) *Coriandrum sativum* Coriander is an annual, 13cm/5in high in its leafy stage and over 45cm/18in high when seeding. The leaves, with their musty curry flavour, make a unique contribution to salad dishes, as do the flowers. It is also grown for the strong-flavoured seeds, commonly used in curries. Coriander grows best in cool conditions, in light soil with plenty of water throughout growth. It tolerates light frost, and stands well in winter under cover.

In temperate climates, it can be sown throughout the growing season, though it may run to seed rapidly in hot weather. Sow in succession outdoors from early spring to early autumn, *in situ*, either densely to cut as cut-and-come-again seedlings or thinning to 15cm/6in apart for larger plants; or multi-sow several seeds per module, planting out 15cm/6in apart. The hard outer seed coat sometimes prevents germination: if so, crack the 'pods' gently with a rolling pin.

Earlier and later sowings can be made under cover, and early sowings can be grown to maturity under fleece. Cut leaves at any stage up to about 12.5cm/5in high. The flavour deteriorates once the plants start running to seed. If you are growing coriander specifically for seed, use varieties recommended for seed, such as the large-seeded Morrocan; these tend to bolt rapidly and have sparse leaf. For leaf coriander, use improved, leaf varieties such as 'Santo' and 'Leisure' where available. Coriander leaf can be frozen but does not dry well.

Dill *Anethum graveolens* This feathery annual is grown for the seeds and seedheads, which are widely used in pickling cucumbers, and for the delicately flavoured leaves, easily chopped into salads.

Grow leaf dill like coriander (see above), using improved varieties such as 'Dukat' where available. Seedlings normally resprout at least once after cutting. For seedheads, and hence the seeds, sow in early summer by broadcasting, or in rows 23cm/9in apart, thinning to 7.5cm/3in apart. Dill is very pretty at every stage from seedlings to seeding. Plants left in late summer will often reseed themselves.

Fennel *Foeniculum vulgare* The herb fennel (unlike Florence fennel, p. 52) is a hardy perennial, growing up to 1.5m/5ft high. The common green form has beautiful gossamer leaves, with a light aniseed flavour; the stunning bronze fennel (*F. v.* 'Purpureum') is milder-flavoured. The chopped leaves and peeled young stalks can be used in salads, as can the seeds.

Fennel tolerates most well-drained soils. Sow in spring *in situ* or in modules for transplanting, spacing plants 45cm/18in apart. Plants can also be propagated by dividing up clumps in spring. Plants tend to run to seed in mid-summer, but for a constant supply keep them trimmed back to about 30cm/12in high and remove flower spikes. Bronze fennel in particular can self-seed prolifically and become invasive – but deserves a place in every decorative potager. Renew plants when they lose their vigour.

Hyssop *Hyssopus officinalis* Hyssop is a short-lived, shrubby, hardy perennial, about 45cm/18in high, though if kept trimmed it makes a neat low hedge. The shiny little leaves have a strong, savory-like flavour, and remain green late into winter. The beautiful blue, pink or white flower spikes attract bees and butterflies.

Propagate hyssop by taking softwood cuttings from a mature clump in spring, or sow indoors in spring and early summer, eventually planting seedlings about 30cm/12in apart. Pinch back shoot tips to keep plants bushy, and prune back hard in spring. Plants need renewing every three or four years.

Lemon balm *Melissa officinalis* This easily grown hardy perennial forms clumps up to 60cm/24in tall. The delightful lemon-scented leaves can be chopped into salad dishes.

Sweet cicely

Winter savory

Raripila mint

Apple mint

Spearmint

Ginger mint

Pineapple mint

Narrow-leaved sage

Variegated lemon balm

Green lemon balm

Lovage

Angelica seed head

Angelica leaves

Curly parsley

Broad-leaved parsley

Lemon balm tolerates a wide range of soil and situations, and is an excellent ground cover plant. Propagate it by taking a rooted piece from an old plant; or sow seed indoors in spring, planting 60cm/24in apart. Cut plants back hard in the autumn. There are pretty variegated and golden forms.

Lovage *Levisticum officinale* This handsome hardy perennial grows up to 2.5m/8ft tall, and is one of the first to emerge each spring. The glossy leaves have a strong but superb celery flavour. Rub them into a salad bowl, or chop them sparingly into salads. The leaf stalks can be blanched like celery.

Lovage thrives in rich, moist soil and tolerates light shade. Sow fresh seed indoors in spring or autumn, eventually planting at least 60cm/2ft apart. (One plant is enough for most households.) Alternatively, divide an old clump in spring, replanting pieces of root with active shoots. Lovage often seeds itself, and young seedlings can be transplanted.

Marjoram and **Origanum** *Origanum* spp. There are many forms and varieties (and much confusion over naming) of these perennial Mediterranean herbs with gentle, aromatic flavours. Several compact forms are only 15cm/6in high, but taller varieties grow up to 45cm/18in. Gold-leaved, gold-tipped and variegated varieties may be less flavoured, but they are very decorative in salad dishes and in the garden. My favourites for salads are the half-hardy sweet or knotted marjoram (*O. majorana*) with its lovely soft leaves; gold marjoram (*O. vulgare* 'Aureum'); the hardy winter marjoram (*O. heracleoticum*), which remains green here in winter; and the well-flavoured pot marjoram (*O. onites*).

Marjorams grow best in well-drained, reasonably fertile soil in full sun, though golden-leaved varieties, which tend to get scorched in hot weather, can be grown in light shade. Some varieties, including sweet marjoram, can be raised from seed, sown indoors in spring and eventually planted 13cm/5in apart. Many others are propagated by softwood cuttings taken in spring, or by dividing established clumps. It is often possible to pot up plants for use indoors in winter. On the whole marjorams dry well.

Mint *Mentha* spp. The majority of the many hardy perennial mints can be used, albeit sparingly, in salad dishes, imparting that special 'minty' flavour. My own favourites for flavour are apple mint (*M. suaveolens*), spearmint (*M. spicata*) and raripila or pea mint (*M. rubra* var. *raripila*). For their decorative quality, I grow the cream and green pineapple mint (*M. suaveolens* 'Variegata') and the variegated, gold and green Scotch or ginger mint (*Mentha × gracilis*). Each mint has its own subtly different flavour: yours to discover!

Most mints spread rapidly in moist, fertile soil and tolerate light shade. The easiest way to propagate is to lift and divide old plants in spring or autumn. Very few are raised satisfactorily from seed. Replant small pieces of root 5cm/2in long, laid horizontally 5cm/2in deep, 23cm/9in apart; or plant shoots with attached roots. Replant mints every few years in a fresh site if they are losing vigour. Plants die back in winter. In autumn, transplant a few into a greenhouse, or into pots or boxes: they will start into growth early in spring. Most mints retain their flavour well when dried.

Mitsuba (Japanese parsley, Japanese honewort) *Cryptotaenia japonica* This hardy, evergreen perennial is a woodland plant, growing about 30cm/12in high. It has long leaf stalks and pale leaves divided into three leaflets, not unlike flat parsley in appearance. Stems and leaves are used raw in salads and have a delicate flavour, encompassing that of parsley, celery and angelica. The seeds can be sprouted. It does best in moist, lightly shaded situations. In the West it is mainly grown as single plants, often edging shaded borders. In its native Japan it is also grown densely, often in polytunnels, to get fine, virtually blanched, very tender stems.

Although perennial, mitsuba is best grown as an annual. Sow *in situ* from late spring to early autumn (optimum soil temperature is about 25°C/77°F), making successive sowings for a continuous supply. Thin plants to 15cm/6in apart. They will be ready for use within about two months. Alternatively, plant under cover in early autumn for use during winter. Plants left in the ground may seed themselves for use the following year.

Parsley *Petroselinum crispum* Parsley is a biennial, growing 10–45cm/4–18in high. Its characteristically flavoured leaves are widely used in cooking and as a garnish. There are two types: curly, and plain or broad-leaved, of which 'French' and 'Giant Italian' are typical varieties. Curly parsley is more decorative, but the plain-leaved varieties are more vigorous, seem to be hardier and are more easily grown. Most chefs consider them better-flavoured.

Parsley needs moist conditions and fertile soil. For a continuous supply, sow in spring for summer use, and in summer for autumn-to-

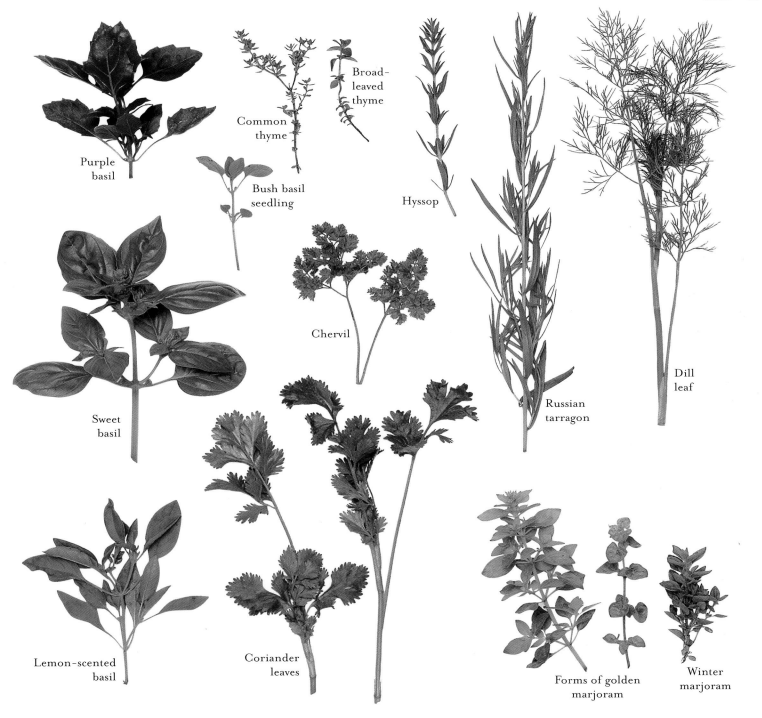

Purple basil

Common thyme

Broad-leaved thyme

Bush basil seedling

Hyssop

Sweet basil

Chervil

Russian tarragon

Dill leaf

Lemon-scented basil

Coriander leaves

Forms of golden marjoram

Winter marjoram

spring supplies. Sow *in situ* or in modules for transplanting when seedlings are still young. Failures with parsley stem from it being slow to germinate. Once you have sown it, take care to keep the soil moist until seedlings appear (see Sowing in Adverse Conditions, p. 105). Thin or plant 23cm/9in apart. Parsley normally dies back in winter after moderate frost. Keep a few plants cloched or plant them in a greenhouse in late summer/early autumn for winter-to-spring supplies. Cut off flowering heads to prolong the plant's useful life.

Sage *Salvia officinalis* The sages are moderately hardy, evergreen perennials, growing 30–60cm/12–24in high. The large, soft, subdued grey-green leaves of common broad-leaved and narrow-leaved sage (*S. lavandulifolia*) are strongly flavoured. Only slightly less so but very decorative are gold sage (*S. o.* 'Icterina'), the less hardy, tricolor sage (*S. o.* 'Tricolor') with pink, purple and white leaves, and the red or purple sage (*S. o.* Purpurascens Group), frequently mentioned in traditional salad lore.

Sages need well-drained, light soil and a sunny sheltered position. For common sage, sow seed indoors in spring, planting out 30cm/12in apart the following spring. With other varieties, propagate from heel cuttings taken in early summer. To keep plants bushy, prune lightly after flowering in late summer and harder in spring.

Sage flowers are edible, the beautiful red flowers of the tender pineapple sage (*Salvia elegans*) being deliciously sweet in salads.

Summer and winter savory *Satureja hortensis* and *S. montana* Summer savory is a bushy annual that grows up to 30cm/12in high with fairly soft leaves, while winter savory is a more compact, hardy, semi-evergreen perennial, with narrow, tougher leaves. Both are almost spicy in flavour, and are said to enhance other flavours in cooking. Use them sparingly in salad dishes.

Savories need a sunny position and well-drained, reasonably fertile soil. Sow in spring indoors, but do not cover the seeds, as they need light to germinate. Plant 15cm/6in apart. Winter savory can also be propagated from softwood cuttings taken in spring. In late summer, pot up a winter savory plant for winter use indoors: they are very pretty when they burst into renewed growth in spring.

Sweet cicely *Myrrhis odorata* Sweet cicely is an attractive, hardy perennial, often growing 1.5m/5ft high; its leaves resemble chervil and have a sweet, aniseed flavour. They are a delight chopped into salad or used whole as garnish, but pick them just before you need them, as they wilt almost instantly. The substantial roots can be boiled and sliced into salads. Sweet cicely starts into growth early in the year, dying back late, so has a long season of usefulness.

It grows best in rich, moist soil in light shade. Sow fresh seed outdoors in autumn, thinning to 8cm/3in apart, and plant in a permanent position the following autumn 60cm/24in apart. Or sow in modules, keeping them outside during winter. Plants can also be propagated by dividing roots carefully in spring and autumn. Replace plants only if they are losing vigour.

French and Russian tarragon *Artemisia dracunculus* and *A. d. dracunculoides* French tarragon is a narrow-leaved, moderately hardy perennial, growing about 1m/3ft high, while Russian tarragon is larger, coarser and much hardier. The aromatic leaves of both have a distinct flavour, but the Russian is widely believed to be less strong. It is adequate for salad dishes, but French tarragon is preferable for flavouring vinegar and in cooking.

Grow tarragon in a well-drained, sheltered position, preferably on light soil. Russian tarragon can be raised from seed sown indoors in spring, but French tarragon rarely sets seed, so propagate it by dividing old plants or from root cuttings. Plant 60cm/24in apart. In cold areas, cover French tarragon roots with straw in winter. Plants decline after a few years and should be replaced.

Thyme *Thymus* spp. The culinary thymes are pretty, creeping and low-growing herbs, sun-loving and mostly hardy perennials. Their tiny leaves can be blended into salads, salad dishes, dressings and vinegar, adding nuances of the essential thyme flavour. The following are varieties I have found rewarding to grow for salads: the traditionally flavoured common and large-leaved thymes (*T. vulgaris* and *T. pulegioides*); lemon-scented thyme (*T. citriodorus*); *T.* 'Fragrantissimus', which has an orange scent; and caraway thyme (*T. herba-barona*).

Grow thyme in a sunny situation on well-drained, but not particularly rich soil. Thymes thrive in dry conditions and do well in containers. Common thyme can be raised from seed sown in spring indoors, on the surface, and eventually planted 30cm/12in apart. Propagate other varieties by dividing established plants in spring or autumn, or taking softwood cuttings in spring or summer. Trim back plants after flowering. Renew them every three years or so once they become straggly. They can be potted up for winter use indoors.

flowers

Using edible flowers in cooking and salads is an ancient, universal tradition. They are often added just for their colour and fragrance, but some – nasturtiums, day lilies and anise hyssop, for example – have real flavour. In the past flowers were collected from the wild, but today the need to preserve wild species is paramount, so pick only where they are abundant and it is not illegal. Or grow your own.

Gather flowers early in the day, when the dew has just dried on them. Pick or cut them with scissors; handle them gently and carry them in a flat basket to avoid bruising. Where flowers are invaded by insects (such as pollen beetle), lay them aside so the insects can creep away! If essential, wash flowers gently, lightly patting them dry with paper towelling. Keep them in a closed bag in a refrigerator until needed. Refresh them by dipping in ice-cold water just before use.

It is mainly petals that are used in salads. With daisy-like flowers, pull them gently off the centre. Small, soft flowers can be used whole, but large flowers may have rough, hard or strongly flavoured parts. Taste cautiously and remove these parts if necessary. Sprinkle flowers or petals over the salad at the last moment, after dressing, as dressings discolour them and make them soggy. Use either one or two types, or a confetti mixture, being careful not to overwhelm the salad. Charm lies in subtlety.

Very many cultivated and wild plants have edible flowers but there is only space for brief notes on a few of them. For cultivation, consult general gardening books. Be sure to identify plants correctly before eating the flowers; some can be toxic. (For identification, consult a field guide – see Further reading, pp. 162–3) They are listed here under common names but alphabetically by Latin names.

Anise hyssop *Agastache foeniculum* A hardy perennial about 60cm/24in high. The tiny flowers in the flower spikes have an almost peppermint flavour. The young leaves are edible raw.

Hollyhock *Althaea rosea* These tall cottage garden plants have beautiful red, yellow, rose and creamy flowers. Petals and cooked buds are used in salads. They are perennial but best grown as biennials to avoid infection with rust.

Anchusa *Anchusa azurea* A perennial growing 120cm/48in tall with bright, gentian-blue flowers, superb mixed with red rose petals in a salad. After flowering in early summer cut back the main stem to encourage secondary shoots to prolong the flowering season.

Bellis daisy *Bellis perennis* The many cultivated rose-, red- and white-flowered forms of the little white lawn or English daisy are all edible. Use the daintier, small-flowered varieties whole, but with the larger, double varieties, use only the petals. Treat them as biennials, sowing in autumn and spring for almost year-round flowers. Lawn daisies close quickly so pick just before use.

Borage *Borago officinalis* This self-seeding annual grows about 120cm/48in high, typically a haze of sky blue flowers all summer though there is a less common white-flowered form. The flowers are delightfully sweet, but remove the hairy sepals behind the petals before eating them. The flowers look wonderful frozen into ice cubes for drinks. We leave a few plants to seed in our polytunnel to give us early spring flowers. Finely chopped young leaves are edible raw in salads.

Pot marigold *Calendula officinalis* The petals of these vibrantly coloured annuals were traditionally used for seasoning and colouring cakes, cooked dishes and salads. Today's varieties are all shades of orange, yellow, bronze, pink and brown, in single and double flowered forms. If regularly dead headed they flower from early spring until the first frost. They often self seed. Flowers can be dried for winter use, and in the past were pickled.

Chicory *Cichorium intybus* Any cultivated or wild chicory plant left to seed in spring produces huge spires of light blue, occasionally pink, flowers. Use the petals or whole flowers in salads: they have a slightly bitter but distinct 'chicory' taste. The flowers close and fade rapidly, often by midday but try picking early and keeping in a refrigerator. They can be pickled: the colour is lost but a faint flavour remains. (For cultivation, see Chicory, p. 18.)

Courgettes, Marrows, Squashes, Pumpkins *Cucurbita* spp. The buttery yellow flowers of these and many oriental gourds have a creamy flavour and crisp texture. They can be cooked, but use them raw, whole or sliced, in salads. Pick the small male flowers once fruits are setting (leave a few for pollination) and spare female flowers, identified by the tiny bump below the petals.

Florist chrysanthemum *Dendranthema* x *grandiflorum* In China and Japan special varieties of the tender, perennial florist chrysanthemum are cultivated for culinary purposes. Petals of other chrysanthemums can be used in salads, but try them first, as some are bitter-flavoured. Before using in salads, blanch the flowers by dipping them into hot water for a few seconds (see p. 144) Flowers of the hardy edible-leaved chrysanthemum (*Xanthophthalmum coronarium*) are also edible (see p. 44).

Carnations, Pinks, Sweet william *Dianthus* spp. The raw flowers of these popular garden plants have varying degrees of fragrance and flavour, from mild to musky to a strong scent of cloves. Sweet william is notably strong-flavoured.

Lavender *Lavandula* spp. In the past salads were served on beds of lettuce and lavender sprigs – but the flowers are strongly flavoured and should be used sparingly. There are blue-, purple-, pink-, and white-flowered varieties.

Jacob's Ladder *Polemonium caeruleum* The sweetly scented flowers of the many species and varieties of these pretty hardy perennials are pleasantly flavoured and colourful in salads.

Day lily *Hemerocallis* spp. The flavour of raw day lily flowers varies widely. American writer Cathy Barash (see Further Reading, p. 163) believes the darker colours tend towards bitterness, while pale yellows and oranges are sweeter. My light orange variety (probably *H. citrina*), from a Chinese research station, has a superb, vanilla flavour and crisp texture. Taste before use – and only eat in moderation!

Sweet bergamot (Bee balm, Oswego tea) *Monarda didyma* The colourful flowers of these perennials have distinct 'mint with hints of lemon' flavours. I love them mixed with borage in salads. Some F1 hybrid varieties are reputedly bitter. Dried flowers are used for a delicately flavoured tea.

Primrose *Primula vulgaris* and **Cowslip** *P. veris* In the past these mild-flavoured flowers were collected from the wild in spring. Today, they, and the many colourful hybrids, can be cultivated for salads. Cowslip flowers used to be pickled.

Rose *Rosa* spp. Most rose petals can be used in salads, but fragrant roses, especially the classic old roses – *R. rugosa*, the Apothecary rose *R. gallica*, and the Damask rose *R. damascena* – are most flavoured. Always try petals before using; some have a bitter aftertaste, often found in the white part at the base of petals.

Sage *Salvia* spp. The blue, white or pink flowers of culinary sage (*S. officinalis*) have a pleasant subdued sage flavour, are fairly firm and stand well in salads. The colourful bracts of clary sage (*S. sclarea*) and painted sage (*S. horminum*) have a faint mint flavour. The sweet, scarlet flowers of the pineapple sage (*S.elegans*) really do have a hint of pineapple in them. For cultivation, see p. 84.

Scorzonera *Scorzonera hispanica* and **Salsify** *Tragopogon porrifolius* The plump flower buds are used cooked and cooled, and the more faintly flavoured petals – yellow in scorzonera, lilac in salsify – are strewn on salads. The flowers may open only briefly in the morning sunshine, then close firmly. If the petals are wanted later in the day try picking when open and keeping them in a closed bag in a refrigerator until needed. (See also p. 76.)

Tagetes (Signet marigold) *Tagetes tenuifolia* The sparkling little flowers of the 'Orange Gem', 'Tangerine Gem' and 'Lemon Gem' varieties have fruity, fragrant flavours. They are easily grown tender annuals with a long flowering season (see photograph on p. 8).

Nasturtium *Tropaeolum majus* These easily grown annuals, with trailing and dwarf forms, are of ancient use in salads. Buds and flowers are piquant, the leaves are peppery and seeds are pickled as capers. For salads grow the dainty, variegated-leaved 'Alaska' varieties: their vibrantly coloured flowers retain a 'spur', which I think keeps them fresh longer once picked than modern spurless varieties. Also pretty is the red-leaved 'Empress of India'. Tuberous-rooted nasturtium (mashua), *T. tuberosus*, has edible flowers. Nasturtiums often reseed profusely.

Society garlic *Tulbaghia violacea* This moderately frost-tolerant perennial has beautiful, fragrant, usually lilac flowers, with a mild garlic flavour. The leaves also are garlic-flavoured.

Broad bean *Vicia faba* See page 78.

Pansy and violas *Viola* spp, **Sweet violet** *V. odorata* All supply colour and texture, rather than flavour, though in the past violet flowers were eaten with lettuce and onions! The tiny heartsease flowers, *V. tricolor*. are delightfully delicate. Winter-flowering pansies meet a need for colour in winter.

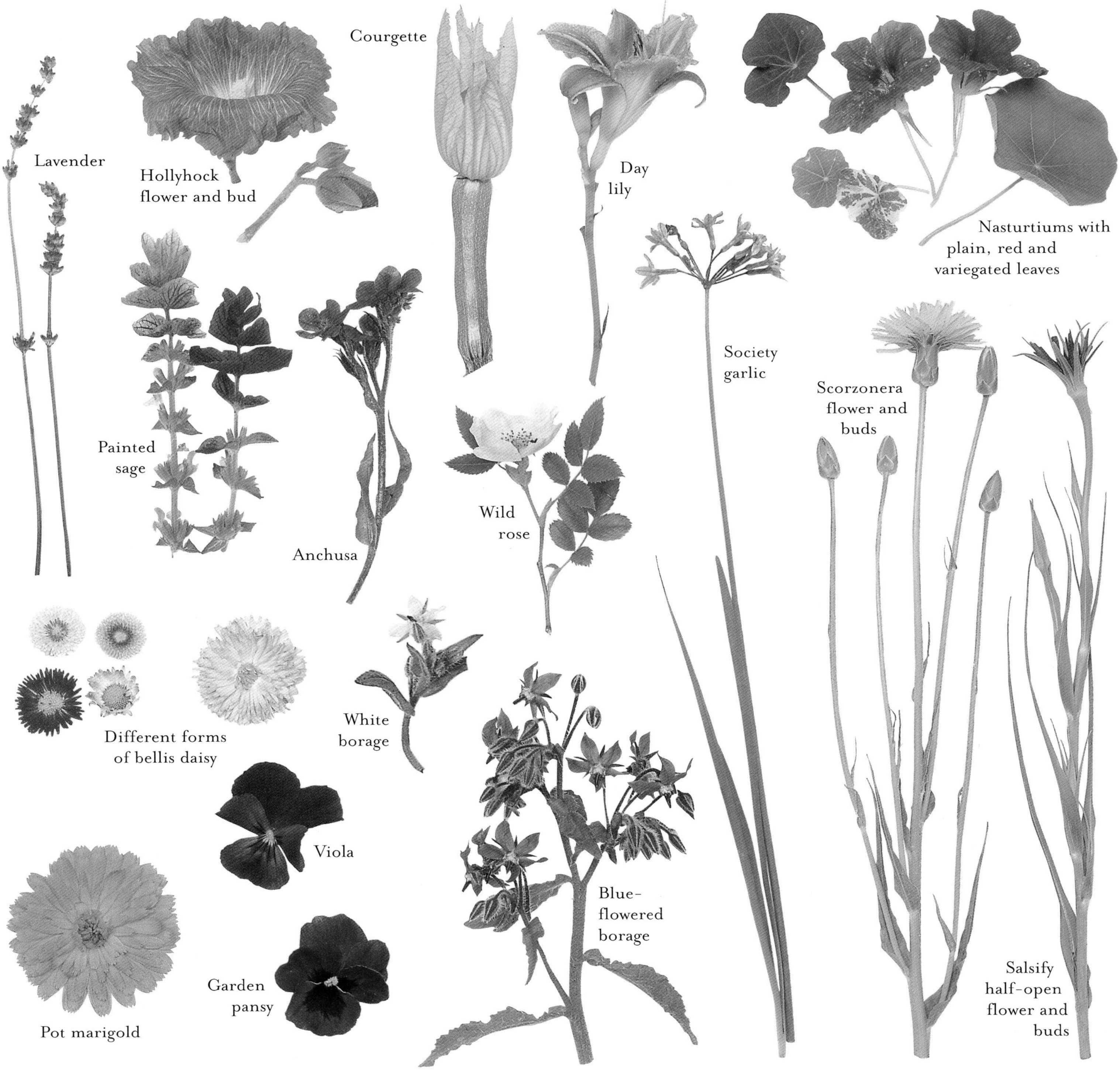

Lavender

Hollyhock
flower and bud

Courgette

Day
lily

Nasturtiums with
plain, red and
variegated leaves

Painted
sage

Anchusa

Society
garlic

Wild
rose

Scorzonera
flower and
buds

Different forms
of bellis daisy

White
borage

Viola

Blue-
flowered
borage

Garden
pansy

Pot marigold

Salsify
half-open
flower and
buds

wild plants

Our cultivated vegetables have all evolved from wild plants, so it is not surprising that the countryside is still a treasure trove of edible plants. Over the centuries some of these wild plants have invaded arable fields and gardens, becoming weeds. In this less competitive environment they grow lushly, providing tender pickings for salads. Many have wonderfully lively flavours that truly enrich a salad. They are probably best worked into mixed salads in small quantities, rather than made into a salad composed entirely of wild plants.

The golden rule with weeds and wild plants is to pick the leaves small and young, as most become tough as they mature. Peasant communities all over the world scour fields and mountains in early spring for those very first leaves. Wild plants have always been valued for their medicinal and 'health-giving' properties; we now know that many are rich in vitamins and minerals.

It is absolutely essential to identify wild plants accurately, as a few are easily confused with poisonous species. Identify them with a good botanical text or, if you have no botanical knowledge, be guided initially by an expert. You will soon get to know the common garden weeds and wild plants in your area. Never go just by a picture in a book. Two people I met did so, confused ground elder with dog's mercury and found themselves in hospital as a result.

Seed of wild plants is now widely available, so it is possible to grow your own. There is only space here for brief notes on a few of the many edible wild plants. They are listed by common name, in the alphabetical order of their Latin names as the common names are often misleading. For identification, consult one of the books listed in Further Reading, pp. 162–3; for seed sources, see p. 163.

Yarrow (milfoil) *Achillea millefolium* Very common weed, remaining green much of the year. Strongly flavoured.

Ground elder *Aegopodium podagraria* Pernicious weed with a delightful angelica flavour. Do not confuse it with the similar but poisonous dog's mercury (*Mercurialis perennis*).

Garlic mustard (Jack-by-the-hedge) *Alliaria petiolata* Common hedgerow weed with appealing, faint garlic flavour.

Wild garlic (Ramsons) *Allium ursinum* and *A.* spp. The leaves have a strong garlic flavour. Leaves, stems, bulbs and flowers of many wild alliums have a mild to strong garlic flavour, including crow garlic (*A. vineale*), keeled garlic (*A. carinatum*) and sand leek (*A. scorodoprasum*).

Wild celery (Smallage) *Apium graveolens* Grows in damp places. Chop leaves and young stems into salads. Do not confuse it with poisonous hemlock (*Conium maculatum*) or water dropwort (*Oenanthe crocata*).

Burdock *Arctium lappa* and **Lesser burdock** *A. minus* Rampant plants, used all over the world cooked and raw. For salads, pick the leafy stems of young shoots in spring, strip off the peel and cut into 5cm/2in pieces. Intriguing flavour.

Horseradish *Armoracia rusticana* For cultivation, see p. 76.

Shepherd's purse *Capsella bursa-pastoris* Very common weed, green much of the year. Basal leaf rosettes and stem leaves are excellent raw; their distinctive flavour is due to sulphur. Cultivated in China for use raw and cooked. Said to be richer in vitamin C than oranges.

Hairy bitter cress *Cardamine hirsuta* Very hardy, ubiquitous little weed appearing in autumn and spring. Cut the tiny, cress-flavoured leaves for salads. Seed pods explode when touched: thin out seedlings to get plants of a reasonable size. Cover them with cloches in autumn to increase their size and tenderness.

Lady's smock (Cuckoo flower) *Cardamine pratensis* Plant of damp meadows; remains green late in winter. The leaves have a watercress spiciness and are excellent in salads.

Red valerian *Centranthus ruber* Red- and white-flowered forms, found on dry banks and walls; often cultivated in gardens. Use young leaves and flowers.

Fat hen (Lamb's quarters) *Chenopodium album* Very common arable weed, often found near manure heaps. Has spinach-like flavour, and is excellent cooked like spinach or raw. American Indians made the seeds into cakes and gruel.

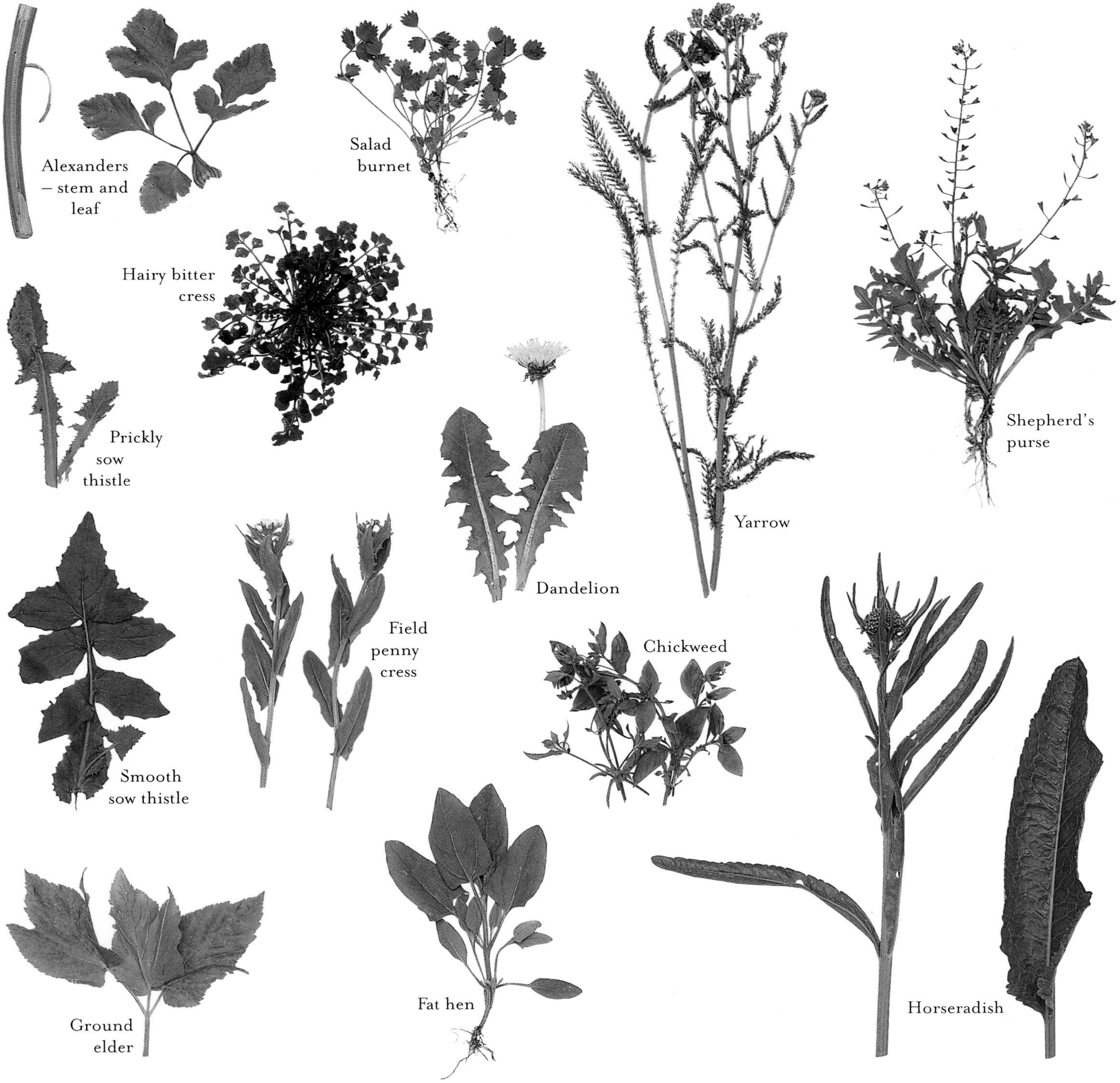

Alexanders
– stem and
leaf

Salad
burnet

Yarrow

Shepherd's
purse

Hairy bitter
cress

Prickly
sow
thistle

Dandelion

Field
penny
cress

Chickweed

Smooth
sow thistle

Ground
elder

Fat hen

Horseradish

Ox-eye daisy (Marguerite) *Chrysanthemum leucanthemum* The young leaves and flowers are used in salads in Italy.

Golden saxifrage *Chrysosplenium oppositifolium* The *cresson des roches* of the Vosges mountains. Found in wet places.

Marsh thistle *Cirsium palustre* A plant of damp places. Use young shoots and the stalks after removing prickles and peeling.

Rock samphire *Crithmum maritimum* Found on cliffs and shingle. Use the fleshy leaves and stems cooked or pickled for salads.

Sea purslane *Halimione portulacoides* Succulent grey-leaved plant of salt marshes. Wash off mud carefully. Use leaves fresh or pickled.

Woad *Isatis tinctoria* The young leaves of this beautiful, easily cultivated plant are pleasant in salads.

Oyster plant *Mertensia maritima* Pretty, seaside perennial. The fleshy leaves are reputedly oyster-flavoured and excellent in salads.

Watercress *Nasturtium officinale* (Confusingly also called brooklime, the common name for *Veronica beccabunga*, a bitter but edible waterside plant.) Grows in running water: never pick from stagnant, contaminated or pasture water because of the risk of liver fluke infection. It is preferable to cultivate it (see p. 46). Older leaves are more flavoured than young.

Common and **Large evening primrose** *Oenothera biennis, O. erythrosepala* The young leaves can be eaten raw; the roots, lifted before the plants flower, can be eaten after cooking.

Wood sorrel (Alleluia) *Oxalis acetosella* The delicate, folded, clover-like leaves are among the first to appear in woods in spring. They have a sharp sorrel flavour.

Field poppy *Papaver rhoeas* Common red-flowered poppy. The leaves are eaten in the Mediterranean, the seeds used to decorate buns. Don't confuse with the toxic red-horned poppy (*Glaucium corniculatum*).

Buck's horn plantain (Herba stella, Minutina) *Plantago coronopus* A pretty perennial. The tough but tasty leaves are at their best in spring and autumn, remaining green well into winter. Blanch briefly in hot water to tenderize (see p. 144). Easily cultivated; sow in spring or late summer, thinning to 13cm/5in apart. (Can be grown as cut-and-come-again seedlings.) Readily seeds itself, but cutting back flowers encourages young leaves for salads.

Redshank (Red leg) *Polygonum persicaria* and **Bistort** *P. bistort* The leaves of redshank, a common arable weed, are used cooked or raw. Do not confuse it with the acrid water pepper (*Polygonum hydropiper*). The late Robert Hart of 'forest garden' fame used the young shoots and leaves of bistort in salads.

Common wintergreen *Pyrola minor* Berried evergreen, found in woods, moors, rocky ledges and sand dunes. The young leaves are used in salads in North America.

Red-veined dock *Rumex sanguineus* Has elegantly colourful but coarse-textured leaves. Soften them by brief blanching in hot water (see p. 144). Easily cultivated, but potentially invasive.

Glasswort (Marsh or Sea samphire) *Salicornia europaea* Primitive-looking plant of salt marshes and shingle beaches. Gather narrow succulent young leaves in summer. Excellent raw or pickled.

Salad burnet *Sanguisorba officinalis* A low-growing, very hardy perennial of the chalklands. The decorative lacy leaves have a faint cucumber taste and remain green for much of winter. Use the youngest leaves raw in salads, but blanch tougher older leaves in hot water (see p. 144). Easily cultivated. Sow in spring, thinning to 10cm/4in apart. Remove flower stems.

Reflexed stonecrop *Sedum reflexum* Succulent perennial found wild on walls and rocks. Use of the leaves of this and other sedums in salads is ancient. Easily cultivated in dry places.

Milk or **Holy thistle** *Silybum marianum* Striking plant with beautiful white-veined foliage. Use young leaves and peeled, chopped stems raw, roots raw or cooked. Easily cultivated.

Alexanders *Smyrnium olusatrum* Tall, striking plant, common in coastal areas. Use of buds, young leaves, stems and spicy seeds (a pepper substitute) in salads is ancient. The stems used to be blanched. Not to be confused with poisonous hemlock and water dropwort (see *Apium graveolens* p. 88), found in similar places.

Perennial sow thistle *Sonchus arvensis*, **Prickly sow thistle** *S. asper* and **Smooth sow thistle** *S. oleraceus* Weeds found commonly on arable land. Pleasant taste, but trim off bristly parts.

Chickweed *Stellaria media* Very common garden weed, growing almost all year round. Use refreshingly tasty seedlings or larger plants if still succulent. (They are often best if grown in the shade.) Cut with scissors and leave to regrow.

Dandelion *Taraxacum officinale* For cultivation, see p. 47.

Field penny cress *Thlaspi arvense* Very common weed with delicious spicy leaves.

salad growing

planning the garden

Soil and site

Most salad plants are eaten raw, so it goes without saying that they must be succulent and tender. If they have to struggle for existence in poor soil, contend with alternating periods of drought and waterlogging, or be buffeted by cold and searing winds, they will inevitably become coarse and toughened. So in planning the vegetable garden four aspects hold the keys to success: fertile soil, good drainage, adequate water supplies and shelter.

The ideal textbook site is open: in other words, not overshadowed by buildings or overhung by trees, reasonably sheltered in that it is protected from strong winds and reasonably flat. So where there is a choice, avoid exposed sites, frost pockets, steep slopes and deeply shaded situations. In practice one normally has little choice about the site. If it has shortcomings, it is a question of working around them and ameliorating them. If, for example, you are faced with a very steep sloping site, consider terracing at least part of it for a vegetable garden.

SOIL

Vegetables can be grown on a wide range of soils, the 'perfect' soil being a medium loam, which generally means a well-drained mixture of soil types with a good level of organic matter in it. In practice, soils range from the extremes of very light sands to heavy clays.

Very light soil, being well drained, warms up rapidly in spring and is therefore excellent for early salad crops. On the other hand, its nutrients (plant foods) are washed out rapidly and in dry weather it is liable to suffer from drought. Clay soil, at the other extreme, is a cold, ill-drained soil in winter and may become baked hard in summer, but it is a rich storehouse of plant foods and can be very fertile once it has been worked and improved. Chalk soils tend to be light, warm and easily drained, but have varying levels of fertility.

The practicalities of creating a fertile soil are discussed on pp. 111–115. In essence, almost all soil types (an exception is very peaty soils) are improved by constantly working in 'organic matter', which is converted into humus, largely through the activity of earthworms. A key feature of organic matter is that it provides food for earthworms. They not only release the nutrients in the organic matter, but in their burrowing and casting make 'cemented' burrows, which create vital drainage and aeration channels in the soil.

The main source of organic matter for gardeners is home-made compost and manure. The implication for planning is that all this heavy material has to be transported around the garden, in wheelbarrows or by some other means. The more accessible the garden and individual beds, the easier this will be.

DRAINAGE

Good drainage is essential in vegetable growing. While a few salad plants, such as celery, fennel and Chinese cabbage, originated in marshlands and can stand fairly wet conditions, for most waterlogged soil is the kiss of death.

A drainage problem is usually obvious. Classic signs are water lying on the surface for several days after heavy rain, or encountering water when digging down, say, 30cm/12in. Absence of earthworms and soil that is greyish, bluish, blackish or mottled rather than brown are other indications of poor drainage.

Poor drainage can be improved, over several years, simply by digging in large quantities of bulky organic matter. This has been borne out by my own experience. When we first moved here our soil was sticky yellow clay and parts of the garden were waterlogged every winter. Constantly working in spent mushroom compost has improved it beyond measure. Where the problem is more persistent it may be necessary to make drains to remove the excess water. The simplest form is a trench drain (see illustration above), Make trench

Trench drains are a practical way of improving poor drainage. To make a simple trench drain dig out a trench about 30cm/12in wide and 60–90cm/24–36in deep. Fill the lower third of the trench with rubble before replacing the soil.

drains across the lower end of a slope, or on either side of a level site. You can incorporate them into a garden path, meandering through the garden. In serious cases it may be necessary to lay a network of drains with clay or plastic pipes, emptying into an outlet such as a ditch, artificial soakaway or sump. Seek expert help on the type of drains to use, their layout, depth and spacing, and the gradient at which to lay them. You can also improve drainage by using raised beds (see p. 94).

Occasionally, poor drainage is caused by an underlying hard pan, possibly due to a mineral deposit or compaction resulting from the use of heavy machinery or continual rotovation at the same depth. Where this occurs, the only remedy is to break up the hard pan with a spade, pick-axe or small mechanical digger.

WATER SUPPLY

Many salad vegetables have a high water content and may need frequent watering, especially during their 'critical' periods (see p. 117). Shortage of water restricts their growth and causes their quality to deteriorate. Under-watered radishes, to take one example, will be cracked, woody and unbearably hot rather than crisp and succulent. The oriental greens are more prone to premature bolting in dry conditions. In areas where water shortage is likely, bear this in mind when siting your salad crops: the shorter the distance that you have to carry cans or trail hoses, the better. Take measures to save rainwater for example, by collecting it off nearby roofs in water butts.

SHELTER AND WINDBREAKS

Gardeners consistently fail to appreciate the value of shelter in vegetable gardens. Research has shown that sheltering vegetables from even light winds can increase their yields by up to 50 per cent. Salad plants are particularly vulnerable to the damaging effects of wind. So in gardens that are at all exposed it is worth erecting some kind of windbreak. In frost-prone areas, leave a gap at the lower end of a slope to allow frost to drain away.

The ideal windbreak should act as a filter to the wind, and should be about 50 per cent permeable. Wind tends to leap over a solid barrier, creating an area of turbulence on the leeward side. Hedges, lath fences (with gaps between the laths), hurdles and windbreak netting battened to posts all make effective windbreaks. In exposed situations it may be worth the expense of surrounding the entire garden. Factors to consider are that hedges compete with crops for nutrients, moisture and light, may create shade and require maintenance. Good modern netting lasts for several years, but it will have to take tremendous strain. Erect the posts securely, reinforcing the corner posts if necessary. In small gardens some kind of fencing, about 1.5m/5ft high, may be more appropriate.

A windbreak is effective for a distance of roughly six times its own height, so a very large garden may require several windbreaks across the site. Where possible, site windbreaks across the path of the prevailing wind. In urban gardens, venomous winds often funnel through gaps between buildings. Any windbreak erected to close the gap should extend several feet/a metre beyond the gap on each side.

Within a garden you can put up smaller windbreaks to make it more sheltered. Strips of netting or hessian sacking about 30–60cm/12–24in high strung between beds or rows of vegetables cut down the wind very effectively. Even plants can make temporary windbreaks. Closely planted sweet corn or maize is grown as a windbreak in Holland; Jerusalem artichokes, sunflowers, even chicory or a 'hedge' of cardoons can be used. Protective films, fleeces and nets, cloches, polytunnels and greenhouses are all devices that shelter plants and protect them from wind (see pp. 120–23).

PRIME SALAD SITES

For as long as salads have been cultivated, a premium has been put on the very early crops, raised in sheltered sites on south-facing slopes. Enterprising market gardeners in the past even created slopes for early salads, while in the large walled kitchen gardens of the European gentry the earliest salads were grown in sunny beds at the foot of the walls. With ingenuity, warm fertile spots can be found or created in most gardens, for growing early – and late – salads.

Garden layout

THE CASE FOR NARROW BEDS

The layout of any vegetable garden is determined by the nature, size and shape of the beds. Whereas in the past vegetable gardens were laid out in large plots (wasteful in terms of space and resources), today the most efficient gardens are divided into small, permanent beds, narrow enough for the centre to be reached from the path. This 'narrow bed' system is widely adopted by organic gardeners.

Its salient feature is that it helps to preserve the fertility and structure of the soil (see p. 111). Good soil structure underpins soil fertility, but is a fragile quality, easily destroyed by digging heavy soil when it is wet, or simply by treading on the soil, again especially when wet. With narrow beds there is no need to walk on the soil, ever, either for cultivation or harvesting.

Another advantage of narrow beds is that all manures, compost and organic mulches are concentrated where they are needed: precisely where the plants are growing. In large beds much is wasted on ground that in practice has to serve as paths or access. It is much easier to build up and maintain fertility in narrow beds. This encourages plants to be deep rooting, which increases their resistance to drought.

Narrow beds lend themselves to the kind of intensive planting that suits the small size of contemporary gardens. Instead of widely spaced rows (where much of the space between rows simply invites weeds to grow), plants are grown at equidistant spacing. Among many benefits (see p. 96), their mature leaves form a blanketing canopy over the soil, inhibiting weed growth.

BED SIZE, SHAPE AND HEIGHT

Narrow beds can be various sizes and shapes. Rectangular beds are probably the easiest to manage and can be any length. Square beds must be kept reasonably small, or it becomes impossible to reach the centre from the paths. Beds can also be round, curved, crescent-shaped, triangular or any irregular shape. One of the charms of the potager approach (see p. 7) is the scope for grouping beds of any shape into aesthetic patterns. A practical width for beds is 90–150cm/3–5ft. The important point is to choose a width that feels comfortable to you. I personally like a width of about 120cm/4ft; this is also a convenient width for the hoops we use for low polythene and net tunnels (see p. 123).

Beds can be level or raised above the ground. Level beds are the easiest to work, though salad plants at ground level tend to get muddied. Raised beds can be anything from 10 to 90cm/4 to 36in high; higher beds are often made on a brick or concrete foundation to provide access for disabled gardeners. Raised beds are usually made by excavating the soil from the path area on to the beds. If you are making raised beds to overcome serious soil problems, such as contaminated or very badly drained soil, you will have to import good-quality soil. The soil in the final bed needs to be at least 30cm/12in deep.

Raised beds can be free-standing or edged, usually with timber. If free-standing, they should be slightly tapered to make them stable. A bed 120cm/4ft wide at the base should be about 90cm/3ft wide at the top. The surface can be flat or rounded. Where beds are oriented in an east–west direction, the south-facing rounded surface (in the northern hemisphere) will attract increased sunlight and radiation.

Kitchen garden beds can be edged with plants – herbs such as chives, parsley, marjoram and thyme are a common choice – or with hard materials. These tend to take less space and, where salad plants are concerned, help to keep them clean. Bricks, tiles, stones and various form of timber are all commonly used. Boards should be of pressure-treated timber; they can be stained with weatherproof preservatives or painted to add a colourful touch.

PATHS

Paths are an important element in any vegetable plot. They should be at least 30–45cm/12–18in wide, with occasional wider paths at least 60cm/24in wide, so that you can manoeuvre laden wheelbarrows comfortably. The choice of surface ranges from bare soil and grass to permanent paths of brick, stone, gravel, stone or paving slabs. Brick paths, perhaps combined with stones or pavers, can be laid in imaginative patterns, making a feature of a practical element. Lay them on a base of sand and black polythene film (see illustration

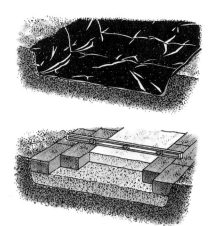

LEFT To make paths, line 10cm/4in deep channels with heavy black polythene film to prevent weeds from germinating. To make a level base, put a 5cm/2in layer of sand over the film, and lay bricks and pavers on top.

RIGHT These 5ft/1.5m-wide potager beds can be reached from the paths. The radishes are being grown for their seed pods.

above). Our kitchen garden paths are bare soil, covered with heavy-duty, weed-suppressing but permeable black fabric, disguised, wherever feasible, with a light layer of bark chippings. It makes a serviceable, firm, clean and well-drained surface.

BED DIRECTION

In the northern hemisphere, to make maximum use of sunshine, beds should theoretically be orientated from north to south for summer crops, and from east to west for early and late crops. In practice this is difficult to carry out. Site tall plants such as sweet corn and climbing beans so that they do not cast shade on low-growing plants.

CROPPING PLANS

To get the most out of the garden, it is worth planning carefully. The traditional starting point is the rotation plan. Rotation is the practice of grouping together closely related vegetables and growing them in a different bed, or different part of the garden, over at least a three-year cycle.

This is to prevent the build-up of those serious soil pests and diseases that attack a limited range of plants in the same botanical family. In practice, many soil pests are fairly mobile, so there is little point in simply moving a crop a few yards away. Moreover some species of eelworm and diseases such as clubroot, can remain in the soil for up to six or seven years, so rotation would have to be practised over a long cycle to be really effective. This is obviously impractical in small gardens.

Nevertheless, without being a slave to rotation theory, it is sound preventive medicine to try to rotate the main groups below over a three- or preferably four- or five-year cycle. It is easier to work out a flexible rotation plan where a garden is divided into several small beds rather than two or three large ones. In the absence of a rotation plan, at least try to follow each crop with one from an unrelated group; and never replant a piece of ground with a crop that is the same as, or closely related, to the crop that has just been cleared.

Main rotation groups:
- *Solanaceae* – potatoes, tomatoes, aubergines, peppers.
- *Leguminosae* – peas, beans, fenugreek.
- Brassicas – cabbages, cauliflower, broccoli, radishes, mustards, turnips, swedes, kohl rabi, oriental greens.
- Alliums – onion, leeks, garlic.

Fit in the many other vegetables wherever there is space.

Detailed planning At the outset, draw up a plan of your beds and decide how many and which to allocate to the main rotation groups. Write on the plan the vegetables you are growing in those groups, with a note of how many months they are likely to be in the ground. (For leafy saladini vegetables, see p. 161). Where space and time allows, follow or precede them with another crop. For example, in the potato bed, you could plant lettuces or cucumbers when you lift the early potatoes in June or July. It is worth putting aside a part of the garden, or a couple of beds, for perennial vegetables such as asparagus, globe artichokes, rhubarb, sorrel and Good King Henry.

Space-saving systems

Vegetable gardens in the twenty-first century are smaller than in the past, many would-be gardeners, especially in urban areas, having to make do with the tiniest of plots. This was brought home to me when I visited community gardens in the USA. In some a piece of ground the size of an average desk was considered 'large'. It was inspiring to see what was produced in these minute gardens. Salad plants have much to offer where space is at a premium, and lend themselves to space-saving techniques such as equidistant spacing and all the forms of intercropping.

EQUIDISTANT SPACING

Scientific research has now demonstrated the inefficiency, in most cases, of the traditional method of growing plants close together in rows, with the rows spaced far apart. Within the rows plants compete fiercely for the limited resources of nutrients and moisture, and in so doing deprive each other of sunlight. Yet in the space between the rows, where there is no competition, weeds flourish.

You can overcome this problem with equidistant spacing. Think of each plant as the centre of a circle, from which it draws its nutrients and moisture, the radius varying with the size of the plant and its demands. A cauliflower, for example, draws from a far greater area than a lettuce. The most economic way of utilizing the soil – the storehouse of both nutrients and moisture – is to space plants so that when fully grown their 'circles' just overlap. You can achieve these effects by planting in staggered rows with equidistant spacing in both directions – that is the same space between the plants in each row as

Equidistant spacing makes optimum use of the ground. Here the spacing between the plants is the same as the spacing between the rows. The dotted circles indicate the area the full-grown plant will occupy, and from which it draws its nutrients and moisture.

there is between the rows themselves (see illustration). The mature plants, each more or less touching their neighbours, form a leafy canopy over the soil. This proves an effective means of weed control, as few weed seeds germinate when deprived of light. The main exception is narrow-leaved plants like onions. In this case keeping the soil between the plants mulched (see p. 118–9), will control potential weeds. Broad-leaved plants can be mulched in their immature stages before they cover the soil.

SPACING AS A TOOL

For the major vegetables, researchers have established the optimum spacing to get the highest yield from a given area. You can also use spacing as a tool, to control the size and quality of vegetables, and the speed with which they mature. With onions, for example, close spacing will produce pickling onions, moderate spacing small cooking onions and wide spacing very large onions. The same principle holds true for carrots, cabbages, leeks and many other vegetables. The quality of calabrese heads and self-blanching celery stalks will, to some extent, be improved by close spacing; tomatoes will mature earlier when grown relatively close.

The most extreme example of close spacing is seedling crops, and the slightly more mature stage known as 'baby leaves'. The archetype seedling crop is garden cress, grown by generations of children on blotting paper on a windowsill and cut about 4cm/1½in high. When cress is sown in ordinary soil rather than on blotting paper it will grow up to 30cm/12in high, and after it has been cut, it will resprout. In fact, depending on the conditions, you can often make several cuts from one sowing.

Many plants can be used at the seedling stage in salads, and the majority, like cress, will produce several cuttings in one season – hence the term 'cut-and-come-again'. This productive method of growing nutritious and tasty salad materials is discussed fully on pp. 127–30. (For the space- and time-saving technique of multi-sowing, where several seedlings are sown together in a module and planted 'as one', see p. 108.)

Here garden cress is sown around young cabbage plants when they are planted. The fast-growing cress may be cut twice before it is uprooted to give the cabbages space to mature.

Small 'Tom Thumb' lettuces are interplanted between multi-sown onions. The lettuces will be harvested long before the onions mature.

INTERCROPPING

The underlying principle of intercropping is that some plants, typically brassicas such as cabbage, grow much more slowly than others. They will not occupy their allotted 'circle' until they have been in the ground for several months. In their early stages, when they are still small, it is possible to grow a fast-growing crop alongside or around them, which will be ready for use and harvested before the entire space is required by the slower-growing plant.

In much the same way, it is not always necessary to wait for a crop to be cleared before sowing or planting its successor. There may be space to sow or plant alongside. By the time the second crop needs more space, the first will be ready for harvesting. For example, towards the end of summer in my polytunnel, I sneak drills of winter cut-and-come-again seedlings between the last of the basil plants.

Intercropping takes various forms. The 'intercropper' can be sown or planted, within existing rows, between rows, or simply around another plant. It has to be said that intercropping is easier to manage when plants are grown in conventional rows rather than when they are at equidistant spacing. Intercropping often results in beautiful patterned effects in the salad garden.

In-row intersowing In this case slow-growing root vegetables such as parsnips are 'station sown' (see p. 104), and a few seeds of a fast-growing crop such as radish, spring onion, salad rocket or a small lettuce are sown between each 'station'. A slightly less precise method is to mix seeds of fast growers with slow growers (such as maincrop carrots or parsnips) and sow them together in the row. The fast growers will act as row markers for the slower developing carrots or parsnips (see also Mixed Patches, p. 98).

Sowing between rows and around plants A quick crop can often be sown between rows of onions, shallots or leeks, whose narrow leaves require little space when first planted (see photograph above). Similarly, where celeriac, beet and brassicas are grown in rows, intercrops can be sown between them in the early stages. Where the main crops are grown at equidistant spacing, there will be room, when they are first planted, to sow a quick-growing crop around them. I often sow salad rocket, radishes, cress or red seedling lettuce in figure-of-eight patterns around Brussels sprouts and cauliflowers. The intercrops must all be harvested before the brassicas overcrowd them. This may seem like stating the obvious, but I have found that it requires quite a lot of will power to uproot the intercrops if they are still being reasonably productive.

An interesting method of double cropping – you might even call it 'top cropping' – is to sow a seedling crop in the ground above potatoes, after they have been planted. You can usually make at least one cut before the potatoes burst through.

Planting between rows and plants Some of the smaller salad plants can be planted between rows, or between individual plants, of relatively slow-maturing vegetables. Appropriate interplants are lettuce, small pak choi, summer or winter purslane, chrysanthemum greens, mizuna greens (if kept cut back hard), corn salad and land cress. All will normally provide a picking or two before they are encroached upon by the main crop. Corn salad, land cress and winter purslane can be planted under Brussels sprouts in the autumn in mild areas, and will grow there happily until spring. They probably even benefit from the extra shelter.

Undercropping This is a form of intercropping where tall plants are combined with ground-hugging or trailing crops. Sweet corn is one of the most amenable plants for undercropping. The leaves create only light shade, so you can plant the ground beneath with a

Climbing plants such as beans and cucumbers that are trained up tepees will shade the ground beneath them when they are fully grown. However in their early stages they can be underplanted or undersown with salad plants like lettuce.

range of crops, some of which will remain in the ground long after the corn is harvested in late summer (see Intercropping Guidelines, p. 100). Asparagus is another plant with airy foliage that casts little shade, so you can use the ground beneath for small plants like corn salad and seedling crops. I have found that parsley does well in an asparagus bed: a few plants left to seed more or less perpetuate themselves.

There is sometimes scope for undercropping climbing vegetables in their early stages, for example climbing beans, the smaller squashes and cucumbers. One year I grew the round South African squash 'Little Gem' up a tepee of four canes, each set at the corner of a 1m/3ft square. I sowed the squashes under jars to help germination, one at the foot of each cane; at the same time I planted a dozen lettuces in the square. While the marrows germinated and started to grow up the canes, the lettuces grew steadily. They were ready for cutting before the marrows had clothed the cane structure and blocked out the light. The foliage of 'Little Gem' squash and of some trailing marrows has pretty grey markings and makes a striking garden feature.

Natural coexistence This is another form of intercropping. It was the late Rosemary Verey, the well-known gardener, who showed me how chervil and dill work well in tandem. Both, once established, self-seed and so keep going on the same spot. The chervil naturally germinates in autumn, normally remains green in winter, and runs to seed in late spring. Just when it is dying down the dill germinates and carries on throughout the summer.

Mixed patches The concept of mixing different seeds and sowing them together is ancient, the idea being that they mature in turn, making optimum use of a piece of ground. The seventeenth-century diarist John Evelyn suggested mixing lettuce, purslane, carrots, radish and parsnips. A simple traditional mixture is radishes and carrots. A common Chinese practice is to mix carrots and pak choi: the pak choi is harvested at the seedling stage, leaving the carrots to mature. (This works well with a ratio of two teaspoons of carrot seed to one of pak choi.) A trick I was taught long ago is to mix carrots and annual flowers such as love-in-a-mist, nemesia and scabious. The annuals flower colourfully, and all the while the carrots are growing inconspicuously (hidden from carrot fly), ready for pulling at the end of the season.

Various examples of intercropping. TOP LEFT Lettuce and early summer cabbages, interplanted together in spring. TOP RIGHT Cress intersown between young kohl rabi plants. CENTRE RIGHT Mizuna greens thrive beneath sweet corn, and will remain there, and continue to be productive, long after the corn is harvested. LOWER LEFT AND RIGHT Seedling mixtures are an extreme example of intercropping. The mixtures here are 'Braising mix' (LOWER LEFT), which is composed of several types of oriental greens, and 'Oriental saladini' (LOWER RIGHT), a blend of oriental greens and kales.

Mixing your own cocktail of seed is something of a gamble, but premixed selections are widely available. Among the most popular are variations of the traditional salad mixes, which we first encountered on our European travels, known as *mesclun* in France, and *misticanza* in Italy. They are often sold as 'saladini' (see p. 140). These mixtures can contain up to a dozen salad plants, typically several types of lettuce and chicory, salad rocket, chervil, endive and corn salad. They can give a continuous supply of salad over many months, different plants maturing in succession. Similarly 'stir fry' mixtures, mustard mixes and blends of oriental greens such as the mixture known as 'Oriental saladini' make lovely salading when cut young.

Last word on intercropping Once tuned into the concept of taking a quick 'catch crop' in a piece of ground that is currently under-utilized, you will find endless opportunities to do so. For help in working out intercropping combinations, see the lists below and the planning chart on p. 159. Base your schemes on your observations of how plants grow in your garden. But be careful not to overdo it. In areas with high rainfall or low light conditions, excessive intercropping may result in rampant, jungle-like growth and an increase in disease. Both sets of crops must have enough space, light, moisture and nutrients to develop fully, and there must be room for necessary cultivation and harvesting. These factors are sometimes overlooked in the excitement of 'getting in as much as possible'. The soil must be fertile and well watered to sustain such intensive use. Once crops are established, it is advisable to water well, then mulch the plants to retain moisture, stifle weeds and keep the plants clean.

INTERCROPPING GUIDELINES

Slow-growing plants that can be intercropped in early stages Brassicas: e.g. cauliflower, cabbage, broccoli, Brussels sprouts, kales, kohl rabi; parsnips, Hamburg parsley, salsify, scorzonera; onions and shallots; celeriac, leeks, beetroot; perennials: e.g. globe artichokes, cardoons.
Tall plants that can be undercropped (climbers in early stages only) Sweet corn, climbing squashes, marrows, cucumbers and climbing beans – all on supports.

Fast-maturing plants suitable for intercropping, and undercropping climbers in early stages Summer radishes; small lettuces such as 'Tom Thumb', 'Little Gem'; early turnips; all cut-and-come-again seedling crops.
Low-growing plants suitable for undercropping sweet corn (as it does not form a dense canopy) Trailing marrows, cucumbers and gherkins; red chicory, endive, corn salad, land cress, salad rocket, mizuna greens, chrysanthemum greens, dwarf French beans; parsley and all cut-and-come-again seedling crops; all fast-maturing crops above.

KEEPING THE POT BOILING

One of the challenges of planning is to have something fresh from the garden all year round. Gluts, so often partnered by shortages, are a waste of space. Bolting lettuce is depressing, however fond you are of lettuce soup.

What you can grow successfully is largely determined by the climate, but you can do a lot to extend the natural season.
• Choose varieties (of lettuce or cabbage, for example) to span the growing season. Make use of varieties that fill gaps: for example autumn-planted onion sets mature in the 'onion gap' in early summer.
• Sow 'little and often', especially salads such as hearting lettuce and summer radish which run to seed or deteriorate soon after maturing. As a rule of thumb, make the next sowing when the previous one has germinated.
• Stagger planting. Plant a crop over several days, so that the plants mature in sequence. Alternatively select seedlings of different sizes when planting. Raising plants in modules (see p. 108), produces excellent plants, which can be held back without damage.
• In cold climates use to the full all forms of cover, from light fleeces laid over outdoor crops, to greenhouses and polytunnels (see pp. 120–23). A 0.5°C/1°F rise in temperature is equivalent to moving 100 miles south (in the northern hemisphere). In spring, sow early cut-and-come-again seedling crops and make early sowings of outdoor crops under cover. In summer, grow heat-loving crops such as peppers and tomatoes. In autumn and winter, use their sheltering effect to improve the quality of winter salads.

plant raising

Seed

Is it worth going to the trouble of raising your own plants, rather than buying them ready for planting out? The answer must certainly be, 'Yes, if you can.' It's fun and satisfying but, above all, it gives you a far greater choice of interesting varieties, as garden centres and nurserymen invariably supply only the most popular varieties. You also avoid the risk of introducing soil-borne pests and diseases, such as vine weevil and clubroot, into your garden.

The majority of salads are raised from seed; the better the seed quality, the greater the chances of a good crop. In most Western countries minimum standards of purity and germination are laid down for the main vegetables, so you can be fairly sure of buying seed that was of reasonable quality when it was packeted. However, seed deteriorates with time and in adverse conditions, losing its viability (ability to germinate).

Wherever possible, buy seed in hermetically sealed foil packets. These safeguard viability much longer than paper packets, but once the packet is opened, normal deterioration sets in. Be wary of packets that have obviously been subjected to damp or very dry conditions: they are unlikely to germinate well.

STORING SEED

Seed should be kept dry and cold. Many germination failures stem from using old seed or seed that has been kept in damp garden sheds or hot rooms. Ideally, seed should be stored at temperatures below freezing: for every 5°C/9°F rise above zero, the storage life of seed is halved.

Keep seed in an airtight tin or jar in a cool room, or, if you have space, in a domestic refrigerator. An additional safeguard is to put a cloth bag or dish of silica gel in the container to absorb atmospheric moisture. Silica gel will need to be dried out periodically. Unfortunately it has become hard to buy in small quantities. An

alternative, suggested to me by the Genetic Resources Unit at Wellesbourne, is to use grains such as wheat or rice. Dry them initially for about an hour on a metal tray in a low oven (to drive out any moisture), then cool them somewhere dry. This is best done in an airtight jar. Seed can then be stored in paper packets in the same jar.

The natural viability of vegetable seed varies according to the species, and is affected by a range of factors. Tomato and legume (the family that includes peas and beans) seed can, under good conditions, keep for up to ten years; brassicas, lettuce, endive and chicory will normally last four or five years, but may fall off after a couple of years; the onion and leek family deteriorate after the second year; root vegetables such as parsnip, salsify and scorzonera lose viability rapidly, so it is advisable to use fresh seed each year.

If in doubt, do a germination test before making your main sowing. Put a piece of foam rubber (to retain moisture) in a dish, cover it with a double layer of paper towelling, lay the seeds on top and put it somewhere warm (see p. 108). If they have not germinated within a couple of weeks, cut your losses and buy fresh seed.

SAVING YOUR OWN SEED

Home gardeners are usually advised against saving their own seed, as it is unlikely to match the quality of purchased seed. Nevertheless, it can be worth saving seed of salads used as cut-and-come-again seedling crops, not least because you will need far more seed than the average seed packet contains. You may also want to save seed of unusual varieties that are difficult to obtain, or of an outstanding plant of your own. Never save seed of F1 hybrids, as they will not come true.

Save seed from only the very best plants, never from diseased plants or those running to seed prematurely. If possible, keep the

Seed is easily saved from salad plants such as cress and rocket. The pods must be dried thoroughly.

plants isolated from other varieties to avoid cross-pollination. Keep them well watered while they are flowering and forming seedheads, but stop watering once the pods are formed. Ripening plants may need staking to prevent them from falling over and soiling the seed pods. It is best to let the seed pods dry naturally on the plant, but in persistently damp weather uproot the plants and hang them under cover until completely dry.

When the pods are brittle, the dry seed can be shaken out on a newspaper and stored in envelopes or jars. I sometimes leave garden cress and salad rocket seedheads in the greenhouse, crumbling the seed pods directly on to the ground when I want to sow.

Seed saving is most successful where the climate is dry when the seed is ripening. Cress, salad rocket, corn salad, chervil, radish and chicory are amongst the easiest to save. To be sure of maintaining quality, it is advisable to start again with commercial seed every few years. (For further reading, see pp. 162–3.)

Choosing varieties

In common parlance gardeners still talk about 'varieties', although the correct term today for 'varieties raised in cultivation' is cultivars.

For keen salad growers, the widest choice of varieties is generally found in mail-order seed catalogues. There are some useful indicators of quality and performance.

F1 hybrid seed Most new vegetable varieties are 'F1 hybrids'. These are bred by crossing two parent lines, each of which has been inbred for several generations. Compared to standard 'open-pollinated' varieties, the resulting hybrid seed is of outstanding vigour, evenness and reliability, often with useful disease resistance. Because F1 varieties are easily patented, their widespread use commercially has tended to erode, and lead to the loss of, some heritage varieties.

Awards of merit As a result of assessment in formal trials, outstanding cultivars are given the Award of Merit (AM) by the Royal Horticultural Society in the UK, and Gold, Silver and Bronze medals in the All America Awards Scheme (AAA) in the USA.

'Suitable for organic gardeners' Regular trials are now being carried out to assess a variety's performance in an organic system. The main qualities looked for are natural vigour (not least to outstrip weeds), and pest, disease and weather resistance. Incidentally, strictly organic gardeners would not use dressed seed, although these chemical treatments undeniably protect seed in the vulnerable early stages of germination.

Forms of seed

Besides ordinary or 'naked' seed, seed is available in various forms.

Pelleted seed Individual seeds are coated with an inert protective substance, making each seed into a small, round ball. This makes them easy to handle and sow with precision. The coating breaks down in the soil, but the pellets must be kept moist until this point, or they may not germinate. Softer-coated pellets, known as 'pills' or 'split pellets', are sometimes available. They are mainly sown under cover, and should be sown shallowly.

Chitted (pregerminated) seed The seeds have already germinated, to the stage of an incipient radicle (root), or with the first 'seed leaves' developed (the first tiny leaves after germination, before the next 'true' leaves). They are posted to customers in airtight sachets, and are pricked out on receipt. The technique is used for seeds that are difficult to germinate.

Primed seed The seeds are brought to the point of germination, then dried before being packeted. Once sown, the seed germinates exceptionally fast – a useful characteristic for early sowings in adverse conditions. Primed seed is advocated for early sowings of carrots, onions and parsnips. Seed has to be sown soon after receipt.

Seed tapes and sheets Evenly spaced seed is embedded in soluble tapes or paper-like sheets, which are 'sown' on the ground or in a seed tray, covered lightly with soil and kept moist until germination. The predetermined spacing means that little, if any, thinning is required.

WHERE TO SOW

There are two main options for sowing vegetables, depending on climate, season and the nature of the crop.

'Outdoors' implies sowing either *in situ* – that is, in the ground where plants will mature, or in a seedbed from which they will be transplanted into their permanent positions. Sowing outdoors is suitable for robust vegetables that germinate easily, for vegetables that dislike being transplanted and for seedling crops that are sown thickly and harvested young.

'Indoors' is a loose term to describe sowing in some kind of seed tray or pot in a protected environment, which can range from a windowsill to a cloche to a greenhouse. Sowing indoors enables plants to be given a head start when conditions outdoors are still unsuitable for sowing or planting. The first lettuces, for example, may be sown indoors early in the year and planted out as soon as conditions allow. In areas with a cold or short growing season, the only chance of growing tender crops like tomatoes and peppers to maturity is to start them indoors, planting outside when they are well developed.

Sowing outdoors

Choosing the right conditions for sowing and preparing the seedbed well are crucial to success when sowing outdoors. A lot of good seed fails to germinate because it was sown when the soil was too cold, too wet, too dry or too lumpy.

THE SEEDBED

The term 'seedbed' is used ambiguously both for the surface of any piece of ground where seed is sown and for an area put aside for raising seedlings that will later be transplanted. The latter, 'nursery' seedbed is primarily a means of saving space for vegetables that have a long growing season or take up a lot of space when mature. In their early stages they can be grown relatively close in the seedbed, during which time you can use the ground they will eventually occupy for another crop.

A nursery seedbed should be made in an open position. Resist the temptation to use an out-of-the-way corner, perhaps near a hedge. This is likely to result in sad, drawn seedlings deprived of light and moisture. The soil does not need to be rich but it must be well drained and if possible, weed-free. Where the soil is likely to be full of weed seeds, prepare the seedbed first (see below), then leave it a week or so for the main flush of weed seeds to germinate. Hoe them off before sowing.

PREPARING A SEEDBED

The surface of the seedbed needs to be free of clods, lumps and stones, and raked to a fairly fine tilth – with the soil particles about the size of breadcrumbs. A fine tilth is important for sowing small seeds, but larger seeds, such as peas and beans, can cope with a

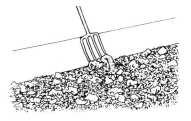

The first stage in preparing a seedbed is to break up the clods of earth with a garden fork.

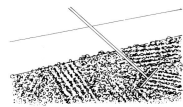

To prepare a tilth rake backwards and forwards in different directions.

rougher surface. The soil should be reasonably firm: where feasible, leave it to settle for a few weeks after it has been dug.

The mechanics of making a seedbed depend on the soil. Sandy and light soils are easily raked down into a good surface in spring, but clay and loam soils are naturally much lumpier. (Some clay soils are unsuitable for seedbeds but can be improved by working potting compost and sand into the surface.) These heavier soils should be dug over in autumn and exposed to winter frosts, which help break down the clods. Once the soil has started to dry out in spring, you can start work on making a seedbed.

It is important to choose the right moment to do so. If the soil sticks to your shoes, wait a few days until it has dried out. Covering the soil with cloches or clear film will make it dry faster. If the soil is too dry, water it before working on it. Start by breaking down large remaining clods with a garden fork or the back of a rake. If this proves difficult, fork the soil over lightly first. Then rake it smooth (see illustration on p. 103), removing small clods and stones.

When to sow

Most vegetables have an optimum temperature for germination. As a rule, the higher the temperature, the faster they germinate, although some seeds (butterhead lettuce and onion, for example) germinate poorly at temperatures above 24°C/75°F. You can find out the soil temperature with a soil thermometer; to obtain a correct reading, insert it 5–8cm/2–3in deep in the soil. Otherwise simply feel the soil. If it feels cold to your touch, delay sowing. There is little to gain by

sowing prematurely in cold soil: the seed is likely to rot or become diseased. If you are unable to sow immediately after preparing the seedbed, cover it with a light mulch of straw or dried leaves to protect it from strong, drying spring winds or heavy rainfall until you are ready to sow.

Methods of sowing

Seed can be sown in drills, broadcast or sown individually.

Sowing in drills A standard narrow drill is a slit made in the soil, normally in a straight line (see illustrations below), at an even depth, which helps prevent erratic germination. The depth depends on the size of the seed. As a rough guide, seeds need to be covered by at least twice their depth. A 'wide' drill, often used for sowing peas or cut-and-come-again seedling crops, is usually up to about 10cm/4in wide, made using the broad blade of an onion hoe or similar tool.

Spacing seeds evenly along the drill is essential, both to prevent overcrowding when the seedlings first germinate, and to minimize subsequent thinning.

This is the purpose behind 'station sowing', where three or four seeds are sown in a group together, at regular intervals or 'stations' along a drill. Where plants will eventually be thinned to stand 20cm/8in apart, station sow at half that distance – that is, 10cm/4in apart. Pelleted seed is very useful for station sowing. Not only does station sowing simplify thinning, but it enables a fast-growing crop to be sown between stations as markers for a slow-growing one (see Space-saving Systems, p. 96).

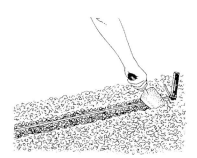

Sowing in a drill
Use the point of a trowel or hoe to 'draw' the drill at an even depth.

Space the seed thinly and evenly along the drill, so that the seedlings are not overcrowded. They will then grow healthily.

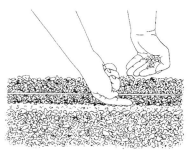

After sowing, press the seeds gently into the bottom of the drill, using a finger or the back of the trowel or hoe.

Cover the seed with soil using the hand or the blade of a hoe. Finally firm the soil gently with the hands or trowel.

Sowing in adverse conditions Seeds germinate poorly if sown in very dry conditions. A useful technique to overcome this is to make the drill and carefully water the bottom of it (not the ground surrounding it) until it is almost muddy. Then sow the seed, press it into the drill, and cover it with dry soil. The dry soil acts as a mulch, preventing evaporation, so the soil remains moist until the seed has germinated. (This tip, which I heard on a radio programme, has saved me from countless fruitless sowings.) To further encourage germination in dry weather cover the seedbed after sowing with a light mulch or with clear polythene film, removing it as soon as the seedlings break through the surface.

To counteract very wet conditions, line the drill with sowing or potting compost, or with well-rotted leaf mould, to make a dry bed on which the seed is sown.

Broadcasting This is the old-fashioned method of sowing by scattering seed over the surface. It is still very useful for seedling crops that require little or no thinning, and for fast-growing salads such as radishes or early carrots. It is economical with space.

Prepare the seedbed as described on p. 103–4, taking special care to ensure that it is free of weeds. Then scatter the seed over the surface as evenly as possible. Crops used at a very young stage, such as garden cress, can be sown thicker than, say, radishes or Sugar Loaf chicory, for which individual seedlings will eventually need more space to develop.

After sowing, cover the seed by raking gently first in one direction, then at right angles. Because the seed is so near the surface, there is a greater risk than normal of it drying out in hot weather, in which case cover the bed with a thin mulch or polythene film until the seed has germinated. Alternatively, sprinkle fine soil, potting compost or sand over the surface.

You can achieve much the same effect by making parallel drills very close together. Make narrow drills about 5–8cm/2–3in apart, and 10cm/4in-wide drills (to take one example) about 10–15cm/4–6in apart. These will be easier to weed than a broadcast patch.

Sowing large seeds individually Very large seeds, such as peas, beans, cucumbers and sweet corn, can be sown by simply making a hole in the soil with the point of a small dibber and dropping the seed into it. Make sure the seed touches the bottom of the hole and is not suspended in mid-air. Sow two or three seeds per

A jam jar can be used as a 'mini cloche' to give seeds an early start. Sow large seeds singly or in a group of two or three, thinning to the strongest after germination. Remove the jar during the day as soon as the seeds are through.

hole, thinning to one seedling after germination. For early sowings, you can use a jam jar as a 'mini cloche', placed over the planted seeds to help warm the soil (see illustration below).

Sowing under fleeces and transparent films To give extra protection against the weather early in the season, sow seeds under fleeces and polythene films (see p. 123). Sow the seed in slightly indented drills, with the films laid over the top. This will prevent the films from slumping on to the germinating seedlings if wet weather ensues.

THINNING

Seedlings grow very rapidly, and if they are overcrowded they become diseased and fail to develop properly. Thin them as soon as they are large enough to handle, either when the ground is moist or having watered gently beforehand. To minimize disturbance to the remaining seedlings, simply nip off unwanted seedlings just above soil level. It is best to thin in stages, each time thinning so that every seedling stands clear of its neighbour (see illustrations below). Be sure to clear away surplus thinnings, as their scent may attract the plant's enemies.

To avoid damaging seedling roots, thin by nipping off surplus seedlings just above soil level.

Thin so that each remaining seedling stands clear of its neighbour. Firm back the soil after thinning.

Sowing indoors

Raising plants indoors is best seen as a multi-stage operation in which certain phases may be omitted or merged with others. The key phases are:

Sowing Seed is sown in a small container, in fine-textured 'compost' or a special growing medium. It is put somewhere warm to germinate.

Pricking out The crowded seedlings are transplanted individually into a larger container with richer, coarser compost. They are spaced out so that they can grow rapidly.

Potting on The by-now small plants are moved into individual pots of richer compost.

Hardening off Plants destined to be grown outside or at lower temperatures are gradually acclimatized before being planted in their permanent positions.

With modern composts and propagators it is deceptively easy to germinate seedlings, and at this stage they take up little space. Once they are pricked out and/or potted on, they need more room, good light and some warmth. It may be difficult to meet these conditions unless you have a greenhouse. It can be several weeks from sowing before soil conditions and temperatures are suitable for planting outside, so beware of sowing more plants than you have room for. If they are kept in overcrowded conditions with inadequate light or heat, they will deteriorate and be prone to disease. If this is the case, consider buying some of the plants you need from garden centres or mail order seed companies, many of whom now supply plants.

SOWING CONTAINERS

Seed trays are the most widely used containers for sowing seeds. They need to be deep enough to hold about 2.5cm/1in of growing medium. You can use all sorts of things, from small clay or plastic horticultural pots 5–7.5cm/2–3in deep to the wide range of containers used in the take-away industry. Whatever the container, it must have some means of drainage (make holes in the base if necessary) or be naturally porous, like cardboard egg boxes.

Modules In recent years the concept of sowing in 'modules' has gained ground and is highly recommended. In essence, a module is any container or 'cell' in which a single seed is sown and grown on until it is ready for planting. This eliminates the need for the pricking-out stage and, because the seedlings have no competition from neighbouring seedlings, results in plants of excellent quality.

Types of sowing container

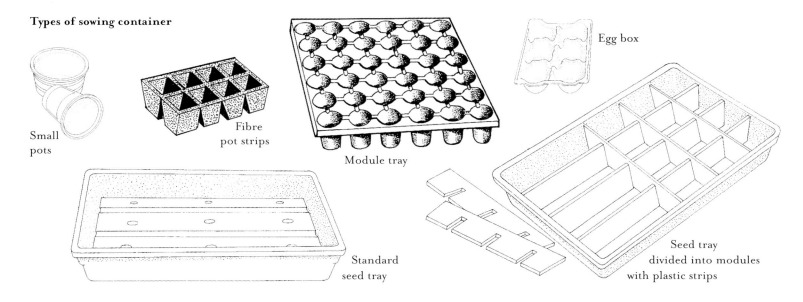

Small pots

Fibre pot strips

Module tray

Egg box

Standard seed tray

Seed tray divided into modules with plastic strips

The cell or module is planted out whole, so there is virtually no root disturbance. The robustness of seedlings grown in modules means you can often plant them under conditions where planting normal 'bare-root' transplants would be impossible. They are also less likely to deteriorate if for any reason you have to delay planting. Plants raised in modules are often known as 'plugs'.

Modules are a useful means of raising a range of plants or a sequence of varieties where garden space is limited. For example, you could sow a dozen or so lettuce modules every week or ten days to provide continuity, or, in theory, sow a large forty-celled module tray with something different in each cell.

The most common type of modules are seed trays of moulded plastic or polystyrene, divided into individual cells. You can convert standard seed trays into modules with interlocking plastic dividers – home-made if necessary. Small pots, if seeds are sown in them individually, are in effect modules. Another form of module is the 'soil block', made by compressing specially formulated potting compost into a compact cube with a block-making tool. The freestanding blocks can be aligned in a standard seed tray. Blocking tools and compost are currently hard to find, so the system, valuable though it is, has fallen out of use. I mention it here in case it reappears in future.

Sowing and potting compost

Ordinary garden soil is unsuitable for raising plants indoors, as it is too coarse and likely to be full of weed seed. Various light-textured sowing and potting composts have been developed for the purpose; most are sterile, so there is no problem with germinating weeds. Sowing composts are very fine-textured, and contain few plant nutrients, so they cannot sustain plants beyond the seedling stage. Potting composts are coarser with a higher level of nutrients, so they can support plants until they are potted on or planted out. In practice, most salad plants can be sown direct into a potting compost or 'multipurpose' compost, unless the seed is exceptionally fine. Alternatively, seed can be germinated successfully in an inert medium such as coarse sand, perlite or vermiculite, or even sifted leaf mould; these have no nutritive value, so seedlings need to be transferred into a stronger compost soon after germination. 'Garden' compost, incidentally, is unsuitable as a growing medium: it is too

rich and using it would result in sappy, disease-prone seedlings.

In the past, two main types of composts were widely used: the soil-based composts made to the John Innes formula, and peat-based composts. Both incorporate chemical fertilizers and both utilize peat. As peat is a diminishing natural resource, its use is discouraged in organic gardening. Finding satisfactory substitutes has been a problem. However, they are now being developed from coir (the natural coconut waste product), from worm-worked compost and from other sources. Use them whenever possible. I also advocate watering sowing or potting composts with a weak solution of seaweed extract or growth promoter. These seem to stimulate healthy growth, and provide nutrients for the developing seedlings.

Propagators

Most seeds germinate best in warm soil, a soil temperature of 13–16°C/55–60°F being suitable for the majority of salad plants. Propagators are a means of supplying 'bottom heat' below the seed tray. They range from very simple units heated with an electric light bulb, to electrically warmed plates or coils placed beneath or within a seed tray, to elaborate automated, self-watering units. A propagating unit can also be installed on a greenhouse bench using insulated electric cables buried in sand. Get professional advice if making a home-made system. Propagators can be designed to run in conjunction with gas, oil and paraffin greenhouse heaters.

A propagating unit should have a cover to retain atmospheric moisture and prevent the seed trays from drying out. As space in a propagator is always at a premium, try to choose containers of a size that will fit into it neatly.

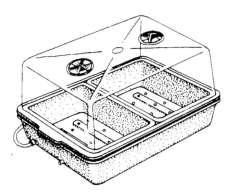

A simple domestic plug-in propapagator, in which the heat source is an electric light bulb beneath the tray. The cover helps retain moisture, while the small ventilators prevent the build-up of condensation, which may lead to damping off diseases. Otherwise remove the cover daily, wiping off any moisture.

SOWING IN CONTAINERS

Fill the containers as in illustration (1) below, with moist but not wet compost. Some peat-based and peat substitutes are hard to re-wet when dry; if so it may be easier to fill the container with dry compost and stand it in a tray of water for an hour or two or even overnight to absorb moisture. See what works best with the materials you have. Once you have filled the container, tap it a couple of times to settle the compost, then smooth the surface with a piece of board or, for a round container, with the bottom of a flower pot or something similar.

Sow the seed thinly on the surface, trying to space seeds at least 12–25mm/½–1in apart. Large seeds can be handled between the fingers; with small seeds it is easier to push them gently off a piece of paper. A useful method of sowing individual seeds is to tip them into a saucer, and to pick them up singly on the moistened point of a piece of broken glass (see illustration (2) below). Dangerous though this sounds, it works beautifully, the seed dropping off as it touches the compost. You can pick up seed on the tip of a darning needle or bodkin, but it does work best with broken glass!

Cover the seeds as in illustration (3) below. If the surface is dry, water gently with a fine rose on the can, or for very small seeds, use a mister. To prevent the compost drying out, put the container into a covered propagator or plastic bag (see illustration (4) below), or cover it with a sheet of glass. Some seed trays have a plastic dome or cover for this reason.

SOWING IN MODULES

Use the same method to sow in modules, but aim for only one germinated seedling in each module. To this end either sow one seed per cell, or sow several seeds and nip out all but the strongest after germination. If you are uncertain about the viability of the seed, do a germination test before sowing (see p. 101). Sow the seed in a small indentation in the centre of each module, made with the finger or a miniature dibber (see illustration opposite.).

Multi-sowing There are cases where several seedlings can be sown in a module, left unthinned and planted out 'as one'. This saves space and time when sowing and planting. The modules are planted slightly further apart than normal to compensate for the number of plants at each station. Onions, turnips, kohl rabi, leeks, and round beetroot all respond well to multi-sowing. The wider spacing enables intercropping in the early stages, such as small lettuces between rows of multi-seeded onions (see photograph on p. 7).

GERMINATION

After sowing, put the containers somewhere warm to germinate – in a propagator, in an airing cupboard, above but not directly on a radiator, or on a windowsill (in which case keep them out of direct sunlight). Examine the seeds daily, removing the covers for a few minutes to let air circulate and wiping off condensation. This helps prevent damping off diseases.

Post germination Most vegetable seeds germinate within four to

Sowing in containers
1 Fill the seed tray to within 12mm/½in of the top, levelling the surface with a piece of board.

2 Sow seeds very thinly on the surface. Here a piece of glass is used to space individual seeds 12–25mm/½–1in apart.

3 Sift a thin layer of potting compost or sand over the seeds to cover them. Press it smooth after sowing.

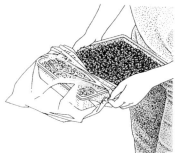

4 Slip the seed tray into a plastic bag to keep the potting compost moist until the seed germinates.

Pricking out
First water the seedlings thoroughly. Fill the seed tray or module into which they are being moved with moist potting compost and level the surface. Use a small dibber to ease out the individual seedlings, holding them by their leaves to avoid damaging the root hairs.

Make a small hole in the compost just large enough for the seedling's roots. Insert the seedling so that the lower leaves are just above the surface.

Firm the soil gently around the base of the stem. Space most seedlings about 4cm/1½in apart and keep them out of direct sunlight until they are well established.

ten days, and once germinated, tend to grow rapidly. Bring seeds that have been germinated in the dark into the light immediately, or they will become weak and etiolated and rarely develop into strong plants. Turn seedlings on a windowsill half a circle daily, so that growth is even. Germinated seedlings need good light (but not direct sunlight) and warmth: in most cases temperatures 3–6°C/5–10°F lower than those needed for germination will suffice during the day; at night, aim to keep them at least frost-free. At this stage remove covers on the containers wholly or partially to give the plants adequate ventilation. Keep the compost moist but do not overwater.

PRICKING OUT

Never allow seedlings to become overcrowded. As soon as they are large enough to handle, generally when they have two or three small leaves, prick them out into potting or multi-purpose compost. They are normally pricked out into seed trays that are about 4cm/1½in deep, or into modules. (For the method, see illustrations above.)

POTTING ON

Many salad plants – lettuce and endive, for example – can be planted out direct from the seed tray after hardening off (see below), once they have developed a good root system and four or five healthy leaves. Plants such as tomatoes, which need to remain under cover longer, or will be grown to maturity in a large pot, need to be potted

on. Never move a plant directly from a small into a very much larger pot: pot it first into a pot of an intermediary size.

Standard potting compost is normally used for potting on (see illustration below), but home-made mixtures can be satisfactory. I make my own, mixing roughly equal quantities of good soil (taken from near the compost heap), well-rotted garden compost, and well-rotted leaf mould or commercial potting compost to lighten the mixture. If using a soil-based compost, fill the bottom third of the pot with drainage material, such as broken crocks, covered with dried leaves or coarse fibrous material (this is unnecessary with proprietary composts, which are well drained). Plants may need supplementary feeding after a few weeks in pots (see p. 124).

Potting on
Water the plant which is being moved, then ease it out of its container. Holding it so that the bottom of the stem is 2.5cm/1in below the rim of the new pot, pack potting compost gently around the roots. Tap the pot on the bench to settle the compost, and finally firm around the stem with the fingertips. Water gently after planting, using a fine rose.

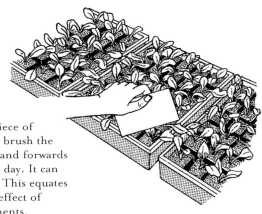

'Stroking' or 'brushing' is an alternative method of hardening off developed by the Japanese to save moving the plants outdoors. Using a piece of paper or cardboard, brush the seedlings backwards and forwards for up to a minute a day. It can be done twice a day. This equates to the 'toughening' effect of exposure to the elements.

HARDENING OFF

Before they are put outside, plants need to be gradually acclimatized to colder, more exposed situations, preferably over a two- to three-week period. Start by increasing the ventilation indoors; then move the plants into a sheltered position outside during the day, bringing them in at night. If you have a cold frame, simply remove the lights during the day and replace them at night. Finally leave the plants out day and night before planting. 'Stroking' or 'brushing' is a method of hardening off which avoids the need to move plants or manipulate their conditions (see illustration left). Hardening off is especially important when plants are raised in peat-based composts, which encourage lush, soft growth, making plants more susceptible to checks, pests and diseases after planting.

Planting

Planting is inevitably a shock and setback to a plant, so whatever you are planting, whether small plants from a seedbed or seed tray or a pot-grown plant, try to minimize the disturbance.

Plants vary in their optimum size for planting. Some, such as Chinese cabbage, transplant badly, though the use of modules helps overcome the problem. As a general rule, the younger plants are when transplanted, the better. Root crops such as carrots and parsnips, though normally sown *in situ*, can be transplanted when very small before the tap roots develop. Always plant in dull weather or in the cool of the evening.

Having already dug over and prepared the ground, rake it smooth. The soil should be pleasantly moist, so in dry conditions, water several hours prior to planting. Similarly water the seedbed or container well in advance. Dig up the plants with a trowel, holding them by the leaves or stem. Remove plants in pots by upturning the pot and tapping it sharply. Make a hole in the ground large enough to accommodate the roots without cramping them. Holding the plant in the hole, replace the soil around its roots (see illustration below). Firm the soil around the stem and check that the plant is firmly anchored by tugging a leaf. If the plant wobbles, replant more firmly. If necessary, water and mulch after planting, provided the plants would not be swamped by the mulch.

In hot weather shade the plant for a few days: simple shades can be made from paper (see below). Leafy plants that are naturally vigorous but wilt in heat, like chicories and spinach, can be trimmed back to a couple of inches after planting to minimize water loss.

When planting, hold the plant by the stem, while filling in the soil around its roots. Both the original container and the soil where it is is being planted should be watered well in advance.

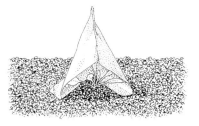

In hot weather plants benefit from shading immediately after planting. Make a simple shading cone from newspaper or a heavy-duty envelope, stapled to a short cane. Small pieces of shading net can also be used.

garden practices

Soil fertility and manuring

The soil is essentially the plant's larder, supplying the elements or nutrients a plant needs and absorbs through its roots. The three major elements are nitrogen (N), potassium (K) and phosphorus (P). A plant needs several other elements in smaller quantities, and 'trace' elements, such as iron, in minute quantities. Broadly speaking, N is important for leaf growth (leafy crops such as brassicas require large amounts), P for early growth, and K for general plant health and ripening. Nitrogen is always the nutrient most likely to be in short supply, as it is very soluble and washed out of the soil in winter; most soils have reasonable reserves of P and K.

The nutrients come from three sources, the first being the mineral particles of sand, silt and clay in the soil, produced over the centuries by the weathering of rocks. The second source is organic matter in the soil. This, through the action of bacteria, is broken down into humus, from which the elements are 'released' in forms plants can use. Thirdly, nitrogen is obtained from atmospheric nitrogen in the soil, which is 'fixed' for plant use by soil bacteria.

So soil bacteria play a vital role. However, they only flourish in soils of suitable acidity/pH (see below), with an adequate supply of oxygen and water. The soil's ability to meet these requirements depends on its structure – that is, its network of soil 'crumbs' and the spaces between them.

In a good soil the mineral particles and humus join together to form tiny but very stable crumbs of varying sizes. The crumbs are separated by air spaces which link to form a network of aeration and drainage channels. After heavy rain, water drains away through the large spaces, which then fill with air, but a crucial reservoir of moisture is retained in the smaller spaces. Soil quickly becomes waterlogged and airless without these drainage channels. The significant fact for gardeners is that humus is a key agent in crumb formation: it both coats sand and silt particles so that they form crumbs, and facilitates the breakdown of large clay clods, ultimately into crumbs. It also absorbs and retains moisture.

Earthworms, who are enormously beneficial in the soil, feed on organic matter. As they plough through the soil, it passes into their bodies, where it is intimately mixed with soil and gums and lime from their bodies. This kickstarts the crucial process of converting organic matter into humus.

For all these reasons, adding organic matter to the soil is the basis of soil fertility. Hence the maxim at the heart of organic gardening: 'Feed the soil, not the plant.' The main sources of organic matter are bulky animal manures, compost and green manuring.

MANURE AND FERTILIZERS

The term 'manure' implies a bulky 'organic' substance, derived originally from plants or animals. The best-known forms are farmyard manure and garden compost. They improve soil fertility as outlined above, and also supply some plant foods. A 'fertilizer' is a concentrated liquid or solid, which contains plant nutrients but is of little benefit to the soil. Typical 'organic' fertilizers are liquid comfrey, seaweed extracts and various proprietary products made from sources such as chicken slurry. These are useful but relatively slow acting. 'Inorganic' or 'artificial' fertilizers are soluble, fast-acting, manufactured chemicals. They will give quick results and high yields, but should be seen as a form of 'force feeding'. The resulting lush growth is 'soft', and prone to pest and disease attacks. It is also easy to give an overdose, damaging the soil and the plant. These are some of the reasons why they are not used in organic gardening.

Organic matter in the soil breaks down fairly fast, especially in hot and wet conditions, so must be regularly replenished to maintain soil fertility. Aim to work some into every piece of ground every year. As a very rough guide, think in terms of 2.75–5.5kg per sq. m/5–10lb

Narrow beds ridged up in winter and covered with
manure, which worms will work in by spring.

per sq. yd, the higher figure being for poorer soil. If you start with poor soil, it will of course take a few years to raise the fertility to a satisfactory level. Liquid fertilizers and seaweed-based stimulants can be used to supply extra nutrients where growing conditions are below par, and to boost growth for hungry crops such as tomatoes.

Finding supplies of organic manure is not as easy as it used to be, especially in urban areas. Don't be shy of collecting vegetable waste from greengrocers and city markets: it all makes excellent compost.

SOURCES OF ORGANIC MATTER

Farmyard and animal manures Ideally the manures should be mixed with plenty of straw or litter. Fresh manure should be composted in a covered heap on a concrete base for about six months before use. This reduces potentially damaging levels of ammonia, and helps to kill weed seeds and pests. Manure mixed with sawdust or wood shavings should be composted eighteen months before use.

Poultry, pigeon and rabbit manures These are very concentrated, so work them into a compost heap in small quantities.

Spent mushroom compost Over the years this excellent product has improved our garden's fertility and solved its drainage problems. It is sterilized, so free of weed seed. The high chalk content is beneficial in clay soils, but makes it unsuitable for alkaline (chalk) soils. Do not use it continuously on the same ground.

Straw and hay Both are good sources of organic matter. Stack fresh material in layers 15cm/6in thick, watering each layer unless it is moist. Keep the heap covered with tarpaulin or old carpeting until required. Hay must be very well rotted to kill the grass seed.

Seaweed This is a rich source of nutrients and can be used fresh, dried or incorporated into a compost heap. If you spread it on the soil, it may attract flies while decomposing; to overcome this, cover lightly with soil.

Recycled municipal waste and treated sewage sludge More of these products are becoming available. They can be excellent. Just make sure they are guaranteed free of heavy metals.

GARDEN COMPOST

I would strongly advise gardeners to make their own compost from garden and household vegetable wastes. Compost can be made in simple heaps, or in purpose-made bins.

Compost heaps This is the simplest way to make compost. Pile suitable waste materials into a heap up to about 1.5m/5ft high, then cover it with black polythene sheeting. In temperate climates it will be ready for use in about a year. To get the best end product, mix different types of material into the heap. Use anything that will rot, including small quantities of the organic matter above. Shred or chop up coarse or woody material, such as cabbage stalks. Just avoid having a solid mass of any one substance, such as lawn mowings or autumn leaves (see p. 113). Do not use diseased plant material, weeds that have gone to seed, or roots of perennial weeds such as ground elder or couch grass, which should all be buried or burnt.

The disadvantage of this method, apart from being slow, is that it does not generate high temperatures, so weed seeds, pests and disease spores may not be killed; nor will coarse material be completely rotted. Nevertheless, organic matter is eventually returned to the soil, and that is what matters.

Compost bins The object of a purpose-built bin is to generate high temperatures, so that waste decomposes rapidly, killing weed seeds, pests and disease spores. The end product is homogenous, and looks like soil. High temperatures are generated only with a relatively large volume of waste material, so bins must be at least 1m/3ft wide and 1m/3ft high, though they can be any length. They should be well insulated. If you make two bins side by side, one can be maturing while the other builds up. A bin is normally a permanent

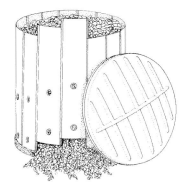

LEFT A patented compost bin is useful for small households, though its capacity is generally too small to generate enough heat to break down very coarse material. Waste is put in the top and several months later removed from the base.

RIGHT A pair of purpose-built compost bins are durable and efficient. See main text below for construction details.

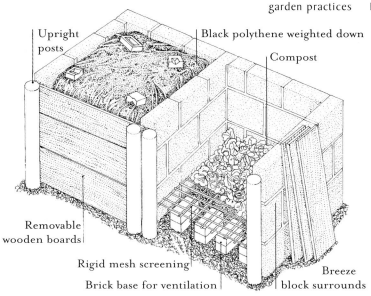

Upright posts | Black polythene weighted down | Compost | Removable wooden boards | Rigid mesh screening | Brick base for ventilation | Breeze block surrounds

construction, sited in an out-of-the-way place on well-drained soil.

The bin must be strong, as the raw material is heavy and bulky. The side and back walls can be constructed of insulating material such as breeze blocks, bricks, timber or straw bales (these, of course, would need to be replaced annually). The front can be made of loose boards slipped behind upright posts. This enables you to build up and dismantle the heap in stages.

If feasible, raise the base of the heap 10cm/4in off the ground for ventilation and drainage. Use a layer of brushwood, rubble, clay drainage pipes or double rows of bricks with 5cm/2in gaps between them. Heavy mesh screening can be laid over the drainage base to hold the compost in place (see illustration above right).

The best way to fill the bin, although it requires discipline, is to pre-mix the materials in a plastic sack, balancing leafy and fibrous material. Either add a sack at a time, or wait until there are enough sackfuls to make a layer about 20cm/8in deep.

The bacteria that bring about decomposition need air, moisture and a source of nitrogen, which is found naturally in leafy green material or animal manure. There will be plenty of nitrogen in a summer heap, but in autumn and winter supplement the nitrogen by adding a bucket of chicken or animal manure, or seaweed extract or proprietary compost activator (at the rates recommended by the manufacturer) to each layer or to pre-mixed wastes.

Nutrients are easily washed out of compost by rain, so when the bin is full cover it with black polythene sheeting, punctured with 2.5cm/1in diameter holes about 30cm/12in apart for ventilation. Either weight this down, or cover it with permeable but insulating material, such as 7.5cm/3in of soil, matting or a layer of straw.

In temperate climates a heap made in summer is normally ready in two or three months, in winter in eight or nine months. Turning the heap 'sides to middle' accelerates the process. Don't worry unduly about composting theory. All compost is valuable; even when partially composed it still provides food for earthworms.

Leaf mould Leaves decompose very slowly and are best composted separately. Pile fallen leaves into a wire-netting enclosure at least 60–90cm/2–3ft high, sited in a dry shady place, or keep them in airtight black plastic bags. They take about two years to turn into a mould that can be used in potting composts or for mulching.

Worm compost Worm compost is made by recycling organic wastes in a home-made or patented 'wormery' or bin, using worms such the red brandling worm, which feed exclusively on decaying organic matter. It is an efficient form of composting, which can be done indoors. The fertile end product can be used as a fertilizer, or mixed into potting composts. (For further reading, see pp. 162–3.)

HOME-MADE LIQUID FERTILIZERS

These simple 'brews' can be used, like proprietary organic fertilizers, to stimulate growth or as a general purpose fertilizer.

'Black Jack' Suspend a sack of well-rotted animal manure mixed with grass clippings in a butt of rainwater. It will be ready a few weeks later. Dilute the liquid to the colour of weak tea before use.

Liquid comfrey Comfrey (*Symphytum* x *uplandicum*) is an easily grown hardy perennial. Use the productive variety 'Bocking 14'. Make the liquid in a barrel or bin, raised off the ground on bricks. Insert a tap near the bottom, or drill a 1cm/½in hole in the base, putting a container beneath to catch the liquid. Stuff the barrel with comfrey leaves, weight them down, then cover the barrel with a lid. Within a few weeks the concentrate will drip through. Use it diluted with 10–20 parts of water. It is rich in potassium, making it an excellent feed for tomatoes. (For further reading, see pp. 162–3.)

Green manuring

Green manuring is the technique of growing crops (often called 'cover crops') that will be dug into the ground to improve soil fertility. Different plants are used for different situations and purposes. Fast-growing leafy crops such as mustard and *Phacelia tanacetifolia* give a quick nitrogen boost; fibrous rooters such as 'grazing' rye increase the organic matter in the soil; various legumes (field beans and clovers, for example) can fix atmospheric nitrogen in the soil. Hardy green manures such as winter tares and field beans can be sown in autumn, protecting the soil and preventing the loss of nutrients in winter. Green manures should never be the sole form of manuring, but sowing even small patches can make a valuable contribution to fertility. (For further reading, see p. 162.)

Incorporating manure into the soil

Bulky manures and compost are either dug into the soil, or spread on the surface, depending on the soil and the state of the manure.

Fresh manure and compost is best spread on the surface, allowing worms to work it in gradually. If it is dug in, there will be a loss of nitrogen from the soil in the early stages of decomposition. Well-rotted manures and compost can be dug in, or used to mulch growing crops. Traditionally heavy soils are dug in the autumn – so that frost action can break up the clods – and manure is dug in at the same time. The soil can be forked over lightly in spring if necessary.

An alternative method is to ridge up heavy soils in winter, and cover the ridge with manure. In my 90cm/36in-wide beds I first fork down the centre of the bed, then spade the soil from each side on to the middle, making a single central ridge (see photograph on p. 112). The ridges ensure good drainage while exposing a greater surface to frost action. By spring, the soil has a beautiful crumbly surface.

Light, well-drained and sandy soils are best covered with manure in winter, but dug over in spring. The manure protects the surface from winter rains, which destroy structure and wash out nutrients. In most years it is adequate simply to fork the soil to the depth of a spade (one spit deep). Every third year or so it is beneficial to dig more deeply. This 'double digging' (see illustration below) breaks up any hard pan that may be forming in the soil and impeding drainage. It enables manure to be worked in at a deeper level, encouraging plants to root more deeply – the best insurance against drought.

Soil acidity

Soil acidity is another factor affecting soil fertility. It is related to the amount of calcium (lime or chalk) in the soil, and is measured on the pH scale. This ranges from 0 to 14, the neutral point being 7. Soils

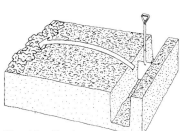

Double digging
Make a trench one spade deep and about 38cm/15in wide across the bed, and remove the soil to the far end of the strip. Keep the manure handy in a wheelbarrow.

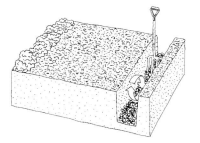

Fork the soil at the bottom of the trench, then put in a good layer of manure or garden compost, or whatever you are using.

Fill the trench with soil from the next strip, then fork soil and manure together so that the manure is spread evenly through the soil.

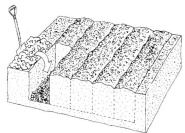

Continue in this way to the end of the strip, then fill the last trench with soil from the original trench. Double digging is normally necessary only one year in three.

with a pH below 7 become progressively more acid, those with a pH above 7 more alkaline. The change from one pH level to the next represents a tenfold increase in acidity or alkalinity. Most vegetables grow best on a slightly acid to neutral soil, with a pH of about 6–6.5.

In extremely acid or alkaline soils plant nutrients become 'locked up' and unavailable to plants, soil bacteria cease to function and earthworms move out. In humid climates soils become increasingly acid, as rainfall washes calcium out of the soil. This is marked on light, well-drained soils and where there is atmospheric pollution.

Don't worry about acidity unless plants are growing poorly, or there are few worms, or the soil looks sour with moss growing on the surface. In these circumstances test the soil with a simple soil analysis kit or pH meter. If the soil is acid, raise the pH level to around 6.5 by adding lime over several successive seasons. Organic gardeners should use ground limestone or dolomite rather than the faster-acting gardener's lime. Apply it in the autumn, but never at the same time as manure. In practice, regular additions of organic matter tend to prevent, and correct, soil acidity problems.

Weeding

The salad lover looks upon weeds with a kindlier eye than most gardeners because many weeds, especially in the seedling stage, make tasty, nutritious additions to a salad. But they compete with other vegetables for water, nutrients, light and space, so must be kept under control. Weeds are either perennial or annual.

Perennials live on in the soil from one year to the next. They may have invasive creeping root systems, such as couch grass (*Agropyron repens*) and ground elder (*Aegopodium podagraria*), or deep, stubborn tap roots, such as the broad-leaved dock (*Rumex obtusifolius*) and dandelion (*Taraxacum officinale*). Use a good wild-plant book (see Further Reading, pp. 162–3) to identify your perennial weeds, and dig them out without mercy. Remove even small pieces of root, and expose them to the sun to wilt before composting them. Most perennials decline when ground is cultivated regularly. Where there is a serious problem, in a previously neglected garden for example, the only solution other than using chemical weedkillers is to blanket the ground with heavy-duty black film, cardboard or old carpet. If necessary, leave this for up to a year, though it may be feasible to start planting sooner through a film or cardboard mulch.

Annual weeds germinate, seed and die within a year, in some cases having several generations a year. A single plant can produce an enormous number of seeds, and some remain viable in the soil for very many years. So in weed-ridden soils there is a huge reservoir of seed, waiting for favourable conditions to germinate.

The most important factor in the war against annual weeds is to prevent them from going to seed in the first place. Shallow cultivation disturbs weed seeds near the surface, destroying about half as a result, either when they germinate and are hoed off, or through exposure to birds or bad weather. After several years' cultivation their numbers will be markedly reduced. There is considerable truth in the old adage, 'One year's seeding, seven years' weeding.' Deeper cultivation brings up seed from lower levels, so in weedy soil confine cultivation to shallow hoeing.

When previously undisturbed soil is cultivated, there is a great flush of weeds in the first year. Hoe them off and, if you have time, let a second crop of weeds germinate before sowing or planting. In fact planting, which gives plants a head start over weeds, may be preferable to sowing. Minimize cultivation during the growing season or only cultivate shallowly (see above). Keeping crops mulched (see p. 118–119) is a very effective means of preventing weeds from germinating. Growing plants at equidistant spacing (see p. 96) rather than in rows also prevents weed germination.

Research has shown that weeds between rows pose much more competition to growing crops than those within rows, so remove them first. Where crops are sown as opposed to planted, weeds start to become competitive about three weeks after the crop has germinated. If time is short, postpone weeding until that point: remember though, that by then it is urgent! My favourite tool for weeding in an intensively cultivated salad garden is a small hand or onion hoe, which enables you to get really close to the plants.

Watering

Plants require a constant throughput of water, taken in through the roots and evaporated through the leaves. They need enough water to keep the leaves turgid – growth is checked once they start to wilt – but it is a fallacy to assume that the more watering the better. Water washes nitrogen and other soluble nutrients out of reach of the roots; it encourages shallow, surface rooting, rather than the deep rooting that enables plants to utilize deeper reserves of nutrients and moisture; and I am convinced it reduces the flavour of vegetables such as tomatoes.

Water mainly stimulates leaf growth, which is what you want for leafy plants such as lettuce and cabbage. With root and bulb crops – radish and onions for example – overwatering may result in excessive leaf growth at the expense of the roots. Requirements also vary according to the stage of development: there are 'critical periods' for watering (see p. 117).

CONSERVING WATER
In regions where water is an increasingly scarce resource, do everything you can to conserve it and minimize the need to water. The following practices all work towards this end:
• Dig in as much bulky organic matter as possible, as deeply as possible. This increases the water-holding capacity of the soil, and is particularly beneficial on light, fast-draining soils.
• Keep the soil surface mulched to prevent evaporation (see pp. 118–119). Far more water is lost through evaporation than drainage.
• On sloping ground, cultivate across rather than down the slope (see illustration below).
• In dry weather, cultivate as little as possible and only very shallowly; deeper cultivation brings moisture to the surface, which then evaporates. Once the top few inches of the soil have dried out, they act as a mulch and the rate of evaporation is slowed down.
• Keep the ground weed-free. Weeds both compete for water and evaporate moisture through their leaves.
• Wind increases the rate of evaporation, so especially in exposed gardens erect artificial windbreaks (see p. 93).
• Collect water from conveniently sited roofs, with a down pipe leading to a lidded rain butt or barrel.
• Where water is scarce, concentrate watering on the critical periods (see opposite).

HOW TO WATER
The golden rule is to water gently and thoroughly. Large water droplets destroy the soil surface and damage fragile plants and seedlings. Water these with a fine rose on the can, the rose turned upwards for the gentlest spray.

The most common fault is to underwater. Even when it looks wet, the soil is often still surprisingly dry. Soil becomes wet layer by layer, and until the top layers are thoroughly wet, the root zone beneath will remain dry. To test how far water has penetrated, push your finger into the soil after watering. Generally speaking, heavy but infrequent watering is far more beneficial than frequent, light watering. However, light soils need to be watered more frequently than heavy soils, though less water is required at each watering.

With established plants, direct water to the base of the plant. Where plants are spaced far apart, confine watering to a circular area around each, leaving the soil between them dry to discourage weed

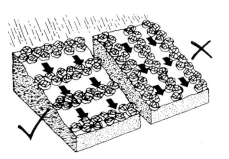

Conserving water
In a sloping garden, plan beds and crops to run across, rather than down, the slope. This cuts down water loss through surface run-off, and helps to prevent soil erosion from becoming a problem.

Watering large plants
An efficient, labour-saving way of watering large plants is to sink a porous clay flower pot into the ground beside the plant and water into the pot. Water seeps slowly through to the roots with minimal moisture loss from evaporation.

germination. Water large plants such as tomatoes and courgettes by sinking a clay pot into the ground near the plant and watering into the pot (see illustration opposite below).

Plants grown close together make heavy demands on soil water and need generous watering. In very arid conditions plants are spaced far apart for this reason. Intensively grown cut-and-come-again crops also need plenty of water.

Wherever possible, water in the evening to minimize evaporation, but allow time for leaves to dry before nightfall.

CRITICAL PERIODS FOR WATERING

• *Germination* Seeds will not germinate in dry conditions, so water ground destined for sowing in advance.

• *Transplanting* This is a delicate stage for plants. Transplant them into moist but not waterlogged soil, and keep it moist until they are established. Root hairs on bare-root plants (as opposed to plants raised in modules) are often damaged by transplanting, so the plant can only absorb a little water at a time initially. Water gently – daily in dry weather – applying no more than 140ml/¼ pint each time.

• *Leafy vegetables* Leafy vegetables such as brassicas, lettuce, endive, spinach, celery and courgette require a lot of water throughout growth. In the absence of rainfall, they will benefit from about 9–14 litres per sq. m/2–3 gallons per sq. yd a week. Where regular watering is difficult, limit watering to a single, very heavy watering – about 18 litres per sq. m/4 gallons per sq. yd – 10–20 days before you estimate the plant is ready for harvesting.

• *Fruiting vegetables* For tomatoes, cucumbers, peas and beans – all vegetables grown, in botanical terms, for their fruits – the critical time for watering is when the plants are flowering and the fruits start to swell. Heavy watering at this stage increases their yields appreciably. (See appropriate crop in Salad Plants, pp. 12–90.)

• *Root crops* These need enough water for steady growth, but too much water encourages lush foliage rather than root development. In the early stages, water only if the soil is in danger of drying out, at the rate of at least 4.5 litres per sq. m/1 gallon per sq. yd a week. They require more water in the later stages as the roots swell.

WATERING EQUIPMENT

In small gardens, a watering can, with a fine rose for watering seedlings, is sufficient. In larger gardens, semi-automatic systems potentially save time and water. Various types of hose or tubing are connected directly to a tap or garden hose running from a tap. These gently water a strip up to 50cm/20in wide. Overhead sprinkler systems are not recommended. They waste water (much evaporates or falls on bare soil), and plants are more prone to disease when water is directed on to leaves, rather than to the roots.

Perforated polythene 'layflat' tube This cheap, flexible, but not very durable hose is laid on the ground between plants. Water seeps out through small holes in the tube.

Porous pipe/seeper hose These stronger hoses are permeable along their length. They can be buried 10–15cm/4–6in deep in the soil in permanent beds or, where more flexibility is wanted, laid on the surface. Covering them with mulch prevents evaporation and the build-up of scale in hard-water areas.

Trickle irrigation Water is delivered to individual plants through nozzles or emitters in fine tubes. Networks can be designed to water large areas, greenhouses and containers. On a large scale, get professional advice and good-quality equipment.

Two types of semi-automatic watering system, connected to a mains tap via a hose.

LEFT A permeable porous pipe or seeper hose. Covering with a plastic film or straw mulch limits evaporation.

RIGHT A trickle irrigation hose. Water is emitted at regular intervals through tiny nozzles in the fine tubing.

Mulching

Mulching is the practice of keeping the soil covered. The mulch can be an organic material, such as compost, leaf mould or even recycled paper or cardboard, all of which eventually rot into the soil. It can also be an inorganic material, such as polythene film, or even stones, gravel and sand – traditional mulching materials in hot climates.

The main purpose of a mulch is to conserve moisture in the soil. This is important, not only because plants need water, but because they can only extract soluble nutrients from moist soil. However, mulches have many other beneficial effects. They help control weeds, both by inhibiting weed seed germination and suppressing subsequent growth; weeds that do germinate are easily pulled out of a mulch. Mulches improve soil structure by protecting the soil surface from heavy rain and desiccating winds, and by lessening the impact of treading on the soil. Most organic mulches are a source of nutrients and provide food for worms which, in turn, contribute in many ways to soil fertility. Mulches beneath sprawling plants such as cucumbers help keep the fruit clean, and prevent disease spores from splashing on to the foliage and fruit. Small mats made of materials such as flax fibre are sometimes sold for the purpose.

Mulches keep the soil cooler in summer and warmer in winter. This slows down frost penetration, making it easier to dig vegetables out of the ground. Stone, gravel and sand mulches in greenhouses radiate heat at night, raising the air temperature.

TYPES OF ORGANIC MULCH

The many suitable materials for organic mulches include animal manures, garden compost, seaweed, old straw, spent mushroom compost, cotton waste, wilted green manures, wilted comfrey, dried lawn mowings, dried leaves, dried bracken, coir and cocoa shell. Various other materials can be used, provided they will rot down and are fairly loose-textured. This makes them easier to spread close to plants and allows rain to penetrate. Fresh lawn mowings form an impenetrable sticky mat – hence the need to dry them out before using as a mulch. Mulching materials should preferably be wilted or partly rotted, or nitrogen will initially be taken from the soil as decomposition starts. Avoid materials that are likely to be a source of diseases or weed seeds, or have been treated with weedkillers.

It is best to avoid using wood derivatives, such as sawdust, wood shavings, and pulverized and shredded bark, and tough leaves such as pine needles on vegetable beds unless they have been composted for several months, alone or mixed with animal manures. They are excellent, however, as path mulches. Newspaper, cardboard, recycled paper and carpet, though of low nutritive value, can be used in appropriate situations for mulching vegetables. Use them like polythene films (see p. 119). The remnants of most organic mulches can be dug in at the end of the season, although by then earthworms will often have done the work.

WHEN AND HOW TO MULCH

A key fact about mulching is that it maintains the status quo of the soil. So don't mulch when the soil is very cold, very wet or very dry – all conditions which discourage plant growth – because the soil will stay that way. Mulch when the soil is warm and moist: the soil temperature should be at least 6°C/42°F and preferably higher.

On the whole, the most suitable time to mulch is when planting. But if planting in spring, make sure that the soil has warmed up before mulching; in summer, water well after planting and then mulch to cut down on subsequent watering. Either plant through the mulch, or mulch after planting. In his book *Square Foot Gardening*, Mel Bartholomew suggests drilling holes in a pile of newspapers or carpet squares and slipping them over growing plants. Or make a carpet mulching pad by cutting a slit from the perimeter to a hole in the centre; you can then ease it around a plant.

It is inadvisable to mulch with loose organic materials immediately after sowing, as birds are likely to scratch around, disturbing seeds and seedlings. Mulch seedlings in stages once they are through the soil, taking care not to swamp the small plants.

As to thickness of mulch, with the exception of films and similar materials, the thicker the mulch the more effective it will be in conserving moisture and suppressing weeds. In most circumstances a mulch 2.5–5cm/1–2in deep is adequate, though tall plants like tomatoes grow well with a mulch 15–20cm/6–8in deep.

MULCHING FILMS

There is a wide range of mulching films, with new forms being regularly introduced.

Impermeable, light, black polythene films These suppress weeds in the short term, but don't allow rainfall to penetrate. They tend to make soils cool. Use them as a short-term weed mulch in vegetable beds. Early potatoes are often grown under black film to avoid earthing up.

Perforated, light, black polythene films These have masses of tiny perforations, allowing some water and air to penetrate – hence their use for longer-term mulches, usually on perennial crops.

Perforated, clear polythene films Primarily used as crop covers (see p. 123), these could also be used to warm up soil.

Impermeable, clear polythene films Use these to warm up the soil in spring. They retain moisture, but will not prevent weed germination.

Opaque white polythene films These reflect light and warmth upwards, so are used to mulch ripening tomatoes, melons, etc. They help retain soil moisture, but do not suppress weeds very effectively.

Double-sided black and white polythene films These dual-purpose films are used as opaque white films above. The black surface is laid downwards to suppress weeds, while the upper white surface reflects light, and therefore heat, up to ripening fruit.

Permeable woven polypropylene black films These heavy-duty films suppress weeds, and are excellent for mulching paths. Their permeability prevents paths from becoming waterlogged. They can be used to mulch large plants, but are apt to chafe them.

Permeable, black fabric This lightweight fabric is warm and soft to the touch. It suppresses weeds, allows some moisture to penetrate, and has a warming effect. It is excellent for mulching winter crops under cover, but can also be used outdoors. It is more expensive than polythene films, but should last several seasons.

Chequered and coloured films Various films deter specific insect pests, but are currently not widely available.

The above films can be anchored into a slit in the soil (see illustration below), pinned with metal 'tent pegs' or plastic pins, or weighted down with bags of soil or sand (see illustrations on p. 123). When mulching individual plants, it is usually easiest to lay the film, then to plant through a cross made in the film (see illustration below). Alternatively plant first, unroll the film, cut openings over the plants and ease them through. Large seeds like sweet corn can be sown through holes punched in film, and the leaves eased through when large enough. Perhaps I should add a warning: polythene films attract slugs. But at least you know where to look for them!

Planting through polythene film
Lay the film on the bed with a little spare film on each side. Use a trowel to make slits in the soil about 10cm/4in deep on each side of the bed.

Bury the film edge, replacing the soil to keep it in place. The film should be smooth but not too taut.

Cut crossed slits (about 8cm/3in long) in the film at suitable intervals for the plants.

Ease the slits open and plant through them.

Protected cropping

Greenhouses, walk-in polythene tunnels (polytunnels), garden frames, cloches, low polytunnels and 'floating mulches' are all means of growing 'under cover' or 'protected cropping'. Essentially, this means giving plants shelter, and, as explained earlier (see p. 93), nothing increases yields and productivity as markedly as shelter from the elements. Moreover with salad plants, it is the combination of low temperatures and high winds that is potentially lethal. If they are protected from wind, they will survive much lower temperatures than would otherwise be the case, and the leaves will remain palatable instead of becoming tough.

USES OF PROTECTION

In cool temperate climates, protection is the main tool for extending the salad season, with a view to having fresh salads all year round. Most plants start to grow when temperatures rise above 6°C/43°F in spring, and stop growing when they fall below 6°C/43°F in autumn. The days between these two points are termed 'growing days', the number of which determine which crops can be grown successfully in any area. Soil protected with glass or polythene warms up sooner in the year and remains warm later, potentially extending the growing season by at least three weeks – twenty-one 'growing days' – at either end of the season.

For example, in spring the very first salads can be cut from early sowings under cover of cut-and-come-again seedling crops (see pp. 127–130). Many summer vegetables can be started under cover in seed trays or modules, for planting outside as soon as soil conditions and temperatures allow. Where the growing season is short, this head start is crucial for the success of heat lovers such as tomatoes, peppers and cucumbers, which cannot be sown or planted outdoors until all risk of frost is passed. These crops can also be grown to maturity in greenhouses and polytunnels – along with tender herbs such as basil. Towards the end of summer, marginally hardy salads such as Chinese cabbage, pak choi, Florence fennel, red chicory, endive, winter purslane and salad rocket can be planted under cover for winter and spring use. So can hardier salads such as oriental mustards, along with cut-and-come-again seedling sowings of kales,

spinach, corn salad, chervil, coriander and so on. All will be far more productive and better-quality when grown under cover.

Heated greenhouses and polytunnels are very costly, and outside the scope of this book, though where facilities are available, they can be turned to excellent use in winter and early spring. Garden frames are relatively easily heated with electric soil-warming cables. However, in my experience in the UK climate, a wide range of winter salads can be grown satisfactorily in unheated forms of protection.

It has to be appreciated that unheated glass and polythene structures will not keep out frost. This can only be guaranteed by heating them. Winter temperatures under cover will be only marginally higher than those outside – the benefits of these structures lie in their sheltering effect. Incidentally, if plants, either under cover or in the open, have been affected by frost, shade them or spray them with water the following morning, before the sun reaches them. This allows them to thaw out slowly and may prevent serious damage.

In hot weather, temperatures under cover can soar, encouraging the rapid build-up of greenhouse pests such as red spider mite and whitefly. So greenhouses and polytunnels must have good ventilation. In hot conditions they should be 'damped down' once or twice a day – that is, plants and soil sprayed with water – to increase humidity and lower the temperature. This discourages greenhouse pests. Good air flow is also important in winter, as disease builds up in stagnant conditions. Overall, the value of good ventilation under cover, especially for organic gardeners, cannot be over-emphasized.

Protected ground is a precious resource, and should be treated as such. Bring the soil to a high state of fertility by working in plenty of well-rotted organic matter. Avoid using farmyard manure in permanent structures, as it may introduce soil pests, such as symphilids, which are hard to eliminate. Weeds germinate and grow rapidly under cover and soil dries out quickly, so keeping the soil mulched is highly recommended (see pp. 118–19). Most forms of protection have to be watered by hand, unless a semi-automatic watering system is installed (see p. 117).

What do the different types of protection have to offer?

A typical modern aluminium-framed greenhouse on concrete foundations. Plants are grown in the soil or in containers. In cold areas greenhouses are used in summer for tender crops and in winter for a range of high-quality salads. They are very easy to manage.

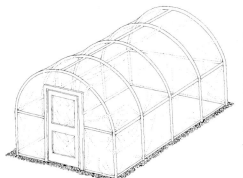

A walk-in polytunnel or hoop tunnel is made by anchoring polythene film over galvanized steel hoops. Polytunnels are cheap and versatile, and are easily moved to a fresh site to avoid the development of soil sickness. They can be used to grow salad crops all year round.

GREENHOUSES

Greenhouses are expensive, permanent structures, but as glass transmits light well and traps heat efficiently at night, they create excellent growing conditions. They can accommodate tall crops such as tomatoes and plants can be grown in the ground or in containers. As solid structures, they are easily ventilated.

Their main drawback is 'soil sickness', a build-up of serious soil pests and diseases which develops where tomatoes and related crops such as peppers and aubergines are grown continuously in the same soil. Unless the soil is sterilized or replaced – both laborious procedures – subsequent crops have to be grown in fresh soil in containers or in soilless systems such as ring culture (which uses bottomless pots filled with compost mix, standing on an inert base such as shingle).

WALK-IN POLYTUNNELS

The typical walk-in polytunnel is a structure 1.8–2.1m/6–7ft high, made by anchoring polythene film over a frame of galvanized tubular steel hoops. Unlike greenhouses, polytunnels need no foundations. After the frame is erected, a trench about 45cm/18in wide is dug around the base, in which the edges of the film are laid and secured by backfilling with soil. This is best done on a warm day, when the film is limp and easily pulled taut. Polythene film can also be used to cover other structures, battened to a wooden frame, for example.

Polytunnels are less sophisticated than greenhouses but a fraction of the cost. Their great advantage is that they can be dismantled relatively easily and erected on a fresh site, so avoiding soil sickness.

Polytunnels are difficult to ventilate. They tend to overheat in summer and are humid in winter, with the attendant risks of pests and disease. Always build in as much ventilation as possible. In a 6m/20ft long tunnel, for example, have a door at each end with a ventilation panel in at least the top half of each door. You can also increase ventilation by cutting semi-circular 'porthole flaps' of 30cm/12in diameter about 45cm/18in above ground level along the length of the tunnel; these can be taped back in place in cold weather.

Always use polythene film treated with an ultra-violet (UV) inhibitor, which extends its life. Some recently introduced films are treated with an anti-condensation or anti-drip agent – a useful development. Depending on the climate, UV-treated 800-gauge film should last at least four years, 720-gauge film for three years. Film life is also prolonged by insulating the outer curved surfaces of the metal hoops with adhesive 'anti-hot-spot' tape. This protects the film from direct contact with the hoops, which can become very hot. Fit the film as smoothly and tightly as possible: the first tears arise where film is flapping or rubbing against a rough surface – though with modern tapes even extensive damage can be repaired. As an organic gardener, I advocate siting polytunnels in a north–south, rather than east–west direction, to minimize the exposure of the long flank to the sun. This helps to keep summer temperatures down.

GARDEN FRAMES

A frame is essentially a miniature greenhouse, covering a couple of square metres/yards of ground. Traditional frames were permanent with solid brick or wood sides and a glass 'lid' or 'light'; they were well insulated. The typical modern frame is portable, and made of aluminium and glass or polythene film; it has less insulation but light is more evenly distributed. Free-standing and lean-to frames are easily made from wood and other materials.

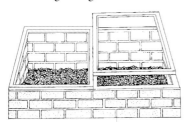

A traditional, permanent, brick-sided frame, with glass lights. It has good insulation.

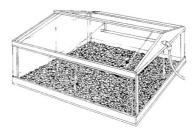

A portable modern aluminium and glass frame, notable for good, evenly distributed light.

Rigid plastic cloche with end pieces made from glass held in place with a cane.

The cheapest form of protection, a low polythene tunnel of thin film laid over wire hoops.

The height of the frame determines what can be grown. A clearance of about 23cm/9in is adequate for lettuce, endive and low-growing salads; about 45cm/18in height is necessary for horizontally trained cucumbers, celery, fennel, bush tomatoes or peppers; upright tomatoes can only be grown in a lean-to frame. However, the lights can be removed to give maturing plants more room. Ventilation is adjusted by raising or removing the lights.

Besides being used in spring for raising seeds, and for early sowings of carrots, beet, lettuce and radish, frames are ideal for hardening plants. An additional use in winter is for forcing Witloof chicory and blanching endive (see also Uses of Protection, p. 120).

CLOCHES

Cloches are small units made from a wide range of materials including glass, fibreglass, rigid and semi-rigid plastics and polythene film. They vary in size from low, 'tent' cloches, only suitable for low-growing salads, to the high-sided 'barn' cloches, which can accommodate larger plants such as tomatoes, dwarf beans and peppers, at least in the early stages of growth. Cloches can be used over single plants or placed end-to-end to cover a row. Never leave them open-ended, or winds funnel through, damaging the plants. If no endpieces are supplied, improvise with panes of glass or rigid plastic, held in place with upright canes.

The main advantage of cloches is their mobility. Glass cloches apart, they are lightweight and easy to move around the garden. To some extent, this is also their drawback, as they have to be moved for cultivation, watering and harvesting. To minimize handling, try to plan the garden so that you only need to move them between adjacent strips of ground – a technique known as strip cropping.

When choosing cloches, consider the following factors:
Materials Glass cloches are the most expensive, provide the best growing conditions, are the most stable and, breakages apart, are the most durable. Opaque corrugated plastics create diffuse light, in which plants seem to grow well. Most plastic materials break down and discolour with exposure to sunlight and should be stored under cover when not in use.
Size The larger the cloche, the more useful it is. Some have extensions which can be raised as the crops grow, or a removable roof. These enable plants that have outgrown the cloche to continue benefiting from side shelter. Large cloches have better air circulation.
Strength Cloches must be robust enough to withstand regular handling and wind. Lightweight cloches may require anchorage of some kind – such as metal pins through a basal flange.
Ventilation Temperatures rise rapidly under cloches, so removable or built-in ventilation panels are useful. (Some have netting beneath the panels to protect crops against birds when the panels are removed.) Otherwise move cloches apart to ventilate them, removing them completely during very hot weather.

LOW POLYTUNNELS

This cheap form of protection typically consists of light (about 150-gauge) polythene film over low wire or steel hoops, the film tied at either end to angled stakes in the ground. Low tunnels are rarely more than 45cm/18in high at the ridge. Hoops can also be made of plastic electric conduit tube or alkathene water pipe. The sides of the films are easily blown up in windy conditions, so they may need additional anchorage. Bury the ends and one side in the soil (leaving the other open for access); run strings or fine wires from side to side over the top and attach them to the hoops at ground level; or weight the sides in any of the ways used for mulching films (see below and p. 119). Films usually last for no more than two seasons, unless heavier, more durable but less flexible films are used.

Low tunnels offer less protection than cloches, but are easily moved and worked. For cultivation and ventilation simply push the film back to one side. In some countries they are ventilated, like walk-in polytunnels, by cutting ventilation flaps along their length.

USES OF CLOCHES AND LOW POLYTUNNELS

Within the limitations of their height, cloches and low polytunnels are useful means of extending the salad season and improving salad quality. Like frames they can be used for hardening off and for early outdoor sowings. They are easily moved to wherever required: in spring on to ground that needs to be warmed before sowing; in summer over maturing crops like onions or tomatoes to hasten ripening; in autumn and early winter over outdoor salads to prolong their useful life. They can also be used inside greenhouses and walk-in tunnels, in winter and early spring, as an extra layer of protection for salad crops.

CROP COVERS

Also known as floating mulches or floating films, these very light films are laid directly on a crop, mainly in the early stages of growth. Their varying degrees of elasticity allow plants to push them up as they grow. They also give some protection against pests. Films are usually put over plants after planting, and anchored by any of the means used for mulching films (see below and p. 119). They are normally removed four to eight weeks later. Do so in dull conditions or in the evening, to lessen the shock of sudden exposure on the 'soft' plants. These films are generally unsuitable for exposed sites, unless very carefully anchored. The main types are clear perforated polythene films and spun bonded polypropylene fleeces. With careful handling they will last a couple of seasons. Buy films with reinforced edges where available.

Perforated polythene films These low-cost films are perforated with small holes or slits, allowing air and some water to penetrate. They give no frost protection, but warm the soil and air quickly. Lay them over the crop with a little slack to allow for plant growth. Restricted ventilation means that once temperatures rise plants can deteriorate rapidly; watch the plants carefully and remove the films if they show signs of stress. You can also use the films over low hoops to cover taller crops like tomatoes, but remove them or slit them open once flowering starts to allow insect pollination.

Fleeces These soft fabrics are gentle in action, and more permeable to air and water, so can be left longer on a crop – up to about eight weeks in some cases. Light fleece (17g) protects against slight frost, heavier fleece (30g) down to about –6°C/21°F. To increase frost resistance, fleeces can also be covered with the fine nets normally used for pest control. Lay fleece fairly taut over the crop, but with the edges folded so that more fabric can be released as plants grow. Fleeces are used on early salads, potatoes and carrots, on overwintering salads outdoors, and as extra frost protection in greenhouses. In cool conditions carrots are sometimes grown to maturity under fleeces, which also protect them from carrot fly. A drawback is the difficulty in seeing the crop beneath the fleece.

Lettuce grown under perforated film anchored into slits in the soil.

Fine netting anchored with weights, two types of plastic pegs and tent pegs.

Fleece anchored with small bags filled with sand, which do not tear the fabric.

Containers

For gardeners restricted to patios, courtyards, balconies or roof gardens, containers are the only means of growing plants. They also provide invaluable supplementary growing space in small gardens, and are the most practical option for tomatoes and peppers where greenhouse soil sickness has arisen (see p. 121).

You can use almost anything as a container, provided it is strong enough to withstand the combined weight of damp soil and a heavy crop. Conventional containers include flower pots, window boxes, tubs, barrels and commercial 'growing bags' – plastic bags filled with potting compost. Less conventionally, all sorts of artefacts can be converted into containers, from watering cans, sinks and bath tubs to rubber tyres and chimney pots. Containers can be mounted on castors to move them around. If growing on a roof, bear in mind the need to limit overall weight.

The larger the container, the better it can withstand the desiccating effects of sun and wind, small containers being most vulnerable. Size largely determines what can be grown. As a rough guide, seedlings and undemanding shallow-rooting herbs can be grown in a soil depth of 10cm/4in; plants the size of lettuce require a depth of about 15cm/6in, while large plants like tomatoes and peppers need containers of at least 23–25cm/9–10in diameter and depth.

Ordinary garden soil is unsuitable for containers as it quickly becomes compacted with frequent watering. Use good-quality potting compost, or garden soil mixed with a roughly equal quantity of well-rotted garden compost, worm compost or potting compost. Smaller quantities of mushroom compost and a handful or so of coarse sand or vermiculite can be added to improve drainage. Water-absorbent granules improve water retention. Earthworms are

beneficial in a container, but will move away if the soil becomes dry. Plants in containers – apart from herbs and cut-and-come-again seedlings – will require regular supplementary feeding during the growing season: use a general purpose or seaweed-based fertilizer. It is advisable to replace the soil every year.

Successful growing in containers hinges on balancing moisture retention with preventing the soil from becoming waterlogged. If necessary, drill drainage holes in the base. They should ideally be slanting (so less likely to get blocked), at least 12mm/½in in diameter and about 7.5cm/3in apart. Cover drainage holes with upturned crocks and a thick layer of coarse drainage material. I sometimes use charcoal. Growing bags filled with very absorbent compost – peat- or coir-based, for example – do not require drainage holes.

Containers need to be watered frequently in the absence of rainfall, and it may be worth installing a drip irrigation system (see p. 117). To conserve moisture and slow down evaporation, keep the surface mulched with loose organic material, mulching mats, or even stones or gravel. Loose mulches can be 5cm/2in deep. Evaporation can be slowed by lining porous clay pots with polythene film (with small drainage holes in it). and in growing bags by planting through small holes or squares cut out of the surface film rather than cutting it away completely. A wick and bucket system (see illustration below) can overcome the watering problem in brief absences. Site containers to minimize exposure to winds or full sun. In summer leafy crops like spinach, lettuce or rocket will grow in light shade.

With ingenuity, you can grow almost any vegetable or herb in containers, but containers are best suited to fast-growing, compact salads. Cut-and-come-again seedlings probably offer the highest returns. Sun-loving herbs such as basil, marjoram and thyme thrive and look decorative, as do edible flowers such as nasturtiums. Tomatoes, peppers, dwarf beans and fennel (if the soil is moisture-retentive) perform well in summer; ornamental kales and some oriental greens flourish in winter containers. Tall-growing, top-heavy plants and climbers are trickier but can succeed if given strong support. Cut-and-come-again seedlings apart, you can make best use of space by planting, rather than sowing, in containers.

A method of watering while away is to make 12mm/½in wide wicks from twisted soft material (such as wool, string or cloth). Place one end in a bucket and the other on the soil. Water seeps along the wick keeping the plant moist.

Pests and diseases

The better plants are grown, the fewer problems there will be with pests and diseases. Time and again it is overcrowded or starved plants, or those growing in an unsuitable climate or the wrong situation, that succumb to attacks which well-grown plants resist or outgrow. So I am not going to dwell on pests and diseases, other than the few most likely to occur in the salad garden. It is far more important to create conditions that encourage healthy growth. (For the identification of pests and diseases, consult any of the books listed in Further Reading, p. 163.)

As an organic gardener, I use only the few chemical sprays approved by the organic standards authorities – currently derris, pyrethrum and pyrethrins, and insecticidal soap and rape seed oil. None of these have long-term damaging effects on the soil or environment. However, any insecticide is potentially damaging, and should be used only as a last resort. Follow the manufacturer's instructions implicitly, and spray only in calm conditions in the evening, when pollinating insects are less active. The case against using more toxic chemicals is that they kill beneficial insects and may leave harmful residues on plants and in the soil, and there is always a risk of harming children and pets.

There are many alternative measures for pest control, such as physical barriers, which deter or keep out pests. 'Biological control', where a pest's natural predator or parasite is introduced to control it, is particularly effective against greenhouse pests. There are practical restraints on implementing biological control; follow instructions carefully. Plant breeders are continually introducing varieties with natural resistance to specific pests or diseases; these are of great value to organic gardeners.

There are few control measures for diseases, so prevention is essential. For example, damping off diseases, where seedlings fail to germinate or die shortly after germination, are usually a result of overcrowding, or sowing in cold, wet or contaminated soil.

The following practices all help prevent pest and disease attacks.
• Make soil fertility your number-one priority – work in bulky organic matter whenever possible. Improve the drainage if the ground is waterlogged, and keep soil mulched where appropriate.

• Practise rotation to prevent the build-up of soil pests and diseases.
• Practise intercropping, which helps to confuse pests.
• Encourage rapid germination by sowing in warm soil. Far better to delay sowing a week or so than to sow in cold or wet soil. Use cloches or transparent film to warm up a seedbed.
• Sow thinly and thin early. Overcrowded seedlings, whether in a seedbed or seed boxes, are the most vulnerable to seedling diseases.
• For indoor sowings, use clean equipment and sterilized composts if available, to prevent damping off diseases. Store composts in dry conditions. Raise plants in individual modules to encourage strong root systems and minimize the transplanting shock. Harden off plants well before planting out.
• When buying in plants, choose the sturdiest and darkest-coloured; examine them carefully for any signs of disease, such as clubroot swellings on the roots of brassicas.
• Grow appropriate plants for your area. For example, if your overwintered lettuce always get infected with mildew, grow endives instead, which are more tolerant of winter conditions. Use varieties with pest and disease resistance where available.
• Encourage steady growth without checks, by ensuring that plants have adequate moisture and nutrients. Remember the organic maxim, 'Feed the soil, not the plants.'
• Grow plants 'hard'. Coddling and overfeeding produce 'soft' vulnerable plants. Forgo the first tomato in the neighbourhood in favour of a later but healthier crop.
• In summer, keep greenhouses on the cool side: over-ventilation is far healthier than under-ventilation.
• Pay attention to garden hygiene. Burn or bury diseased – especially virused – plants. (They tend to be stunted with mottled leaves.) Clear away debris, weeds and old brassica stalks, which harbour overwintering pests that emerge in spring. Keep water tubs and tanks covered; wash pots and seed boxes after use.
• Handle storage vegetables such as carrots, garlic and onions gently. Storage rots almost invariably start with cuts and bruises, which may be invisible to the naked eye.
• Inspect plants regularly for signs of trouble. It is easy to squash

caterpillar eggs or a clutch of newly hatched caterpillars; far harder to track them when they are foraging deep in a plant.

CONTROL MEASURES FOR COMMON PESTS

Birds Sparrows and other small birds attack seedlings and young leafy plants such as lettuce, spinach and beetroot. Protect seedlings with a single strand of strong black cotton about 5cm/2in above the row or grow them under bird nets or fine horticultural nets anchored over low polytunnel hoops (see photograph below). Large birds such as pigeons cause serious damage to peas and brassicas, especially in winter and spring. Protect crops with humming wire stretched over the beds about 1.2m/4ft high. Birds tend to get used to most scarecrow devices unless they are moved frequently. A permanently netted cage may be the only solution to serious bird problems.

Slugs and snails These night feeders attack a wide range of salad crops and can be very damaging. You can treat small areas of soil with a nematode parasite, which controls slugs for up to six weeks. This becomes expensive on a large scale. Protect individual plants by covering with plastic containers with the bottom removed, pushed into the soil. But the most effective, though laborious, control is to go out at night with a torch and collect slugs while they are feeding. I push them into empty beer cans and kill them, I hope instantaneously, by pouring boiling water on them. Slugs can often be found during the day hiding under mulching mats and debris.

Soil pests Various soil pests, including wireworm, cutworm and leatherjackets, are immature forms of flying insects. They attack roots and stems, often nipping off plants at ground level. They tend to be more active in spring. Many are night feeders and can be caught, like slugs, by torchlight at night. If young plants wilt unexpectedly, dig them up and examine the roots carefully: the responsible pest can often be found.

Caterpillars The cabbage family are the main target for common caterpillars, the larval forms of moths and butterflies. Destroy eggs and caterpillars by hand, or young caterpillars by spraying with derris or pyrethrum. Alternatively use the biological control spray *Bacillus thuringiensis*. Growing plants under fine-mesh horticultural nets gives very effective protection from the egg-laying adults. The nets must be well anchored at soil level with pegs or weights, so there are no gaps. See pp. 119 and 123.

Aphids Various species of aphid attack a wide range of outdoor crops; mealy aphids and whitefly attack brassicas. Control by spraying with derris, pyrethrum, insecticidal soap or rape seed oil. Or grow plants under fine horticultural nets (see caterpillars above).

Flea beetles These tiny insects nibble small round holes in seedling leaves in the brassica family, particularly radish and salad rocket. Control by spraying with derris, or grow plants under ultra-fine horticultural nets for the first four to five weeks. Keeping the soil moist deters attacks.

Root flies Carrot fly attacks carrots, and cabbage root fly all brassicas. Eggs are laid at ground level, and the hatching maggots burrow into the stem and severely damage the plant. Protect brassicas with 13cm/5in-diameter collars made from rubberized carpet underlay. Cut a hole in one side to the centre, and slip these around the stems at soil level when planting. Or slip a plastic cup or bottle with the base removed over the plant, pushing it into the soil. Protect carrots by growing them within a 60cm/2ft-high film or net barrier, or grow them under horticultural nets (see aphids above).

Greenhouse pests Glasshouse whitefly and red spider mite are the most serious, attacking various crops including tomatoes, cucumbers, peppers and French beans. Keep them to manageable levels with biological controls: *Encarsia formosa* for whitefly and *Phytoseiulus persimilis* for red spider mite. Interplanting with French marigolds (*Tagetes* spp.) appears to discourage whitefly.

Other pests and diseases and control measures are covered under the relevant crops in Salad Plants, pages 11–90.

Bird net over hoops protects plants from birds.

salad techniques

Cut-and-come-again

People tend to think of vegetables as 'one-offs': they are picked or cut when ready, and that's that. But many leafy salad vegetables, if they are not uprooted when cut, will regrow, allowing two, three and occasionally more subsequent cuts.

'Cut-and-come-again' is a useful umbrella term for this happy ability to resprout, which saves the gardener much time, space and effort. Depending on the plant, cutting can be carried out when plants are at the seedling stage, half-grown or mature.

SEEDLING CROPS

A seedling crop is one where seeds are sown relatively thickly and the very young leaves are cut, generally between 2.5cm and 10cm/1in and 4in high (often marketed as 'baby leaves'). They are not only succulent, tasty and wonderfully fresh-looking, but highly nutritious: they can have twice the vitamin content of mature leaves. Seedlings can be cut just once, or where conditions allow, used as cut-and-come-again crops. (See also Space-saving Systems, pp. 96–110.)

The use of seedlings goes back a long way. Over 250 years ago, the English writer Richard Bradley, in his book *New Improvements of Planting and Gardening*, gave advice on the cultivation of seedlings, or 'small herbs cut in seed leaf' as he called them. He listed a wide range of plants grown for their seedlings: lettuce, chicory, endive, several types of cress, spinach, radish, turnip, mustard, salad rape – even the seedlings of oranges and lemons, which were much in vogue in the seventeenth and eighteenth centuries. These seedlings, often forced on hot beds of fermenting manure in frames or in greenhouses, kept the gentry supplied with fresh 'salading' from winter and spring. People with ample supplies of fresh manure can still make hot beds for early crops, but today heating frames with electric soil-warming cables is a more likely approach.

WHERE AND WHEN TO SOW SEEDLINGS

Seedlings can be grown inside or outdoors, according to the time of year. Bradley remarked that those grown outdoors were better-flavoured; I would suggest that they are more tender if grown under cover, especially in winter.

Seedling crops are probably best value in autumn, winter and spring, when salad greens are most scarce. In high summer, unless sown in light shade, many have a tendency to run straight to seed, quickly becoming coarse and, in the case of mustards and salad rocket, very hot-flavoured. For a continuous supply, a good rule of thumb is to make the next sowing when the previous sowing has emerged through the soil. See also the chart on p. 159.

Seedlings are an excellent means of utilizing vacant ground under cover, again from autumn to spring. Patches of fast-growing cress, salad rape or salad rocket, sown in late autumn, may allow one cutting before low winter temperatures stop their growth. They will probably look miserable by then, especially if they have been touched by frost. Yet as soon as day temperatures rise they burst into renewed growth, providing fresh salad very early in the year. Slower-growing crops sown under cover a little earlier, in early autumn, will provide pickings right through to late spring. Here in East Anglia I make these sowings in my polytunnel in the first week of September. The crops I have found productive for this purpose are the oriental greens mizuna, mibuna, standard and rosette pak choi, komatsuna and several types of mustard; various kales; spinach, corn salad, Sugar Loaf chicory, leaf radish, buck's horn plantain and Texel greens.

Cut-and-come-again seedling crops give such quick returns (cutting sometimes starts within two weeks of sowing) that it is even worth sowing patches as small as 30cm/12in square. They are ideal 'catch crops' on temporarily vacant pieces of ground before the main crop is sown or planted, and lend themselves to intercropping (see

p. 97–100). Because they are small and relatively undemanding, they are suitable for container growing.

Seedlings like cress, mustard, salad rape, rocket, leaf radish, peas, coriander and fenugreek can be grown in shallow seed trays of light soil or potting compost on a windowsill – though in most cases they will only give one cutting. A quick way to resow is to scrape off the stalks after cutting, sprinkle fresh soil or compost on top, and sow on it. Spent growing bags can be sown with a seedling crop once the main crop is finished; as most of the nutrients will have been exhausted, supplementary feeding may be necessary if you want several cuts. These seedling crops can also be grown on windowsills on an inert base (see p. 136).

CULTIVATING SEEDLING CROPS
Prepare the seedbed in the normal way (see p. 103). It is very important that the soil is weed-free: seedlings are easily smothered by weeds, and once both have germinated, weeding is virtually impossible. If necessary, prepare the seedbed in advance to get rid of the first flush of weeds (see p. 115).

Seedlings can be broadcast, or sown in narrow drills 5–10cm/2–4in apart, or sown in broad drills 7.5–15cm/3–6in wide. It can be hard to judge how thickly to sow. Instinct is to sow too thickly, so apply a moderating hand. Allowing for the fact that some seeds will fail to germinate, aim to space seeds about 1.2cm/½in apart. For a continuous supply, start cutting when the seedlings are an edible size, using sharp scissors or a knife. If you want several cuttings, always cut above the lowest seedling leaves. New growth will develop from this point. Remove any loose leaves or debris, as they will rot and soil the seedlings beneath. Seedling patches must be well watered in dry weather to sustain their rapid rate of growth. Patches that have been growing for several months may need supplementary feeding. I would use a seaweed-based feed.

The lifespan of a seedling patch varies from a few weeks to several months, depending on growing conditions (see the chart on p. 159). Unless cut frequently, many quickly outgrow the true seedling stage, though in most cases the leaves can still be eaten at a later stage, either raw or cooked. Sometimes a patch can be thinned – or virtually 'thins itself' in a kind of survival of the fittest – to allow a few plants to grow to maturity. Sugar Loaf chicory is a good

example. A patch which starts as a seedling crop in early spring can be yielding several large plants by winter.

As soon as seedling leaves become tough, the crop should be uprooted. The frequency and number of cuts that can be made depend on the crop and the growing conditions, early spring sowings probably being the most naturally productive. In cool climates this is the best time to leave a few plants to save your own seed (see p. 102). This is only advisable with crops that naturally run to seed at this time of year – not with oriental greens, which would be bolting prematurely. Occasionally gardeners are blessed with a self-sown seedling patch of corn salad, salad rocket, summer or winter purslane, or even weeds like chickweed (*Stellaria media*) – which are at their tastiest at the seedling stage.

Seedling mixtures The traditional French *mesclun* and Italian *misticanza* mixes and our saladini mixtures of salad seeds (p. 100) make excellent seedling crops. Other mixtures available now include oriental saladini (see p. 37), stir fry and braising mixes, mustard mixes, and mixed green and red lettuce (see photograph, p. 4). All give rise to instantly varied salads and are fun to grow.

DECORATIVE PATTERNS
There is a lot of scope for creating colourful effects with seedlings. Think of them as a means of embroidering on the ground. Use narrow drills to outline patterns or 'enclose' a single plant – usually a slow-growing brassica. Seedlings can outline squares, rectangles, circles, semi-circles or triangles, or weave across beds in zigzags or wavy lines, overlapping, interweaving or criss-crossing for heightened effects. Alternatively, infill an outline with broadcast seedlings or seedlings sown in wide parallel drills. Once established, adjacent drills merge to give the impression of a dense carpet. You can sow adjoining patches with seedlings of contrasting colours and textures to create a patchwork effect; changing the direction of the rows, from one patch to the next, makes the pattern more striking. Different-coloured varieties – such as green and red summer purslane, 'Lollo' or 'Salad Bowl' lettuce – grow at the same rate, so are ideal for this treatment.

Seedlings lend themselves to intercropping between rows of longer-term vegetables, most dramatically between coloured plants such as the scarlet-leaved 'Bull's Blood' beet. Use cress, coriander

LEFT Sowing seedling crops in parallel shallow drills in dry weather. Seed is sown in moist drills and covered with dry soil.

RIGHT A wheel pattern made with 'spokes' of red and green 'Lollo' lettuce infilled with gold purslane.

BELOW A selection of productive seedling crops.

Green-leaved summer purslane

Red and green orache

'Rhubarb' Swiss chard

Buck's horn plantain

White-stemmed pak choi

Black Tuscan kale

and dill for a light-textured foil; perpetual beet for a bold impact; purple mustard and red lettuce for a red contrast; and 'Red Russian' and 'Tuscan' kales for subtle shades of purple and blue.

For further information on cut-and-come-again seedling crops and their characteristics, see the chart on p. 159.

REGROWTH IN MATURE PLANTS

While many plants resprout at the juvenile stage, a few do so when cut at maturity. In good growing conditions, red, spring and early summer cabbages may produce a second crop of four or five small heads. Making a shallow cross in the stump seems to accelerate the process. Some varieties of lettuce make a second head after the first is cut. I have known this happen with the overwintered greenhouse lettuce 'Kwiek', and with looser-headed red-tinged varieties such as the semi-hearting 'Marvel of Four Seasons'. It is most likely to succeed in spring; secondary heads in summer may become bitter.

Far more commonly, plants will produce more leaves, but not a tight head, after the first head or mature leaves are cut. This is the case with the Salad Bowl range of lettuce, Chinese cabbage, pak choi, mizuna and mibuna greens, komatsuna, broad and curly endive, and Sugar Loaf and red chicory. These plants are often grown for use in autumn and early winter, and, mizuna apart, are not considered hardy. What is interesting is that once their large, leafy, frost-vulnerable tops have been removed, the stumps, with whatever leaf has been left, will survive much lower temperatures than would normally be the case. When warm weather returns they start back into growth, providing welcome early salad leaves. If they are planted in late summer/early autumn under cover – whether in polytunnels, frames or cloches – the effect is accentuated. The plants remain in good condition longer, recover earlier and are more productive. They can make a major contribution to filling the spring 'salad gap'.

Spring cabbage ABOVE cut in early summer and BELOW with four new heads forming six weeks later.

Salad Bowl lettuce ABOVE cut in early summer and BELOW with regrowth three weeks later.

Mizuna greens ABOVE cut in mid-summer and BELOW with regrowth six weeks later.

Blanching

Blanching – literally meaning 'to make white' – is one of the refinements of salad growing. The stems or leaves of certain vegetables are blanched by excluding light to make them crisper, sweeter, whiter and more delicately flavoured. Bitter leaves such as chicory and dandelion are far more palatable when blanched.

Blanched leaves can be beautiful, too. White, pink-tipped blades of 'Red Treviso' chicory, jagged creamy dandelion leaves tinged with yellow and the frothy white leaves of blanched curly endive all look superb on the plate.

Blanching was once a widely practised art: our gardening forbears blanched celery, cabbage, endive, fennel, cos lettuce, cardoons and seakale, as well as the spring shoots or 'chards' of globe artichokes, scorzonera and salsify; and many wild plants including dandelion, alexanders and wild chicory or succory. Blanching is now less fashionable. Perhaps it is less necessary – some modern varieties are naturally sweeter – and we may be subconsciously aware that vitamins are lost in blanching. Or we are just lazy! But it's fun to do and the end result is rewarding.

Blanching is often coupled with forcing, where crops are brought into earlier growth in a dark environment, mainly in winter and early spring. Once blanching is completed, plants deteriorate fairly rapidly. So in most cases it is advisable to blanch a few at a time in succession and use them as soon as they are ready.

The essence of blanching is to exclude light, either *in situ* or by moving the plants into a darkened environment. Whatever method you use, high humidity in a close environment means there is a risk of plants rotting. To lessen the risk, foliage should be as dry as possible. Cover plants with cloches several days beforehand if necessary and remove all dead, rotting or diseased leaves.

In situ blanching methods

Tying The simplest method of blanching tall or long-leaved plants is to bunch up the leaves and tie them with raffia, string or even elastic bands about two thirds up the plant. The outer leaves will not be blanched, as they are exposed to light, but the central leaves will be crisp and pale within ten to fifteen days. This is a quick and simple way of blanching mature dandelions, the more upright endives and wild chicories.

Covering Light is excluded by covering the whole plant, leaves often being tied up first to keep them off the ground. Sea kale was traditionally blanched under purpose-made rounded clay pots and in China, Chinese chives under narrow, chimney-like clay pots. Alternatives include upturned flowerpots with the drainage holes blocked to exclude light, wooden boxes, and cloches, hoops, frames or any framework covered with black polythene film. I have seen rows of endive boxed over with what looked like miniature coffins, and also with low, tent-shaped wooden frames. Whatever you use, allow space for air circulation to keep plants healthy.

Blanching *in situ*
Curly endive can be partially blanched by tying up the head. The central leaves will become paler and sweeter within ten days or so.

Sea kale forced and blanched under a clay blanching pot

Endive blanched under a light-proof bucket

LEFT Mature, low growing curly-leaved endive blanched by covering with a plate.

RIGHT Within about a week the central leaves (see left-hand plant) are blanched. The plant on the far right has yet to be blanched. As plants tend to deteriorate rapidly after blanching, it is best to blanch them in succession. Leaves must be dry when the plant is covered, or they will rot during the process.

Purpose-made blanching caps are used to cover low plants such as curled endive. The job can also be done by simply placing a dinner plate on the plant. The soft, black permeable mulching fabrics (see p. 119), folded several times to make them lightproof, are excellent for blanching. Anchor the edges with weights or pins. Straw and hay are more traditional blanching materials, used in a layer 15–20cm/6–8in thick, kept in place with metal hoops, canes or wire netting.

Plants can be forced *in situ* in an old method used for Witloof chicory, dandelion, scorzonera and salsify. In early winter they are allowed to die back, or are cut back to about 4cm/1½in above soil level, and are then covered with a ridge of soil, sand or leaves. In spring the blanched shoots push through, and the covering is scraped aside to cut them.

TRANSPLANTED BLANCHING METHODS

Plants are transplanted for blanching for convenience, and when there is a risk of frost damage if they are left in the open.

In frames Traditionally, frames were widely used for blanching,

Witloof and red 'Treviso' chicory being blanched in winter in a polytunnel. Here they are planted in the ground under the staging, and a darkened area is made by anchoring black polythene film over low hoops.

especially for marginally hardy plants such as endives. Dig up mature plants in autumn before the first frosts, and replant close together in the frame. The foliage must be dry, and plants handled carefully, as any cuts or tears in the leaves invite rots. Water the soil moderately beforehand, so that no further watering is necessary.

Frames can be darkened by covering with matting, boards, black polythene film or carpeting. Alternatively, cover the plants themselves with several layers of soft black fabric (see above) or a thick layer of straw, hay or dried leaves. In the past sand or sometimes even soil or ashes were sifted over plants. Keep a watch out for mice: they will be attracted to such cosy corners.

In greenhouses Plants can be forced and blanched by transplanting them into greenhouses and polytunnels, then covering them in any of the ways suggested for *in situ* blanching above. Outdoor plants can also be potted up into large pots, and brought under cover for blanching. It saves space to make a lightproof area under the staging, either with boards, or with black polythene film over low hoops (see illustration left). By the same token a low polytunnel inside a greenhouse can be covered with black film for blanching. In all these cases, replant the plants fairly closely in the soil, if feasible, planting in succession to prolong the cropping period. In spring temperatures can rise dramatically, and remaining plants may deteriorate rapidly or be attacked by aphids. Inspect regularly and if plants have been attacked, use them up quickly.

In cellars Cellars, the *caves* of the French-speaking world, were once widely used for blanching and forcing. Ventilation is good and they maintain a steady temperature of about 5°C/41°F. Plants were either potted into boxes or pots which were put into the dark cellar – no further covering was necessary – or planted into beds of soil in the cellar. In an old Belgium system a 30cm/12in-wide stack of soil was piled against the cellar wall in layers 10cm/4in or so thick. Dandelion and chicory roots were laid close together on each layer, their necks protruding over the edge. The blanched leaves were cut when ready. The roots were left in the heap to make further, less vigorous but useful growth during the rest of the winter.

Forcing Witloof chicory Witloof chicory is one of the most popular of the blanched crops. Roots are lifted and forced under cover in darkness to produce conical creamy white chicons. One of the easiest systems for gardeners is to pot roots into a large flower pot (see illustration right). (See also Witloof Chicory, p. 22.)

Forcing chicory in pots
To force Witloof chicory indoors, lift the roots in late autumn and trim to within 2.5cm/1in of the crown. Pot five or six roots into a large flower pot, covered with an inverted pot of the same size, with the drainage hole blocked to exclude light. If kept at about 10°C/50°F, the white chicons will be ready in about three weeks.

Seed sprouting

Seed sprouting is a highly intensive form of food production. Not only is it possible to sow on Monday and 'harvest' on Wednesday, but the seeds can increase their weight tenfold in the process. No soil or garden is required: just the simplest equipment and a windowsill or somewhere fairly warm to put the seeds.

Sprouted seeds can be used in salads, raw or cooked, and can also be incorporated into soups, stews, omelettes, breads and all sort of dishes. A word of caution about eating raw legume sprouts, such as beans, peas, alfalfa and fenugreek: they contain toxic substances which could be damaging if eaten regularly in large quantities – that is, more than about 550g/20oz daily. Presoaking, sprouting and cooking all reduce toxin levels, but it is a complex story. Soya and mung beans are the least toxic of the sprouted legumes, French and broad beans the most toxic.

A great many seeds can be sprouted. The following lists some of the most commonly available, but there are many others. Most are used when sprouts are 1.2–2.5cm/½–1in long as many tend to get bitter if they grow longer. The development of bitterness seems to vary, depending on sprouting conditions and even on the variety of seed used. It is a case of seeing what works best with you. Those that can be left and eaten as young seedlings are indicated.

Legume family Azuki bean (*Phaseolus angularis*), lima bean (*Phaseolus lunatus*); mung bean (*Phaseolus aureus*), soya bean (*Glycine max*), whole, not split lentils (*Lens esculenta*), chickpea (*Cicer arietinum*). Also edible as seedlings: alfalfa (*Medicago sativa*), clover (*Melilotus altissima*), fenugreek (*Trigonella foenumgraecum*), peas (*Pisum sativum*).

Brassicas and related species Brussels sprouts (*Brassica oleracea* 'Gemmifera' Gp), cabbage (*B. o.* 'Capitata' Gp), cauliflower (*B. o.* 'Botrytis' Gp), kale (*B. o.* 'Acephala' Gp), the oriental leafy greens (see pp. 31–7); radish (*Raphanus sativus*); cress (*Lepidium sativum*), black mustard (*Brassica nigra*), salad rape (*Brassica napus*). All are edible as seedlings.

Cereals and grains Barley (*Hordeum vulgare*), buckwheat (*Fagopyrum esculentum*), maize/sweet corn (*Zea mays*), rye (*Secale cereale*), brown, unpolished rice (*Oryza sativa*), wheat (*Triticum vulgare*). These are only eaten as small sprouts.

Other garden crops Sunflower (*Helianthus annuus*) and pumpkin (*Cucurbita* spp.): in both cases de-hulled seeds or naturally hull-less varieties sprout best. Edible also as seedlings: coriander (*Coriandrum sativum*), leeks (*Allium porrum*), onion (*Allium* spp.).

The best sources of seeds are health food shops and seed firms. Always buy untreated seed intended for consumption, rather than ordinary garden seed, which is often chemically treated. Remember that seeds for sprouting are viable seeds, and must be stored in dry, cool conditions to maintain their viability until sprouted.

Seed sprouting mixtures are sometimes available. The concept is appealing, but unless they have been carefully blended, germination tends to be uneven.

Sprouting uses a lot of seed, so it can be worth saving your own where practicable. Radish is one of the easiest and worthwhile: sprouted radish is deliciously piquant. Allow a few plants to run to seed in spring or summer, and collect the pods when dry (see p. 101). Seed of large mooli and winter radish is best for sprouting, as the seeds, like the roots, are large. Sunflower and pumpkin seed can be saved quite easily.

What, in fact, are sprouted seeds? They are seeds that have germinated and grown – usually for twenty-four hours to a few days – until the 'sprouts' are between 6–40mm/¼ –1.5in long, depending on the species. Up to this point they draw on internal resources. To develop further, and virtually become a seedling crop, they would need to be sown in the ground or on some kind of substrate.

In the germination process, the fats and starches stored in the seed are converted into vitamins, sugars, minerals and proteins. This makes sprouted seeds exceptionally nutritious, notably rich in vitamins and minerals. They are tasty and crisp-textured. However, they develop rapidly and once past their peak they deteriorate from both the nutritional and flavour points of view. For a constant supply, sprout small quantities at regular intervals. Once ready, they can be kept in a fridge for a couple of days in a bowl of water or wrapped in film; rinse daily to keep them fresh. Bean sprouts should be kept for only about twenty-four hours, ideally at a temperature of about 4°C/39°F, as they are prone to bacterial infection.

SPROUTING TECHNIQUES

There are many ways of sprouting seeds, and I would advise beginners to start with one type of seed and sprout it by several methods to see what suits them best. Success or failure in sprouting turns on the fact that seeds need moisture and warmth to germinate, and in germinating they themselves generate considerable heat. This combination of warmth and moisture provides perfect conditions for moulds to develop. So sprouting seeds rot and go 'sour' unless cooled by regular rinsing with cold water.

Seeds can be sprouted loose in a container, or on a base. When sprouted loose there is no wastage as the entire sprout is used.

Sprouting on a base results in some wastage, as the sprouts normally have to be cut off the base. However sprouts on a base remain in good condition longer, and if necessary can be left to develop into small seedlings. Growth is probably somewhat faster in a container.

Whatever system is used, there are a few golden rules:
• Use clean equipment.
• Remove cracked, discoloured and unhealthy-looking seed beforehand.
• Keep seeds fresh and cool by rinsing frequently.
• Keep seeds slightly moist – neither swamped with water nor dried out.
• Grow seeds as fast as possible.

Seeds can be sprouted in the dark or the light: it is a matter of choice, though most seeds sprout faster in the dark. Sprouts grown in the dark are white and crisp – typified by Chinese bean sprouts – but less nutritious than the softer, greener spouts which develop in full light. Where sprouts are being grown on to the seedling stage, start them in the dark, but move them into the light once germinated. To sprout in the dark, put the seeds in a drawer or cupboard – an airing cupboard is ideal in winter – or cover the container in aluminium foil. Windowsills can be used for sprouting in the light, but avoid direct sun.

The container method Various containers can be used, but they must be large enough to allow the seeds to expand their volume seven to ten-fold, as happens in some, but not all cases. Ideally they should be self-draining, a feature in most patented seed sprouters. A cheap and efficient sprouter can be made by drilling holes in the base of a plastic carton - effectively converting it into a sieve (see illustration on p. 136). Seeds are then rinsed simply by holding it under a tap, and letting water run through. Jam jars can be covered with plastic mesh, and seeds rinsed by pouring water in and out through the mesh. Muslin is sometimes substituted for mesh: I personally find that it is awkward to use and that the muslin discolours rather unpleasantly. Sprouting seeds grow more evenly in wide, rather than deep, containers such as jars, unless these are laid on their side.

The basic procedure is to remove damaged seeds, then rinse the seeds with fresh water in a sieve or in a self-draining sprouter. Drain the seeds and put them into the container, in a layer generally no

RIGHT Examples of different types of seed, before sprouting, sprouted on a base and sprouted in a jar.

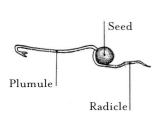

Seed

Plumule

Radicle

ABOVE When put into warm and moist conditions, the seed swells up and after a few days the embryonic root, or 'radicle', breaks through the seed coat. Shortly afterwards, the 'plumule', which eventually becomes the shoot and stem of the plant, emerges. At this stage, two tiny 'seed leaves', remnants of the seed coat, may still be attached, but they will float off if the seeds are put into a bowl of water.

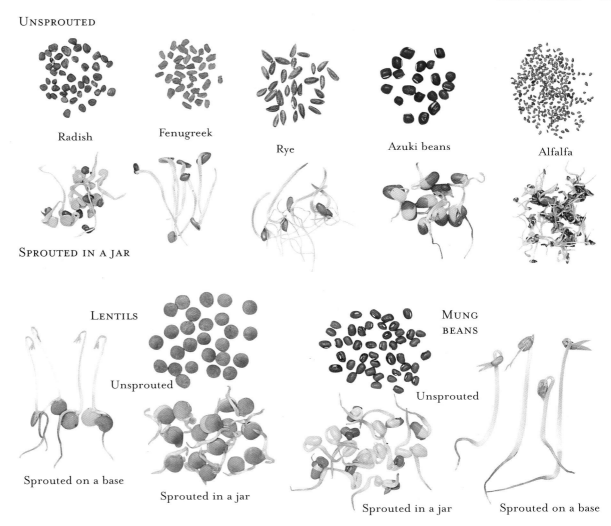

UNSPROUTED

Radish

Fenugreek

Rye

Azuki beans

Alfalfa

SPROUTED IN A JAR

LENTILS

Unsprouted

Sprouted on a base

Sprouted in a jar

MUNG BEANS

Unsprouted

Sprouted in a jar

Sprouted on a base

more than 6mm–1.3cm/¼–½in deep. The larger the seed, the deeper the layer can be. If the container is unlidded, the seeds can be covered with a damp cloth to keep them moist. Some seeds, beans for example, sprout faster if they are presoaked overnight in water.

For most seeds the optimum temperature for germination is between 13 and 21°C/55 and 70°F, though temperatures up to 24°C/75°F can be used. In warm weather seeds can be sprouted at room temperature; otherwise put them somewhere warmer. Seeds should always be germinated quickly: lingering seeds are the most susceptible to disease.

Rinse the seeds at least twice a day – morning and evening – and more frequently if necessary, until they are ready for use.

My 'patent method' of sprouting mung beans in containers My early attempts at mung bean sprouting failed to produce the long crisp sprouts of Chinese restaurants. A research station in Taiwan revealed one of the keys to success: pressure. Whether grown in traditional Chinese clay sprouting jars, or in modern metal bins, the sprouting seeds are subjected to tremendous pressure as they expand against the sides of the vessel. I have found that this pressure can be replicated by simply putting a weight on the

Sprouting mung beans by the 'weight' method
Mung beans being sprouted in a home-made container, with
holes punched in the base. A plastic beaker was used for the
photograph, so that the process could be seen, but it would have
to have been wrapped in foil or put into a cupboard for seed
sprouting in the dark. The mung beans were soaked overnight and
rinsed, then put into the beaker in a layer 13mm/½in deep. They
were then covered with a damp cloth and a 450g/1lb weight. The
cloth and weight were removed night and morning for rinsing
under a tap (LEFT). The sprouted beans were ready for eating
four days later (RIGHT).

germinating seed. I use a 900g/2lb weight in a 3cm/5in-diameter
container, with 13mm/½in of seeds in the bottom. To spread the
weight evenly, place it on a saucer, removing both for rinsing. In nine
cases out of ten, this system produces excellent results. See
illustrations above.

Sprouting on a base Seeds can be sprouted on an inert moist
base such as paper towelling, cotton wool, flannel or other fabrics –
the time-honoured way of growing mustard and cress for eating at
the small seedling stage. These materials can all be laid over a foam
base to retain moisture. Salad rape, radish, coriander, alfala,
fenugreek, lentils, peas, Texel greens and mung beans are among
many others that can be sprouted this way. All can be used as sprouts
or, slightly later, as young seedlings. The seeds quickly root into the
base, standing upright and making an attractive dish.

Spread the rinsed seeds evenly in a single layer over the moist
base. If necessary, put them somewhere warm to germinate, in either
the dark or light. If you intend to use them as young seedlings, start
them in the dark (see p. 134). Rinse them daily by running cool water
over them, holding the seeds in place with the back of a spoon until
they have rooted into the base. If the base is very clean, pull up the
seedlings by the roots and eat whole; otherwise, cut them off at the
base. If kept moist and cool, seedlings may remain in good condition
for two weeks before cutting.

Growing seedlings in soil Any seeds sprouted on a base can
also be sown in a seed tray of finely sieved leaf mould or potting
compost, which would supply some nutrients. Two or three cuttings
of seedlings can usually be made, making a useful windowsill
'harvest'.

LEFT Mangetout peas sprouted
on a foam base covered with
several layers of paper towel.
They reached this stage in eight
days. Mangetout peas seem to
make particularly sweet-
flavoured sprouts.

RIGHT Mung beans sprouted
on a moist cotton-wool base.
They were covered with tinfoil
to exclude light. The far dish is
ready for use.

salad
making

creative salads

Salad making is an easily mastered art, but, like any art, it demands good-quality materials and the expenditure of a little time, skill and that magical ingredient, creativity. So often salads are made for the wrong reasons: to avoid cooking, to save time, or to use up leftovers. And oh, the salads that result – wilted lettuce, soggy coleslaw, dried mounds of grated carrot, gelatinous faded rings of egg white. Such sorry salads are a world away from what can be created with plants picked fresh from the garden. Salad plants offer a richness of flavour, colour, texture, even fragrance beyond the dreams of a salad maker restricted to what can be bought in a shop. Add fresh herbs, delicately flavoured dressings and carefully chosen garnishes, and you will have not only food for the body and the soul but also a feast for the eyes.

The art of salad making has spanned centuries and continents. In Europe it reached extraordinary heights in the 'crowned sallets' of Elizabethan times. These were elaborate constructions. Sometimes a complete head of celery would be the centrepiece, mounted in a pot and surrounded by layer upon layer of sliced meats, eggs, shredded vegetables, nuts and fruits. Or the salad could take the form of a pastry castle with 'towers' and 'ramparts' of carrots, turnips and beetroots, and 'courtyards' planted with herbs and flowers.

One of the most articulate exponents of the art of salad making was the seventeenth-century writer and diarist John Evelyn. His book *Acetaria: a Discourse of Sallets*, which he wrote in 1699, is full of wisdom and observation, most of it as pertinent today as it was 300 years ago. (For the past twenty-five years, it has been within arm's reach of my desk!) Here is how he summarized the 'art' of composing a salad:

> *Every Plant should come in to bear its part, without being overpower'd by some Herb of a stronger Taste, so as to endanger the native Sapor and Vertue of the rest; but fall into their places like the Notes in Music, in which there should be nothing harsh or grating; and though admitting some Discords (to distinguish and illustrate the rest), striking in the more sprightly, and sometimes gentler Notes, reconcile all Dissonances and melt them into an agreeable Composition.*

John Evelyn's garden at Says Court was organized so that a mixed green salad could be put on the table every day of the year.

Perhaps the finest examples of contemporary salad making are to be found in the Middle East, in the wonderful *mezze* tradition, which stretches from Morocco to Afghanistan and from Greece to the Yemen.

Mezze can be anything from a simple snack to a banquet of forty to fifty dishes. They are exquisitely prepared and presented salads, served in tiny bowls. Stuffed peppers, courgettes or vine leaves might be cut in slices; crisp raw vegetables set against creamy fragrant dips; black, purple and green olives contrasted with chopped egg, aubergines served in yogurt, tomatoes in olive oil; and dried lentil and bean salads decorated with cucumber and tomato wedges.

Whatever the inspiration, the approach to any salad dish will be influenced by its role in the meal. If it is to be a starter or appetizer, it may take the form of crudités, though indeed almost any light salad could be served as an opener. The exception is the simple green salad, which is best served between courses to freshen the palate. Where a salad is an accompaniment to a main dish it should contrast or harmonize with it – a colourful marinated pepper salad, for example, to set against the pale flesh of chicken. Alternatively a salad dish can be substantial enough to be a meal in itself. Here the potato and dried bean salads come into their own, as do 'composé' salads, in which vegetables are mixed with another fairly substantial ingredient, such as pasta or rice.

A simple salad of bronze and green lettuce, garnished with lemon balm leaves and blue borage flowers.
(For recipe, see page 152.)

Types of salad

Most salad plants can be treated in various ways, and part of the fun of growing your own, especially the more unusual plants, is deciding how to use them to best advantage. Don't be afraid to follow your instincts and use your imagination, but bear in mind that the quality and flavour of home-grown 'salading' is usually so good that it will need only the minimum 'treatment' – just enough to enhance, but never to disguise or conceal, the natural flavour. Salads may be broadly divided into groups according to their ingredients and the way they are prepared. (For recipes, see pp. 151–8.)

RAW SALADS

I firmly believe that, wherever possible, salad plants should be eaten raw. Not only are the subtleties of flavour, texture and often colour lost in cooking, but the vitamins are destroyed. The most basic raw salads are crudités, 'simple salads' have limited ingredients, and mixed salads and 'saladini' are more complex.

Crudités The classic French crudités are very finely grated, pristinely fresh vegetables, served in delicate mounds with a sprinkling of sea salt. Freshness and quality, of course, are the essence of crudités. Besides being grated, vegetables can be very finely sliced, diced or cut into matchsticks – a perfect way to treat fennel, celery and Beauty Heart radish. Small vegetables, such as summer radish, spring onions and baby carrots, can be left whole. The idea is to eat them with your fingers as an *hors d'oeuvre*, perhaps dipping them into one of the vinaigrettes, mayonnaises or creamy dressings on pp. 148–50 or into dips. Suitable dips include vegetable purées such as puréed aubergine (steamed or cooked in light oil until soft), tahini, hummus, or yogurt flavoured with chopped mint or garlic.

Crudités should look, as well as taste, wonderful. Blend colours and textures to maximum effect, and serve them in attractive dishes with, for special occasions, finger bowls of rosewater and scented geranium leaves. Some – radishes and spring onions, for example – are best chilled before serving; keep them in iced water in the refrigerator. Keep any that discolour once cut in acidulated water (see p. 143).

While all kinds of salad vegetables can be treated as crudités, a few – asparagus for example – are only palatable when very young. Cauliflower is appetizing raw only if broken into tiny florets: trim them to look like bonsai. Root vegetables, on the whole, are best grated. Small tomatoes, cucumbers, gherkins, mature sweet peppers all make appealing crudités, as do the small, dainty leaves of any leafy salad plant. While peas, especially the pods of sugar peas, are delicious raw, avoid eating broad beans and green French and runner beans raw, as the raw seeds contain toxins.

Simple salads The simple salad is made of one or at most only a few raw ingredients, which are dressed and garnished. It is essentially the classic green salad – a few fresh, very crisp lettuce leaves or hearts, tossed in a vinaigrette dressing just before serving. As already mentioned, the time-honoured purpose of this superb but simple salad is to refresh the palate.

Vary a simple lettuce salad by adding a few leaves of chicory, endive, purslane, dandelion or spinach, or any other appropriate salad plant. Or make a simple salad with any of these alone, or in simple combinations. Change their nature again by using different vinegars and oils in the dressings, and garnishing with herbs, flowers, nuts, sprouted seeds or seedlings.

Simple salads can also be made with non-leafy plants such as tomatoes, dressed just with basil and the lightest of vinaigrettes; or with lightly dressed bean sprouts on a bed of endive; or with purslane mixed with salad rocket. Almost any salad vegetable, in fact, can be treated 'simply'. Unpretentious and quick to make, these simple salads depend on the quality of their ingredients for their excellence.

Mixed salads and saladini Mixed salads have many more ingredients and, often, more complex dressings than simple salads, but they must still be subtly balanced and blended so that they have character – not merely nondescript diversity for diversity's sake. Into this category of salads falls 'saladini', the modern incarnation of the sixteenth-, seventeenth- and eighteenth-century salads in which twenty or thirty ingredients were combined.

The term 'saladini' arose from our travels in Europe in the late 1970s. In the northern Italian markets we had seen seedlings of lettuce, endive, chicory, salad rocket and corn salad being sold alongside baskets of small wild plants. The idea was to buy a few handfuls of each and mix them into a salad at home. These small leaves were called *insalatine*, a diminutive of *insalata*, the Italian word for salad, but my untuned ears misheard it as 'saladini'. We liked the word – it was associated in our minds with the Continental plants we began growing and using in mixed salads on our return – and we adopted it as our own to describe our mixed salads.

Virtually all the plants covered in this book can be used in saladini (and see the chart on p. 160–1). Like John Evelyn with his green salads, it is possible to serve a freshly picked saladini every day of the year. Midsummer saladini are very different from those in midwinter but, however bizarre and diverse the individual plants, it is always possible to achieve an end result of harmony of colour, taste and texture.

In mixing saladini we always try to balance flavours, contrast textures, and include a few ingredients for their form and colour alone. When I started reading the gardening classics I discovered that their authors did the same. John Evelyn divides salad plants, or salad herbs, as he calls them, primarily into 'blanched herbs' (therefore pale) such as chicory, celery, fennel, various types of lettuce and endive, and 'green herbs', which include lettuce, corn salad, purslane, assorted cresses, sorrel, the seedling leaves of radish, turnip and mustard, and wild plants. He suggests the proportions in which available salad plants can be mixed in each month of the year – for example, 'a pugil or handful of lamb's lettuce, three parts of radish, two parts of cresses'. He also suggests that they should be enlivened with 'furnitures', by which he means 'all hot and spicy herbs, mixed with the more cold and mild, discretely to temper and give them relish'.

The eighteenth-century gardening writer Batty Langley, in his *New Principles of Gardening*, divided salads into 'raw sallets', 'boiled sallets' and 'pickled sallets', then further classified plants according to the strength of their flavour. For example, among 'hot and dry' plants cress was a mere '2nd degree' on his scale of hotness, while garlic and mustard were fourth degree. Elaborate classifications like these are, of course, unnecessary, but when you are making saladini, keep a balance in mind: make sure that nothing is overpowering. Very strong or bitter plants such as chicories and mustards can be shredded (even blanched in boiling water for a second), and offset with mild, sweet or succulent leaves, such as the purslanes.

Use chopped herbs and flowers in mixed salads and saladini as a means of creating further variations (see p. 79 and p. 85).

COOKED SALADS

Vegetables do not have to be used raw in salads. Many can be cooked, then incorporated into salad dishes when cool.

Of the root vegetables, potatoes, of course, are inedible raw; others, including parsnip, salsify and scorzonera, are generally more palatable cooked. Kohl rabi and Jerusalem artichoke are among those with a markedly different, and I think improved, flavour after cooking.

Many legumes, including green and dried French and runner beans, broad beans and various pulses must be cooked, as they are toxic in varying degrees when raw. Again, to some palates cooked dried beans taste even better when eaten cold.

A number of vegetables can be used raw when very young, but on the whole taste better cooked, then eaten cold. Asparagus, cauliflower, courgettes, calabrese and leeks come into this category.

When cooking vegetables for salads, it is crucial not to overcook them and, as far as possible, not to destroy their texture or natural crispness. Cooked leftover vegetables often make excellent salads, though they may need to be jazzed up with a little extra seasoning, dressing or garnish. While any dressing can be used with cooked vegetables, your choice should be influenced by what else is being served in the meal. If the main course has a creamy sauce, an *hors d'oeuvre* or salad dish dressed with a rich mayonnaise or cream dressing would be inappropriate.

Salads with hot dressings – and 'hot salads' The best-known hot dressing is the French *aux lardons*: essentially hot bacon pieces and juice mixed with salad leaves, which are eaten immediately. There are permutations on the theme, but this dressing is always used for bitter, sharp and strong-flavoured leaves such as dandelion, endive, wild chicory, spinach and oriental mustards.

The Italian *bagna cauda* is another classic hot dressing or dip. Its key ingredients are garlic, anchovy and oil. Piedmontese in origin, it is used with popular Italian vegetables like cardoons, artichoke, celery and endive.

In China and Japan the term 'hot salad' describes vegetables that are stir-fried for no more than half a minute – just long enough to take the edge off their rawness. While still warm, they are tossed in a dressing and immediately brought to table. Sprouted seeds and any of the oriental greens or mustards can be treated this way. Stir fry them in a mix of cooking and sesame oil, then use one of the Chinese dressings on pp. 149–50.

COMPOSÉ SALADS

The original French composé salads were mixtures of raw or cooked vegetables. In their modern form the net is cast wider, and they can be mixed with, say, a staple such as rice, pasta or grains, or alternatively fish, meat, chicken or even cheese, or any combinations of these, dressed and garnished as necessary. Take care when making composé salads: such mixtures, it has to be said, can be dire in the wrong hands.

Meat, chicken and fish should be chopped into pieces of small but discernible size. Do not use a food processor. To prevent pasta from becoming lumpy, moisten it with oil, not butter, as soon as it is cooked and before it has cooled. With rice, for preference use long-grain brown rice, American or Spanish rice, as the grains separate nicely and absorb dressings well. Patna and Basmati rice tend to congeal into a solid mass when cold, but this can be avoided by rinsing thoroughly with cold water after cooking.

Other examples of composé salads are the various forms of Salade Niçoise, in which tuna is combined with salad vegetables, combinations of beans and peas with tagliatelle, or tomatoes provençale and *pain bagna*.

PICKLING

Before the advent of deep freezes and year-round availability of almost everything, pickling – in which vegetables are marinaded in vinegar – was one of the most important means of preserving food to enliven dull winter diets. A trawl through old gardening books reveals an extraordinary range of plants that were commonly pickled for salads – globe artichokes, beet, French beans, cucumbers, leeks, mushrooms, onions, purslane, radish seed pods, herbs such as summer savory and tarragon, the buds of broom, elder and nasturtium, and the flowers of chicory, cowslip, elder, scorzonera

Broad bean, pea and pasta salad.
(For recipe, see page 158.)

(goat's beard), salsify, clove-scented pinks and nasturtiums. Nasturtium seeds were pickled too.

Today there is no longer the same necessity to make pickles, but a few salad plants are still worth pickling, simply because they acquire such a good flavour in the process. Among them are shallots, onions, gherkins, sweet peppers, globe artichokes, small beets and nasturtium seeds. And it's fun to make a few old-fashioned pickles such as radish seed pods and glasswort.

In essence pickling implies conservation in a spiced, clear vinegar such as cider, wine, rice or distilled malt vinegar. In some cases the plants are initially sprinkled with salt or soaked in brine to dehydrate them. For further reading, see p. 162–3.

Quite different are the delicious Asiatic 'quick pickles', which are eaten within hours or at most a couple of days. They are widely used for Chinese cabbage, spicy oriental greens, root vegetables and cucumbers. Essentially the vegetables are sprinkled with salt, and left, depending on the vegetable, for anything from thirty minutes to overnight. In some cases they are pressed under a weight. They are then rinsed before use. For further reading, see my book *Oriental Vegetables*.

Preparing salads

Tools

A few good kitchen tools make the preparation of salads easier and more efficient.

For chopping and shredding, have a good selection of sharp knives, including a paring knife and a medium-sized chef's knife. A Japanese vegetable knife, which is rather like a lightweight cleaver, is a very versatile tool, excellent for shredding cabbage and chopping herbs. Always buy the best-quality knives you can afford.

Chopping boards should be large and made of good hardwood. To clean them, scrub them with salt rather than washing in detergent. Use food processors with great discretion, as their action on vegetables is harsh and apt to destroy their crisp texture; however, they are good for shredding and grating carrots and beetroot. For other root vegetables, an ordinary hand grater is preferable.

Use a good-quality pottery pestle and mortar for pounding garlic, mustard seed, herbs and spices, and for making dressings. A Japanese *sunibachi*, which has a grooved mortar, is excellent for grinding herbs. Use a garlic press for crushing and squeezing garlic.

For drying salads, a collapsible, hand-swung salad basket and a centrifugal type of salad spinner are useful, particularly for small quantities of leafy salad. However, there is nothing wrong with swinging washed salad in a thin piece of muslin and then patting it dry with another clean cloth. For cleaning muddy roots, a stubby Japanese vegetable brush is excellent.

Gathering

Whenever possible, pick leafy salads and flowers just before you use them. In hot weather, it may be necessary to collect them early in the day before they wilt and to keep them in a plastic bag in a refrigerator until required. Remove coarse and dirty outer leaves, but otherwise the less you wash leafy salads, the better. I have consistently found that unwashed salads keep longer. It is preferable to wipe them clean with damp kitchen paper. If washing is really necessary, pull the leaves apart and wash them quickly in cold salted water: this encourages insects and slugs to detach themselves. Calabrese and cauliflower heads tend to harbour well-concealed caterpillars, so leave them in cold salted water for at least ten minutes. Small roots such as radishes desiccate easily and are best kept in a bowl of cold water in a refrigerator until needed. Wilted lettuce can be crisped up just before use in a bowl of ice cubes.

Peeling

Skin or peel salad vegetables only when it is essential to do so. Home-grown tomatoes, peppers, cucumbers, courgettes, young carrots, kohl rabi and new potatoes are all best unskinned, as the skin is nutritious and colourful, and adds texture. With celery and fennel it may be necessary to peel off very stringy parts; the same is true with some varieties of string beans and elderly sugar peas. Some roots are difficult to peel: beetroot bleeds, salsify and scorzonera discolour and are fiddly, and Chinese artichokes are exceptionally fiddly. Cook all these whole without peeling; it is easy to remove the skins as they start to cool. If using beetroot raw, peel it thinly, as the raw skin is unsightly and unpleasant to eat. Large potatoes will need peeling. Prepare globe artichokes by trimming off the stalks, the tough basal bracts and the pointed tips of the upper bracts.

Cutting

How you cut salad vegetables has a bearing on both their taste and appearance. It is important to cut to a uniform size. Vegetables look very attractive in matchstick slivers (*à la julienne*), diced – that is, cut into cubes of about 1cm/½in diameter – or sliced. Do not slice too thinly; it is good to get a sense of substance with each bite. Ultra-thin cucumber slices, for example, are sorry things. Gently tear leaf vegetables rather than cutting with a knife, which is inevitably a brutal action; treated kindly they will look more appetizing, will be less damaged and discoloured, and will keep better.

Roots such as celeriac, salsify and scorzonera, once peeled, become unpleasantly discoloured on contact with air. To prevent this, slice them into water acidulated with a few drops of vinegar or lemon juice, and leave them until required. Rub the cut surfaces of globe artichokes with lemon to prevent discolouration. Once roots have been blanched or cooked, there is no need for acidulation.

Softening and tenderizing

Fibrous elements in leaves, stems and roots are unpleasant in salads, but can be rendered palatable and digestible by blanching in hot water, or very brief cooking, exemplified by stir frying.

Blanching Add a little crushed garlic, chopped onion, salt and pepper, and if handy, a piece of ginger to a saucepan of water. Bring the water to the boil, then reduce it to a simmer. Plunge vegetable leaves into it for no more than a couple of seconds, and roots for a minute or two. Take care not to overdo it. Immediately afterwards, plunge them into cold water, or turn them into a strainer and run cold water through them so that they cool rapidly and retain their flavour. This cold plunging is a good way of treating any vegetables that you are cooking in advance, whether you are going to use them cold or re-heat them, as it conserves their flavour and prevents discolouration.

Stir-frying This is an excellent way of preparing oriental vegetables. Preferably use a wok; alternatively use a deep frying pan. Cut vegetables into 2.5–5cm/1–2in lengths. Heat the wok until it starts to smoke, then put in roughly one tablespoon of mild cooking oil per handful of greens. When the oil is sizzling hot, add the greens, starting with the thickest pieces. Toss them around as they cook. They need to be tender but still crisp; this normally takes only two or three minutes. With more substantial vegetables it may be necessary to add a little water and to cover the pan for another minute or two until they are ready. Stir-frying preserves flavour and most nutrients, and gives vegetables a lovely crisp texture.

Garnishes

Garnishes can be purely decorative or add a new element to a salad dish. There is infinite scope for creativity in these finishing touches, using leaves, flowers, seeds or seed pods from the garden, or spices and other ingredients from the store cupboard. Here are a few suggestions.

Coloured and spicy powders Cayenne and chilli pepper, sumac (a purple-red powder made from sumac seed), ground mustard seeds, cumin and sweet paprika all look good sprinkled on creamy dressings.

Whole seeds Sesame, caraway, pumpkin and sunflowers are just some of the distinctly flavoured seeds available. Crisp them up by toasting them for a minute in the oven, or under a grill lightly sprinkled with oil.

Nuts All sorts of nuts (except salted peanuts) can be used, whole or chopped, preferably lightly toasted.

Hard-boiled egg This looks best chopped rather than cut in rings. You can make patterns by separating the white and yolk, sieving them, and sprinkling them in alternate bands of yellow and white on colourless salads such as celery. Chopped hard-boiled egg goes well with leeks, asparagus, lentils, beetroot, and green and dried bean salads.

Croûtons Bake or fry cubes of bread with a little garlic and olive oil, and scatter them over the top of the salad. Or lightly dress cubes of stale bread with oil and garlic, and put them in the bottom of the salad bowl.

Flowers Flowers make colourful and appealing garnishes. Use individual petals or the whole flower – whichever is most appropriate. Always sprinkle them over the salad at the very last moment. (For the gathering and use of flowers, see p. 85.)

Herbs Herbs are often integral to a salad dish. Besides adding flavour when scattered through a salad, freshly cut herbs make a wonderful garnish, as whole leaves or finely chopped. Below are some ideas on matching herbs and salad plants. For cultivation, see pp. 79–84.

Using herbs

Angelica A delicate, unique flavour is found in the leaves and stems. Use in green salads and as a garnish.

Basil Powerful, distinctive herb, the most widely used varieties having a clove-like flavour. Unsurpassed as an accompaniment to tomatoes, peppers and aubergines and the key ingredient in the Mediterranean sauce 'pesto'. Use small leaves whole and tear, rather than cut, large leaves to preserve their flavour.

Chervil Faint aniseed flavour. The delicate leaves can be used in many salads. With tarragon, chives and parsley, it is one of the ingredients in the famous French *fines herbes* combination.

Green salad with hot bacon dressing. This treatment is ideally suited to sharp-flavoured leaves such as endive, sorrel, spinach and dandelion. (For recipe, see page 157.)

Chives Delicate onion flavour. Chopped chives make a refreshing garnish, suitable for most salads but especially good in potato dishes, as do garlic chives, which have a pronounced garlic flavour.

Coriander A unique, musty, curry-like flavour. Use chopped as liberally as parsley on *mezze* and *hors d'oeuvres*, in yogurt dressings, and with cucumber and courgettes.

Cresses All are peppery and so enliven bland dishes. Watercress combines well with Witloof chicory and oranges.

Dill An unmistakable, indescribable, gently unique flavour. Fresh dill blends well in potato, cucumber, egg, bean and courgette salads; dried dill in sour cream dressings for cucumber and beetroot salads.

Fennel Aniseed flavour. Suitable for tomato, cucumber and salsify salads. It makes a delicate garnish on asparagus.

Horseradish Hot and pungent. A teaspoon of grated root blended with cream or yogurt is superb mixed into root vegetable dishes, cooked or cold. It combines well with chives in mayonnaise made with a light oil.

Hyssop Strong flavour. Use young leaves cautiously with cucumber, onions and pickles.

Lemon balm Delicious, refreshing, slightly sweet lemon scent. Wonderful contrast to bitter-leaved plants such as sorrel, chicory and endive.

Lovage Unique but dominating celery flavour. Use very cautiously in saladini and composé dishes. Rub a wooden salad bowl with a lovage leaf to impregnate it with the flavour.

Marjoram Sweet marjoram is fragrant, blends with most Mediterranean vegetables and enlivens a plain lettuce salad. Pot and winter marjoram are closer to the pungent wild marjoram of the Mediterranean; marjoram is also used with sweet peppers, tomatoes and aubergines.

Mints The stronger mints go well with potato, cucumber, carrots, and bulgur wheat salads. Chop sweeter, more perfumed mints on to green and fruit salads or mix with parsley in mayonnaise.

Parsley Mild but distinctive flavour, widely used in generous quantities in and on many salad dishes. It mitigates the smell of raw onion and garlic.

Sage One of the strongest-flavoured herbs. Use with discretion in fresh salads. It blends well in cooked salad dishes, for example of potatoes or broad beans.

Savory Strongly flavoured. Use like hyssop.

Sweet cicely A sweet aniseed flavour. Use like fennel. Add to water when cooking old carrots, as it rejuvenates them.

Tarragon Its distinctive, fairly strong flavour is best used in cooked dishes and in flavouring vinegar.

Thyme Varieties have many fragrances and strengths. Strip the leaves from the stalks and scatter them on aubergine, tomato, carrot, courgette, lentil and bean salads.

SALAD DRESSINGS

A Wise man should gather the Herbs
An Avaricious man fling in ye salt and vinegar,
A Prodigal the Oyle.

John Evelyn quoted this ancient ditty on salad making approvingly in 1699, and it is equally apt in the twenty-first century. However excellent the salad plants you pick from the garden, a dressing mollifies any plain rawness in the leaves and brings out their natural flavour. In most cases the simplest and lightest dressing is all that is needed. But from time to time a vegetable cries out for more sophisticated treatment. The cry may come from a bulging white globe of fennel, an outstanding crop of tomatoes or some perfectly ripened sweet peppers. Respond in the spirit of adventure. A selection of basic dressings follows on pp. 148–50, with suggested variations, modifications and uses. But there are no rules. Intuition, imagination and experience are the cornerstones of the art of salad dressing.

The principal ingredients in a dressing are oil and vinegar – and it goes without saying they should be of good quality. The satirist Boileau, when attached to Louis XIV's court, described a dinner in which two salads were served – one of yellow purslane, the other of wilted greens. Both, he related, smelt of rancid oil and were swimming in strong vinegar. It can still happen!

The quickest way to make dressings is to put all the elements straight into a jar, close the lid, and shake them as you would a cocktail. Keep several jars handy for the purpose. Oil-based dressings keep for at least a week in an airtight container in a cool place; mayonnaise and dressings made with yogurt or cream will keep for a day or two in a refrigerator.

Oils There are many types of oil. Try to match the oil to the salad by first tasting it on a small piece of bread. This is also a good way to test the flavour of the final dressing.

In the past olive oil was the preferred oil for most salad dressings. To today's palate its distinctive flavour and 'heaviness' often seem too strong, overpowering most salad leaves. So lighter oils are more widely used in salad dressings. If you are an aficionado of the unique olive oil flavour, consider adding just a few drops of the 'real thing' directly to the final vinigrette or directly to the salad. Of the various kinds of olive oil the strongest flavoured are dark, fruity, unrefined oils, labelled 'extra virgin' or 'first cold pressing'. Cheaper refined olive oils, labelled 'pure' or 'fine', can be used where 'lighter' dressings are required.

Walnut oil is a distinct and delightfully flavoured oil that is less dominating than olive oil. It can be used alone in a vinaigrette or blended with olive oil. It is especially good with bitter salad plants. Sunflower, groundnut and soya oil are all light, neutral-flavoured oils, which allow delicate salad flavours to express themselves. They can be blended with olive oil or used alone to produce a much lighter dressing. Sesame oil's strong, distinctive flavour imparts an authentic note to dressings for oriental vegetables.

Vinegars As with oils, there are several types of vinegar, all with rather different flavours. Wine vinegar is a pleasant, relatively gentle vinegar that blends well with any oil in a standard vinaigrette dressing; use it also to make mayonnaise. Cider vinegar is a delicately flavoured vinegar that makes a good light dressing. Sherry vinegar has just the right edge for a vinaigrette for Chinese vegetables, with a few drops of soy sauce added. Balsamic vinegar is a richly flavoured, traditional Italian vinegar, with a superb fruitiness originating in grape must. Use in dressings for leafy salads, and on its own, sparingly, with chicories, root vegetables, cucumber or onions.

You can make subtly flavoured vinegars by steeping herbs, fruit, flowers or shallots in good, light wine vinegar. They are usually ready for use after a few weeks and keep for at least a year. They impart unusual flavours to salad dressings, but must be mixed with a light oil or their flavour will be lost. You can make rose-coloured vinegars with raspberries (just add half a dozen raspberries to a small bottle), and with sprigs of purple basil or red perilla ('shiso'), again, simply put into the pickling jar. Tarragon, rosemary, thyme and green basil are among my favourite herb vinegars. Nasturtium flowers, chive flowers and rose petals all make pleasant attractive vinegars. It is advisable, though not essential, to strain them after about three months, as the ingredients tend to discolour.

Mustards Mustards are a common component of salad dressings. They vary considerably in strength and flavour.

Of the well-known mustards, the mild-flavoured Dijon mustard is the most suitable for standard salad dressings. English mustard has a sharp strong flavour, so it is best restricted to dressings such as rémoulades and ravigotes, used on the more substantial cooked or root vegetables. Meaux mustard (Moutarde de Meaux), an aromatic mustard with partly ground mustard seeds in it, is excellent in potato mayonnaise. You can chop fresh herbs into mustards to add colour and flavour, the flavour varying according to the herbs you use, and use these herb mustards to add an extra quality to a vinaigrette.

SERVING SALADS

The final touch of artistry lies in the choice of dish or bowl in which the salad is served. Mixed leaf salads and colourful vegetables like peppers look marvellous in a glass bowl, but the glass becomes streaky after tossing, so toss the salad in another bowl, then turn it into the glass bowl to serve. Salads are always best tossed in a large bowl, as gently as possible to avoid bruising. Chopsticks are the ideal tool for tossing salads. They are also in my view far more elegant and practical for eating a salad than knives and forks.

When serving salads, use wooden salad bowls only for salads that are tossed in a vinaigrette dressing; never use them for salads dressed with mayonnaise, creamy dressings or dressings made with animal fats, which impart a rancid smell to the wood. Before using a new bowl, season it by rubbing it hard with salt and oil. Wipe wooden bowls clean – never wash them.

While leafy salads are best served in bowls, mixed and composé salads, and salads with heavy dressings, are often better served in platters and shallow dishes, in which the ingredients are clearly visible, giving scope for artistic decoration. Consider also the suitability of dishes for different types of salads. You might feel, for instance, that soft-coloured salads look best in soft-coloured dishes; that blue and white dishes are the perfect foil to brightly coloured salads; that asparagus looks dramatic in tapered dishes – and so on.

salad recipes

This section gives an idea of the diversity of salads that can be made with the plants described in this book. It makes no claim to be comprehensive. Feel free to interpret all the recipes freely. In the art of salad making, perhaps more than in any other aspect of culinary art, it is the spirit, not the letter of the law, that counts. Precise quantities are only given when essential to the balance of the recipe. This is also true of the basic dressings below, which can all be varied according to taste and the salad you use them with.

Salad dressings

VINAIGRETTES AND RELATED DRESSINGS

Basic vinaigrette (French dressing)
For use with green salad, any leafy or crisp raw or cooked salad, thin-leaved kales
1 part wine vinegar or lemon juice, crushed garlic, salt and pepper, 4 parts light oil
Mix the vinegar or lemon juice, garlic and seasoning in a jug or jar. Add the oil slowly, stirring vigorously. A few drops of olive oil can be added to the final vinaigrette for heightened flavour.

Thickened vinaigrette
For use with coarser leaves, cooked root vegetables, oriental greens
ingredients as for a basic vinaigrette, plus mustard and a tablespoon of yogurt or thin cream
Make the dressing as above, adding the mustard after the oil, and stirring it in until the whole mixture is thickened. Add the yogurt or cream to make a richer dressing.

Sauce ravigote
For use with cooked root vegetables
Make a thickened vinaigrette, then add a tablespoon of chopped green herbs (such as chives, tarragon, parsley and chervil), half a teaspoon of chopped onions and a few capers, chopped anchovies and gherkins.

Honey vinaigrette
For use with bitter chicories, sorrel, mustards
yolk of one hard-boiled egg,
1 tablespoon raspberry (or another fruit) vinegar,
3 tablespoons olive oil,
1 teaspoon single cream or yogurt, 1 teaspoon honey
Pound the egg yolk. Add the vinegar. Stirring all the time, add the oil, drop by drop at first, then, once the mixture starts to thicken, in a thin stream. Finally add the cream or yogurt and honey. Note: raw egg yolks may pose a health risk to vulnerable groups such as invalids, the elderly and infants. The yolks of hard-boiled eggs can be used instead.

Eastern dressing
For use with Chinese vegetables, bean sprouts and other sprouted seeds, kales
ingredients for a basic vinaigrette,
1 tablespoon light soy sauce, ½ teaspoon grated ginger, cumin, salt and pepper,
2 tablespoons finely chopped shallots,
1 tablespoon ground sesame seeds,
1 finely chopped garlic clove,
2 tablespoons thinly sliced sweet red peppers (optional), fresh leaf coriander
Make a basic vinaigrette in a small bowl. Gradually beat in the soy sauce, ginger, shallots, sesame seeds, cumin, garlic and seasoning. Sprinkle the dish with sweet peppers, adding the fresh coriander after dressing.

Green vinaigrette
For use with tomato, potato, carrot, pasta salads
Make a thickened vinaigrette, adding chopped basil, mint or thyme and a final sprinkling of olive oil.

Aromatic vinaigrette
For use with any fresh or cooked vegetables
Make a thickened vinaigrette, using an aromatic fruit, herb or balsam vinegar.

MAYONNAISE AND CREAMY DRESSINGS

Basic mayonnaise
For use with cooked vegetables, crudités
2 egg yolks, 1 teaspoon Dijon mustard, salt and pepper, 300ml/½ pint light oil, 1 tablespoon lemon juice or wine vinegar
Put the egg yolks, mustard, salt and pepper into a good-sized bowl, and stir to a smooth paste. Add the oil slowly, drop by drop, whisking as you go, until the mixture thickens. Then add the rest of the oil, stirring continuously. Sprinkle in a few drops of wine vinegar or lemon juice and whisk briskly. Taste and add more seasoning or vinegar if necessary. Should the mixture curdle, break another egg yolk into a clean bowl and beat the curdled mixture into it. Mixtures that have become too thick can be thinned with a few drops of lemon juice.

Mayonnaise is straightforward to make by hand, but can be made in a blender or food processor. The raw egg yolk can be replaced with hard-boiled yolk (see honey vinaigrette). Pound the egg, mix it with mustard, then proceed as above.

Sauce verte (Green mayonnaise)
For use with cooked or raw root vegetables, tomatoes, celeriac

To a basic mayonnaise, add a few finely chopped fresh herbs or a little puréed spinach; alternatively, pound a mixture comprising a few sprigs of chervil, tarragon, watercress and a couple of spinach leaves in a mortar and add it to the mayonnaise.

Rémoulade
For use with celery, celeriac, cardoon, potato and other cooked root vegetables
1 tablespoon prepared mayonnaise,
1 large clove garlic, 2 cooked, chopped shallots,
2–3 anchovy fillets, 1 tablespoon capers,
1 small gherkin, about 6 pitted olives,
parsley and chervil,
1–2 tablespoon tarragon vinegar, salt and pepper
Chop and pound all the solid ingredients. Blend with the mayonnaise and sharpen by adding the tarragon vinegar. Season to taste.

Sauce aïoli (Garlic mayonnaise)
For use with celery, celeriac, cardoon, potato and other cooked root vegetables

To a basic mayonnaise, add several cloves of crushed garlic.

Skordalia
For use with beetroot, potato, aubergine, courgette

This is considered a Greek form of aïoli. Make an aïoli, substituting a well-mashed floury potato for the egg yolk in the mayonnaise to produce a lighter dressing.

In another version, stale white bread, moistened with water and then squeezed, is substituted for the egg. Before making the mayonnaise, pound together the bread and garlic and add ground almonds.

Sauce rouille
For use with cooked salads such as potatoes (still warm), cooked carrots, crudités

To a basic mayonnaise, add crushed garlic and a little chilli powder.

Mousseline
For use with green salads, beetroot, cucumber

Fold one or two whipped egg whites into a basic mayonnaise. This makes a very light dressing that can replace a basic mayonnaise in any recipe.

Spicy mayonnaise
For use with cooked root vegetables, rice-based salads

To a basic mayonnaise, add a few drops of hot West Indian sauce.

Piquant mayonnaise
For use with tomato, beetroot, cooked root vegetables

To a basic mayonnaise, add a little grated horseradish and some paprika. Then fold in an equal quantity of whipped cream.

OTHER DRESSINGS

Plain yogurt dressing
For use with many salads, especially chicory, cucumber, sorrel, dandelion, beet, spinach
300ml/½ pint yogurt, ½ tablespoon light oil,
juice of one lemon, 2 crushed garlic cloves,
small bunch of finely chopped mint, salt and pepper
Mix the yogurt, oil and lemon juice together, then add the garlic, mint and seasoning. Dill or fennel can be substituted for the mint.

Ken Toyé's light yogurt dressing
For use with many salads, especially chicory, cucumber, sorrel, dandelion, beet, spinach
This is one for weight watchers!
300ml/½ pint low-fat yogurt,
½ tablespoon balsamic vinegar, a little mustard,
salt and pepper, tomato purée (optional),
mint (optional)

Stir all the ingredients together. To colour with a hint of red, stir in a smidgen of thinned tomato purée; for green, add very finely chopped mint. Ken adds that serious weight watchers can even make a passable dressing from salted water and ground pepper.

Sour cream dressing (1)
For use with chicory, sorrel, spinach, dandelion, endive

Mix 300ml/½ pint sour cream with one teaspoon each of fresh fennel or dill and chopped mint.

Sour cream dressing (2)
For use with chicory, sorrel, spinach, dandelion, endive
1 tablespoon wine vinegar or lemon juice,
300ml/½ pint sour cream,
½ teaspoon celery seed or finely chopped leaf celery
Add the vinegar or lemon juice to the other ingredients, drop by drop.

Green sour cream dressing
For use with cucumber, beetroot, aubergine
300ml/½ pint sour cream, juice of half a lemon,
4 tablespoon sliced green onions,
purée of parsley, basil or sorrel, salt and pepper
Mix the sour cream with the lemon juice, and add the onions, purée and seasoning.

Sour cream dressing variations
Sour cream can be substituted with light crème fraîche or yogurt. Other possible additions include: hot crispy bacon pieces, thin strips of anchovy, tuna pieces, cooked then sliced mushrooms, roast cumin or coriander seeds, thinly sliced brassica leaves (the hotter flavoured the better), crushed black olives with grated orange zest and garlic, chopped fresh herbs.

Simple Chinese dressing
For use with Chinese vegetables

Mix together 3 parts of sesame oil and 1 part of wine vinegar. Add a dash of light soy sauce, then a crushed garlic clove and a teaspoon of crushed sesame seed.

Chinese sweet and sour dressing

For use with Chinese vegetables

1 tablespoon sugar, juice of one lemon,
salt, a little soy sauce,
1 tablespoon sesame oil (or tahini),
1 tablespoon wine vinegar,
a little sliced fresh ginger root

Make a syrup by warming the sugar in a little water. Add the lemon juice and salt until a sweet/sour balance is obtained. Mix in the soy sauce, sesame oil, wine vinegar, ginger and a pinch of sugar.

Green basil dressing

For use with tomatoes

handful of chopped fresh basil,
2 crushed garlic cloves, 2 tablespoons lemon juice,
6 tablespoons olive oil

Pound the basil in a mortar with the garlic and lemon juice. Add the oil slowly, as for basic mayonnaise, until it reaches a good pouring consistency.

Hot bacon dressing

For use with dandelion, spinach, endive, sorrel, chicory, lettuce
See Green Salad with Hot Dressing, p. 157.

Irish salad dressing

For use with grated vegetables, tomato, cucumber

yolk of one hard-boiled egg,
300ml/½ pint light oil or single cream,
a little vinegar to taste, salt and pepper,
pinch of mustard

Pound the egg yolk and mix in the oil or cream with the vinegar. Add seasoning and mustard.

Tomato and mozzarella cheese with green basil dressing. (For recipe, see page 158.)

Raw salads

SIMPLE SALADS

Korean bean sprout salad with Chinese dressing

Put some mung bean sprouts in a large salad bowl, pour in a Chinese dressing and toss the sprouts until they are evenly covered. Chill thoroughly before serving. Suitable for all sprouted seeds.

Cabbage coleslaw

Finely shred white cabbage and dress with mayonnaise. Add strips of finely sliced red pepper to garnish. Mix in a little sour cream (optional).

Carrot

Finely grated carrots are excellent dressed with a vinaigrette flavoured with chopped chervil, chives, parsley or fennel and salt.

Raw cauliflower

Grate a very fresh, small, raw cauliflower. Finely chop a few carrots, a small bunch of parsley, a bunch of spring onions and a bunch of chives; slice a few radishes into thin circles. Mix together with a bunch of watercress and toss well with vinaigrette. Scatter with fresh chervil before serving.

Cauliflower and hyssop

Mix a fresh cauliflower broken into florets with one tablespoon each of finely chopped hyssop, parsley, apple and chopped carrot. Toss well with a simple yogurt dressing.

Celeriac rémoulade

Peel a large celeriac, cut it into large pieces and blanch in boiling water with vinegar or lemon juice added. Drain and shred the celeriac, dress with a rémoulade and garnish with chopped capers and gherkins. Suitable also for salsify, scorzonera, kohl rabi, cardoon and any other cooked vegetables including potatoes.

Chinese cabbage coleslaw

This makes an excellent accompaniment to duck or pork. Finely shred a medium-sized cabbage, and add a small amount of thinly sliced fresh ginger root, a crushed garlic clove and a tablespoon of soy or Tamari sauce. Toss with a vinaigrette made with sesame oil and wine vinegar. Suitable also for any oriental brassicas, spinach or chard.

Sugar Loaf chicory seedlings

A refreshing early spring salad of chicory seedlings. Garnish the seedlings with a small quantity of finely chopped or sieved hard-boiled egg. Eat plain or with a light vinaigrette dressing.

Red and Sugar Loaf chicory

Tear the larger leaves of red and mature Sugar Loaf chicory into manageable pieces; keep the smaller central leaves whole. Dress with a well-flavoured vinaigrette with a tablespoon of yogurt or thin cream beaten in. Suitable also for lettuce hearts and endive.

Witloof chicory and oranges

This delicious salad hardly needs a dressing – just a sprinkling of light vinaigrette. Arrange the spears of a couple of crisp Witloof chicons like flower petals on a round plate. Slice a mild Spanish onion and two peeled, seedless oranges as thinly as possible and arrange in the centre, with some whole black olives. Garnish with chopped coriander. Suitable also for Sugar Loaf chicory and curly-leaved endive.

Witloof chicory with piquant mayonnaise

Finely slice Witloof chicons, and dress them with horseradish-flavoured mayonnaise. Garnish with chopped parsley, chervil or winter savory.

Celery and fennel

Although celery is generally best as a crudité or served with cheese, it is also good in salads. Finely slice a few celery stalks and a large bulb of fennel and

mix together. Dress them with a vinaigrette with a few tablespoons of blue cheese blended into it.

Corn salad in Salade Lorette

Mix several heads of corn salad with about the same amount each of thinly sliced celery and sliced or chopped boiled beetroot. Dress with vinaigrette. Celeriac could be substituted for the celery.

Courgettes and red lettuce

Thinly slice a few young courgettes, including some with yellow and striped skins if available, and arrange them on a bed of red lettuce. Dress with a light vinaigrette and garnish with chopped red pepper, onion, broad-leaved parsley and a few black olives.

Cucumber salad

Choose a medium-sized cucumber. Peel it if you dislike the skin, although the peel adds flavour. Slice the cucumber fairly thinly, but not too thinly. Arrange on a flat dish, sprinkle with fine salt and leave for an hour. Then drain and rinse with cold water, drain again and pat dry on paper towelling. Arrange on a shallow dish and pour over a yogurt dressing flavoured with chopped mint and garlic, or a sour cream and dill dressing. Chill well before serving.

Cucumber and nasturtium leaves

Mix peeled, sliced cucumber with plenty of small, variegated and red nasturtium leaves. Dress with a thick, mustard-flavoured vinaigrette and garnish with a few nasturtium flowers and buds.

Dandelion

Tear the green leaves of dandelions into small pieces and mix with equal quantities of blanched dandelion, endive or Witloof chicory. Rub the salad bowl with garlic before adding the mixed leaves and toss with a vinaigrette. Garnish with olives. Suitable also for sorrel, salad rocket, young spinach and all types of chicory.

Endive, watercress and oranges

Remove the leaves from a curly-leaved endive and a bunch of fresh watercress, and crisp them in the refrigerator for several hours. Make a vinaigrette with light or walnut oil, mustard, garlic, lemon juice and the zest of a large seedless orange. Remove the orange pith and slice the flesh thinly, or divide the orange into segments and add to the watercress and endive. Toss the ingredients well in the dressing before serving.

Endive and flower salad

Wash and dry a curly-leaved endive. Cut into very thin strips. Add a tablespoon each of finely chopped celery leaves and parsley, and some olives. Toss in a plain vinaigrette. Finally add violet and/or pansy petals and mix gently into the salad before serving.

Fennel, avocado and pink grapefruit

Slice a large bulb of fennel thinly; cut a couple of ripe, but not too soft, avocados into strips (acidulate with lemon to prevent discolouration). Remove the pith from two grapefruits and divide them into segments. Arrange the ingredients in circles on a shallow dish, and garnish with watercress and fennel fronds, if available. Sprinkle with a raspberry-flavoured vinaigrette made with walnut oil. Chill before serving.

Glasswort (Marsh samphire)

Freshly picked, clean young glasswort can be eaten raw. If it is muddy, wash it thoroughly. Otherwise blanch it in hot water for a minute or steam it lightly, then drain it, arrange it on a plate and dress with a vinaigrette made with light oil and lemon juice. Optional garnishes are sieved hard-boiled egg and bronze fennel. Serve with slices of lemon. Enjoy eating it with your fingers, slurping the leaves off the stems, which come away surprisingly easily. This may be a case where finger bowls are needed.

Iceplant with raspberry vinegar

Arrange iceplant in a dish and toss with a vinaigrette made with raspberry vinegar and walnut oil.

Kales with Glorious Garnish dressing

Use young leaves of tender kales raw; otherwise steam or stir fry them first. Dress with 5:1 mixture of vegetable oil and light soy sauce, to which plenty of crushed garlic has been added. Oriental mustards can be treated the same way. The dressing can be made up in advance, and will keep well in a screwtop jar in a refrigerator.

Land cress

To a bunch of land cress add some sliced radishes and a few chopped stalks of celery. Arrange the cress in a dish, with the radishes and celery mixed together in the centre. Pour over a vinaigrette to which plenty of ground black pepper and a teaspoon of soy sauce have been added.

Lettuce and borage flowers

Tear the leaves of a large, fresh red or bronze lettuce and a green lettuce heart, toss in a walnut oil vinaigrette and garnish with variegated mint, lemon balm and borage flowers. (Illustrated on p. 139.)

Oriental greens

This is a very flexible recipe as far as ingredients are concerned. Use any sharp-flavoured leaves, such as oriental mustards, torn or shredded into small pieces, with leafy pak choi, chrysanthemum greens and mitsuba stems. Incorporate a few mild-flavoured leaves such as summer and winter purslane for a contrast. Mix them together and toss in a large bowl with a thick vinaigrette, which will cling to the glossy leaves. Garnish with chopped fresh herbs or the flowers of Chinese chives.

Sweet pepper salad

Arrange rings of different-coloured mature sweet peppers on a bed of crisp lettuce leaves. Garnish with olives, coriander leaves and quarters of tomato. Pour over a vinaigrette made with good olive oil and plenty of garlic. (Illustrated on p. 153.)

Purslane and flowers

Arrange young purslane leaves in a flattish bowl and sprinkle with chicory, nasturtium and bergamot

flowers and a few rose petals. Then add chives, marjoram, and green and purple basil, and decorate with a few sprigs of red currants. Finally splash with a light vinaigrette made with walnut oil. The succulent yellow-green purslane leaves make a perfect foil for flowers.

Radish

Summer radishes are best eaten whole as crudités. Winter radishes can be grated and mixed with a mayonnaise dressing. Alternatively, lightly stir-fry them and incorporate them into any recipe for Chinese vegetables.

Salad rocket, purslane and broad beans

Mix a few handfuls of rocket leaves with a handful of purslane leaves and a small quantity of very small blanched broad beans. Dress with a basic vinaigrette. Garnish with a little sieved or chopped hard-boiled egg or chive flowers.

Sorrel, dandelion and red lettuce

Toss torn leaves of more or less equal quantities of sorrel, dandelion and lettuce in a garlic-flavoured vinaigrette. Garnish with a few olives and some toasted sesame seeds.

Raw spinach

Use tender young spinach leaves. As they tend to be gritty, wash them several times, then shake dry. Make a thickened vinaigrette, well flavoured with garlic and mustard, and pour over the leaves. Garnish with quartered, hard-boiled eggs and sliced onion. Suitable for all types of spinach, sorrel and amaranthus, or for lettuce and spinach mixed in equal quantities.

Tomatoes with pesto dressing

This is one of the simplest but very best ways of serving tomatoes. Make a basic pesto by pounding together basil leaves, garlic cloves, pine nut kernels and Parmesan cheese with salt and ground pepper, then slowly beating in olive oil. Cut well-flavoured tomatoes into fairly thick slices and cover with the dressing. The tomatoes can also be dressed simply with olive oil flavoured with salt, pepper and fresh marjoram or coriander.

Hungarian tomato salad

Use small sweet tomatoes. Skin them (having dropped them into boiling water for a minute to loosen the skins) and chill. Place the tomatoes whole on lettuce leaves and cover with a piquant mayonnaise. Garnish with paprika and chives.

Portuguese tomato salad

450g/1lb tomatoes, 1 large onion,
a bunch of chopped coriander,
2 large garlic cloves, crushed,
basic vinaigrette

Slice the tomatoes thickly and the onion finely and put in a bowl with the coriander and garlic. Pour over the basic vinaigrette, and mix well. Any tomatoes can be dressed in this simple way, but the recipe really calls for meaty beefsteak or Marmande types, ideally mixing yellow- and red-fleshed varieties.

Watercress with sour cream dressing

Watercress (and land cress) has such a sharp peppery taste that it normally requires little dressing. It is, however, good with a sour cream dressing, especially if combined with winter purslane. Crisp the cress in the refrigerator beforehand.

Sweet pepper salad garnished with olives, quartered tomatoes and coriander. (For recipe, see page 152.)

MIXED SALADS

Mixed cabbage

equal quantities of red cabbage, Chinese cabbage, kohl rabi, and fennel, thickened vinaigrette, finely chopped spring onions, red peppers and toasted sesame seeds to garnish

Shred the red and Chinese cabbage finely, and cut the kohlrabi and fennel into julienne strips. Keep the red cabbage separate, but mix the other ingredients together. Toss both sets in a full-flavoured vinaigrette. Put the green vegetables in the centre of a plate and frame with the red cabbage. Garnish with finely chopped spring onions, red peppers and toasted sesame seeds. (Illustrated below.)

Baby raw vegetables

equal quantities of baby carrots, turnips, beetroot, kohl rabi and radishes, green vinaigrette, handful of crisp lettuce leaves

Shred the vegetables, leaving the beets to last to avoid staining. Toss each vegetable separately in a green vinaigrette. Line a shallow bowl with lettuce, and place separate piles of vegetables on top.

Marie Stone's mixed vegetable salad

equal quantities of carrots, turnips, celeriac, Jerusalem artichokes, kohl rabi, beetroot, red and white cabbage hearts, radishes, seakale, thickened vinaigrette or sour cream dressing

Cut the vegetables small, blanch them and dress with any of the suggested dressings.

Onion, carrot, Hamburg parsley and mint

1 small onion, sliced or grated, 25g/1oz fresh mint leaves, 2 heaped tablespoons grated carrot, 2 heaped tablespoons grated Hamburg parsley, a little lemon juice, salt and pepper

Pound the onion finely with the mint. Add grated carrot and Hamburg parsley. Mix well, and add the lemon juice, salt and pepper.

BELOW Mixed Chinese and red cabbage salad. (For recipe, see this page.)

BELOW RIGHT Aubergine and yogurt salad on a bed of red oak-leaved lettuce. (For recipe, see page 155.)

Cooked salads

Asparagus salad

Tie young, well-trimmed and scrubbed asparagus into bundles of about ten spears. Preferably steam, otherwise cook in boiling salted water, until tender. Dress with a lightly flavoured mayonnaise or a basic vinaigrette.

Aubergine and yogurt salad

Peel an aubergine, slice it thinly and sprinkle it with salt. Leave for up to an hour, then wash off the salt and squeeze out any excess moisture. (This enables the aubergine to be fried in less oil.) Drain and pat dry on paper towelling. Fry in oil until crisp. Place on a flattish dish and pour over a dressing made with yogurt, lemon juice, a little olive oil, a pinch of fenugreek leaves and a large clove of garlic. Sprinkle with sumac or paprika. (Illustrated below.)

Green French bean, pea pods and pea salad

Cook equal quantities of whole sugar pea pods, shelled green peas, shredded green beans and diced carrots until just tender. Line a bowl with chilled red lettuce leaves and arrange the vegetables on top. Make a sour cream or yogurt dressing flavoured with mint and garlic. Mix well and pour over the salad. Garnish with a few finely chopped dill or fennel leaves.

Italian French bean salad

Cook green French beans until just tender, drain, season, and mix with a vinaigrette and finely chopped onion or shallot. Leave to cool. Serve piled on lettuce leaves, garnished with chopped hard-boiled egg, Parmesan cheese and chive flowers. Add chopped fresh coriander, parsley, basil, thyme, marjoram or black olives to taste.

Dried and fresh bean salad

Use any attractive flageolet and dried beans, such as pinto, Dutch brown or blackeye. Soak them overnight in separate containers, and cook separately until soft but not mushy. Drain and mix with an equal quantity

of lightly cooked fresh green beans (broad, runner and French). Dress while still warm with a vinaigrette flavoured with garlic. (Illustrated right.)

Turkish beetroot salad with yogurt

4 medium-sized beetroots, salt and pepper,
300ml/½ pint yogurt, garlic, crushed,
caraway seeds, paprika to garnish

Preferably bake the beetroots in foil until tender; or boil them. Allow them to cool and rub off the skins carefully. Slice or dice them, season with salt and pepper and arrange in a dish. Beat the yogurt with crushed garlic, a little salt and a few caraway seeds and pour over the beetroot. Garnish with paprika.

Ken Toyé's sweet and sour cabbage en salade

1 large finely chopped onion,
2 tablespoons light oil, 2–3 cloves chopped garlic,
1lb/500g firm cabbage, chopped (red, green or white, or a mixture of types),
2 tablespoons white wine or cider vinegar,
½ teaspoon sugar, 2 tablespoons water,
½ teaspoon salt, ground pepper

Soften the onion in light oil in a heavy saucepan. Add the garlic and chopped cabbage. Stir well until the cabbage has absorbed the oil and garlic. Add the wine vinegar and sugar, and salt and pepper to taste. Simmer gently, adding the water if it is becoming dry. When it is cooked *al dente*, check the sweet/sour balance, adding more vinegar or sugar as necessary. Turn it into a dish and dress with a thickened vinaigrette. Serve warm.

Cardoon

Cut blanched stems (blanched by excluding light when growing) into 8cm/3in lengths, tied in bundles like asparagus, and steam until tender. Cool, and serve with a piquant rémoulade sauce or a thickened vinaigrette made with plenty of mustard.

Chard with sour cream dressing

Wash chard leaves and stems well, drain and cut roughly into fairly thick slices, using the white part as well as the green. Steam for a few minutes until tender. Drain very well, put in a shallow dish and

season well. Mix with a sour cream dressing and garnish with a pinch of cayenne, chopped chives and dill seed. Suitable also for any of the spinaches.

Chinese artichokes

Scrub the tubers (which are normally small). Cook them in boiling salted water for a few minutes or fry them lightly, or steam them until just soft. Cool and serve with a well-flavoured vinaigrette or light creamy dressing, and garnish with chopped green herbs.

Globe artichoke salad

Before cooking artichokes, clean them by soaking them upside down in cold salted water for an hour or so. Remember that in young plants the top of the stem is also tender and delicious. Cut back the points of very tight heads to make them open up and cook faster. Rub any cut surface with lemon to prevent discolouration. Steam or boil for about twenty minutes, until tender. Drain and cool. The simplest and best way to eat artichokes is slowly, dipped into melted butter or a vinaigrette. Starting at the bottom,

Dried and fresh bean salad. The lightly cooked fresh broad and runner beans are mixed with a range of cooked dried beans. (For recipe, see page 155.)

pull off the leafy bracts one by one, dip the base into the dressing and suck it clean. Discard the fibrous 'choke' and keep the succulent, exquisite fleshy base to the last.

Jerusalem artichokes

Scrub a few artichokes very well. Boil them in salted water until just tender. Drain and peel them while still very hot or, if preferred, leave them unpeeled. Slice them evenly and dress them while still warm with a sauce ravigote or a vinaigrette to which a little tomato purée has been added.

Spring and Welsh onion vinaigrette

Wash and trim a bunch of spring onions, tie them into a bundle and cook in boiling salted water until just tender. Chop a bunch of Welsh onions and steam until just tender. Dress both when nearly cool with a vinaigrette well flavoured with herbs. Serve on a flat dish and garnish with chopped chervil and tarragon.

Parsnip salad

Peel three or four parsnips and steam them until just tender. Remove the core and slice the parsnips into thinnish rings. Lay in rows on a flat plate and, while still warm, dress with a vinaigrette made with light oil and lemon juice. Garnish with parsley, decorate with capers and peppercorns, and serve after an hour or so, when the flavours have had a chance to mingle. Suitable also for most cooked root vegetables such as celeriac, salsify, scorzonera, Hamburg parsley and Jerusalem artichokes.

Potato salads

All potato salads are best made with small, waxy potatoes. They should always be cooked with the skins on and peeled while still warm. Potatoes can be dressed according to taste, but vinaigrette dressings are best added while the potatoes are still hot. Cube or slice the potatoes evenly, and turn gently in the dressing. 'Extras' such as olives, chopped spring onions, crushed garlic or herbs may be added later when the salad is at room temperature. Potato salads do not chill well; nor do they keep well in a refrigerator. If you prefer a mayonnaise or sour cream dressing, add a little vinaigrette to the potatoes when hot, then add the dressing later. Chopped hard-boiled egg may be added to a potato salad along with the mayonnaise or sour cream dressing. A good sauce ravigote or anchovy-flavoured mayonnaise is excellent with potato salad. Potato salads make a suitable accompaniment to a main dish, particularly when served with a green salad. Chive flowers are my favourite garnish.

Potato and dandelion

Thinly slice some cooked potatoes while still hot, and season. Add some chopped shallots and torn dandelion leaves. While still hot, dress generously with a thickened vinaigrette. Garnish with chopped chives and dill. Delicious hot or cold.

Potato salade cressonière

Prepare the potatoes as above, and mix with watercress leaves, chopped parsley and chervil and hard-boiled egg. Dress with a vinaigrette.

Warm potato salad with horseradish

6 good-sized cooked waxy yellow potatoes,
2 bunches spring onions, finely chopped,
425ml/¾ pint mayonnaise,
2 tablespoons Dijon mustard,
1 tablespoon grated horseradish,
cooked bacon, finely chopped (optional),
salt, pepper and paprika to taste

Cube the potatoes while still hot. Mix with the chopped spring onions – both green and white parts – and seasoning. In a pan stir together the mayonnaise, mustard and horseradish, and heat for two or three minutes. Pour the sauce over the potatoes. Mix the bacon in well with the other ingredients. Season with salt and pepper and sprinkle with paprika before serving warm.

Summer Tourangelle

225g/½lb French beans,
350g/¾lb cooked new potatoes,
60g/2oz blanched carrots,
60g/2oz grated kohl rabi,
600ml/1pt garlic mayonnaise,
black olives to garnish

Steam the beans, cut diagonally into 2.5cm/1in pieces, until tender; cook the potatoes. Drain and refresh with cold water. Slice the potatoes and carrots. Mix the ingredients together with the kohl rabi and dress with a little of the mayonnaise, thinned with warm water. Arrange in a salad bowl, decorate with olives, and serve with a bowl of garlic mayonnaise.

Winter Tourangelle

Make as above, using celery, blanched celeriac, or blanched winter radish instead of beans.

Marinated sweet peppers

a mixture of differently coloured sweet peppers,
salt and pepper, fresh coriander, cumin and paprika
to taste, good-quality oil, 3 crushed garlic cloves

Put the peppers under the grill at mid-heat. Keep turning until the skin is black and blistered, and the insides are well cooked. Remove from the grill and wrap in kitchen paper for ten minutes. The skins will then come off very easily. Cut in half, remove seeds and chop into thin strips. Add salt and pepper, a little coriander, cumin and paprika.

Mix the olive oil with the garlic and pour it over the peppers. Leave them to marinate overnight. Serve garnished with chopped parsley and lemon wedges.

SALADS WITH HOT DRESSINGS

Bagna cauda

This traditional Piedmontese dressing – literally 'hot bath' – is a rough-and-ready hot sauce into which vegetables are dipped. Widely used for cardoons, it is also excellent for celery, endive, sweet peppers with skins removed after charring, globe artichoke hearts, Witloof and red chicory and any bitter leaves. Alternatively leaves can be finely shredded, and the bagna cauda poured over them. (White truffles are used in the authentic Piedmontese *bagna cauda*.)

5 tablespoons butter or 5 tablespoons olive oil,
3 cloves garlic, crushed, 4 anchovy fillets, mashed,
225g/½lb mushrooms, chopped

Put the butter and oil into a heavy pan with the garlic and anchovies. Cook gently over moderate heat until garlic turns yellow. Add the mushrooms and simmer until just tender.

Green salad with hot dressing

equal quantities of red lettuce, spinach, sorrel,
endive, dandelion and very young beet tops,
a few pieces of crispy bacon, wine or cider vinegar,
a few pumpkin seeds, croûtons

Choose leaves as small as possible, or tear them if large, and place them in a glass bowl. To make the dressing, cube streaky bacon and cook in a pan until the fat runs; remove the crispy bits and add them to the salad. Add a little vinegar and pumpkin seeds to the fat in the pan, and cook for two minutes. Then pour over the salad. Decorate with croûtons. Serve immediately. (Suitable also for any bitter leaves such as chicory. The vegetables can be on their own or mixed.) (Illustrated on p. 145.)

Composé salads

Broad beans, peas and pasta salad
450g/Ilb fresh green, white and pink tagliatelle –
equal quantities of each colour,
equal quantities of broad beans, sugar peas and
green peas, olive oil, garlic mayonnaise,
fresh basil, fennel and tarragon, chopped
Cook the pasta *al dente*. Blanch the broad beans, sugar peas and green peas. When the pasta is cooked, season and moisten with oil, then add the garlic mayonnaise, mix well and arrange on a platter. Scatter the vegetables on top. Sprinkle with a few drops of olive oil and garnish with the chopped herbs. (Illustrated on p. 142.)

Beetroot and buckwheat salad
Bake in foil or boil a round red or 'Chioggia' beetroot and a yellow beetroot until tender. Cook some roasted buckwheat in water for about ten minutes. Drain. Steam fresh chopped beet stalks until tender. Stir-fry torn beet tops with spring onions, ginger, garlic and chives for two minutes; then add a little light soy sauce. Arrange the stalks on top of the buckwheat. Cube the beets or cut into thin circles. Dress with a garlic vinaigrette and arrange on the top of the salad. The dish may be decorated with chopped coriander or parsley. (Illustrated right.)

Sweet peppers in Salade Marocaine
I large onion, 900g/2lb red and green peppers, oil,
a little tomato purée, 900g/2lb tomatoes, skinned,
crushed garlic to taste,
pinches of paprika, chilli powder, cumin, salt and
pepper, lemon juice,
fresh coriander and parsley, chopped, mixed olives,
lemon wedges or Moroccan preserved lemon
Chop the onion and thinly slice the peppers. Fry them in the oil until just soft, then add the tomato purée, skinned tomatoes, crushed garlic, and paprika, chilli powder, cumin, salt and pepper. Cook for about ten minutes. Cool, then add the lemon juice. When ready to serve, cover with the coriander, parsley, olives and lemon pieces.

Salade Niçoise
450g/½lb green beans, lightly cooked,
450g/½lb cooked and sliced new potatoes,
small handful cooked dried beans,
4 tomatoes, quartered, some black olives,
a few hard-boiled eggs, quartered,
I small can tuna fish, drained, a few anchovy fillets,
basic vinaigrette made with full-flavoured olive oil
and plenty of garlic, a few crisp lettuce hearts
Put the vegetables in a bowl, and arrange the olives, egg, tuna fish and anchovies on top. Add the vinaigrette, then the lettuce hearts for decoration.

Pain bagna
This is the classic Provençale sandwich. Prepare it a couple of hours in advance, so that the juices have time to sink into the bread. Slice a large flat soft roll or pitta bread in half, and sprinkle the bottom half with olive oil and crushed garlic. Cover it with thinly sliced tomatoes, chopped onion, pitted black olives and strips of anchovy. Sprinkle with fresh chopped herbs such as basil or oregano. Before replacing the top half, sprinkle with a vinaigrette dressing.

Tomato and mozzarella cheese
Slice beefsteak tomatoes with an equal quantity of sliced mozzarella cheese. Arrange in alternate layers and pour over a green basil dressing. Garnish with fresh basil leaves. (Illustrated on p. 150.)

Greek salad
I crisp lettuce, small bunch of broad-leaved parsley,
handful of corn salad, 3 quartered tomatoes,
half a sweet pepper, 2 small onions, fresh basil,
225g/½lb feta cheese, crumbled, a few black olives,
garlic-flavoured vinaigrette, fresh chopped herbs
Tear the lettuce and parsley. Thinly slice the pepper and onions. Add the rest of the ingredients, toss in the vinaigrette. Garnish with the chopped herbs.

Beetroot and buckwheat salad. (For recipe, see left.)

Cut-and-come-again seedling chart

Use this chart to plan for a continuous supply of young salad leaves, and to plan intercropping. For cut-and-come-again seedling crops, see p. 127.

	GERM'N TIME	NO. OF CUTS	LASTS (MONTHS)	WHEN TO SOW
Amaranthus spp. Leaf amaranth	√	2	2–3	W
Atriplex hortensis Orache	√√	3	3	*
Beta vulgaris Cicla Gp Perpetual spinach	√√	3+	6+	*
Brassica carinata Texel greens	√√	2	2–3	C
B. juncea Red mustard	√	2	2–3	*
B. napus Salad rape	√	3–4	3–4	*
B. oleracea Acephala Gp Curly kale	√√	2–3	6–8+	C
B. oleracea Acephala Gp Fine-leaved kale §	√–√√	3–4	6–8+	*
B. rapa Chinensis Gp Pak choi	√	2–3	2–4	C
—Rosette pak choi	√	2	2–4	C
—*v. nipposinica* Mibuna greens	√√	2	3+	C
—Mizuna greens	√√	3–4	4+	C
var. *perviridis* Komatsuna	√–√√	3-4	4+	*
Cichorium endivia Curled endive	√√	2–3	3–4	*
C. intybus Sugar Loaf chicory	√√	2–3	3–4	*
Eruca sativa Salad rocket	√	3–5	2–3	C
Lactuca sativa Salad Bowl and cutting lettuce	√√	2–3	3–4	*
Lepidium sativum Garden cress	√	2–5	1–2	C
Medicago sativa Alfalfa (lucerne)	√	2–4	12+ §§	*
Montia perfoliata Winter purslane	√–√√	2–3	2–3	C
Plantago coronopus Buck's horn plantain	√	2	6–8	*
Portulaca oleracea Summer purslane	√√	2–3	2	W
Raphanus sativus Leaf and seedling radish	√	2	1–2	*
Spinacia oleracea Spinach	√√	3–4	2–5	*
Valerianella locusta Corn salad	√	2–3	3+	C
Oriental saladini mix §§§	√	3–4	2–5	C
Saladini/mesclun mix §§§	√√	2–3	3–4	*

KEY

Germination time

√ = less than a week; √√ = 2–3 weeks; √√√ = 3 weeks
This is the average time (under favourable conditions) before the seedling appears above ground. Most are then large enough to eat within 2–3 weeks

Number of cuts

The average number of cuts from one sowing. This will vary according to the season. Most cut-and-come-again crops run to seed rapidly in hot weather, and grow more slowly in cold weather, limiting the number of cuts

Lasts

The average period in months during which the crop can provide tender leaves

When to sow

* = can be sown throughout the growing season
C = best sown in cool conditions
W = requires warm conditions

NOTES
§ e.g. 'Pentland Brig', 'Hungry Gap', 'Red Russian'
§§ Alfalfa is perennial, but leaves become coarse unless plants are cut back regularly
§§§ Performance will depend on the actual seed mixture

Other seedling crops

Brassica campestris Rapifera Gp Turnip *see Brassica napus* Salad rape
Brassica oleracea Acephala Gp Tuscan kale *see* Fine-leaved kale, though it can be cut as cut-and-come-again leaves for 7–8 months
Brassica rapa Pekinensis Gp Loose-headed Chinese cabbage *see Brassica rapa* Chinensis Gp Pak choi
Chenopodium giganteum 'Magentaspreen' Tree Spinach *see Atriplex hortensis* Orache

Some seeds suitable for sprouting

The seeds in this chart are a sample of the many that can be sprouted. None included normally requires rinsing more than twice a day. All can be eaten raw, though legumes should not be eaten raw in large quantities. Sprouting times vary with temperature: those given are for the sprouts reaching an edible size; some can be left longer and eaten at a more advanced or seedling stage.

COMMON NAME	LATIN NAME	AVERAGE NO. OF DAYS TO SPROUT	LENGTH OF SPROUT WHEN EDIBLE
Beans			
Azuki	*Phaseolus angularis*	4–5	12–25mm/½–1in
Lima	*Phaseolus lunatus*	3–5	12–38mm/½–1½in
Mung	*Phaseolus aureus*	3–5	12–75mm/½–3in
Other legumes			
Alfalfa (lucerne)	*Medicago sativa*	1–4	very tiny and 2.5–5cm/1–2in
Clover, crimson	*Trifolium incarnatum*	2–5	very tiny and 2.5–5cm/1–2in
Fenugreek	*Trigonella foenum-graecum*	3–5	12–50mm/½–2in
Lentil	*Lens esculenta*	2–4	6–20mm/¼–¾in
Peas	*Pisum sativum*	6–8	37–75mm/1½–3in
Brassicas			
Kale †	*Brassica oleracea*	3–5	12–25mm/½–1in
Radish	*Raphanus sativus*	2–4	12–25mm/½–1in
Grains			
Barley	*Hordeum vulgare*	3–5	very tiny
Rye	*Secale cereale*	3–5	very tiny or 25–37mm/1–1½in
Wheat	*Triticum vulgare*	3–4	very tiny
Buckwheat	*Fagopyrum esculentum*	2–4	20–25mm/¼–1in
Sunflower	*Helianthus annuus*	1–3	12–38mm/½–1½in
Sweet corn	*Zea mays*	2–3	6–12mm/¼–½in

† Many brassicas sprout similarly, e.g. broccoli, Brussels sprouts, cabbage, cauliflower, mustard

Note on climate and seasons

Climate In very broad terms, climatic zones are divided into tropical, semi-tropical and temperate – which includes the British Isles, and much of Europe and the USA. The planning charts and other data in *The Organic Salad Garden* are based on my experience in East Anglia, in the British Isles, a 'cool' temperate climate, as opposed to the milder, Mediterranean climate. I have used the term 'temperate' to equate with the conditions here as outlined below (roughly US Zone 8), and 'warm climate' for regions with longer, hotter summers, where tender vegetables are easily grown outdoors.

Here at Montrose Farm the average annual minimum winter temperature is about –7°C/20°F, and this is rarely maintained for more than a few days. In practice crops like spring cabbage, spinach, Brussels sprouts, kale and corn salad overwinter successfully outside. We expect our first frosts in early October, and can get frost as late as the first week in June. So I rarely plant tender crops outside until late spring/early summer. Average mean temperature in the hottest month (usually July) is about 15.6°C/60°F. Success with the more tender summer vegetables like tomatoes in the open is never guaranteed – hence my extensive use of unheated polytunnels. I hope gardeners in warmer and cooler climates can extrapolate from this.

Seasons To enable the book to be interpreted elsewhere, I have throughout used 'seasons' instead of calendar months. The chart below indicates the equivalent month in each hemisphere. Consider seasons a rough guide to the timing of garden operations. In practice the dividing line between seasons is blurred; weather patterns vary not just from one year to the next, but within climatic zones, and even within each locality.

Daylength In some plants development is governed by the hours of daylight. 'Long-day' plants flower after the longest day in mid-summer; 'short-day' plants flower before the longest day. Daylength-sensitive edible plants, such as onions and oriental brassicas, must be grown in the appropriate period to avoid the stimulus of flowering.

Hardiness Term used in temperate zones for a plant's ability to survive winter outdoors without protection. Broadly, 'moderately hardy' plants survive at least –5°C/23°F; fully hardy plants to –15C/5°F. Half-hardy (tender) plants do not survive frost (temperatures of 0°C/32°F) in the open.

SEASON	NORTHERN HEMISPHERE	SOUTHERN HEMISPHERE	SEASON	NORTHERN HEMISPHERE	SOUTHERN HEMISPHERE
Mid-winter	January	July	Mid-summer	July	January
Late winter	February	August	Late summer	August	February
Early spring	March	September	Early autumn	September	March
Mid-spring	April	October	Mid-autumn	October	April
Late spring	May	November	Late autumn	November	May
Early summer	June	December	Early winter	December	June

Year-round saladini chart

The salad lover wants not just fresh salad all year round, but a variety of salad plants, epitomized by the mixtures we call 'saladini' (see p. 140). A well-balanced 'saladini' has four main elements. The backbone is bulky, mild-flavoured leaves, but variety is created with smaller numbers of sharp or distinctly flavoured leaves, some crisp or textured elements, and lastly colourful and decorative elements, including edible flowers.

The chart opposite divides some of the most popular plants for saladini into these four categories, indicating the main season in which they are harvested fresh. So a glance down each column indicates the range available for a saladini at any time of year. A few plants fall into several categories. These, along with a few others there was not space to include fully, are indicated at the side. Herbs, sprouted seeds and most root vegetables have been omitted.

Use the chart to plan your own salad garden, so that you will have a supply of varied salad ingredients all year round. The chart is largely based on records kept in my own garden in the British Isles (see climate note left). If you are gardening in a warmer climate, the season for tender vegetables such as tomatoes and cucumbers will be longer, and of course the reverse will apply in cooler climates. To be sure of quality salads all year round, especially in the leaner winter months, I make extensive use of protection or cover. In my case this is unheated polytunnels; it could equally be cloches, frames or protective fleeces. The chart shows how the season can be extended with the use of protection.

In some cases successive sowings must be made to maintain a supply during the potential harvesting period. To help in planning, the first column indicates the average number of weeks from sowing to maturity – though it must be stressed that this will vary widely, depending on local climate, the season, methods used and varieties grown. For cultivation details, see Salad Plants, pp. 12–90. Plants are listed in the order in which they appear in the text.

Where do I start? – a note for novice gardeners

If you are new to gardening, the choice of salad crops can be bewildering. I would suggest starting with just one or two from each group, then extending your range as you gain confidence. The following are some of the most easily grown.

Bulky and mild Salad Bowl lettuce, Texel greens; fine-leaved kales† (see p. 159), pak choi, komatsuna and salad rape seedlings.

Sharp Rocket, sorrel, radish, curly endive seedlings.

Crisp or textured 'Little Gem' lettuce, Tuscan kale, mizuna greens.

Decorative Red lettuce, winter purslane, mibuna greens, nasturtium and calendula flowers.

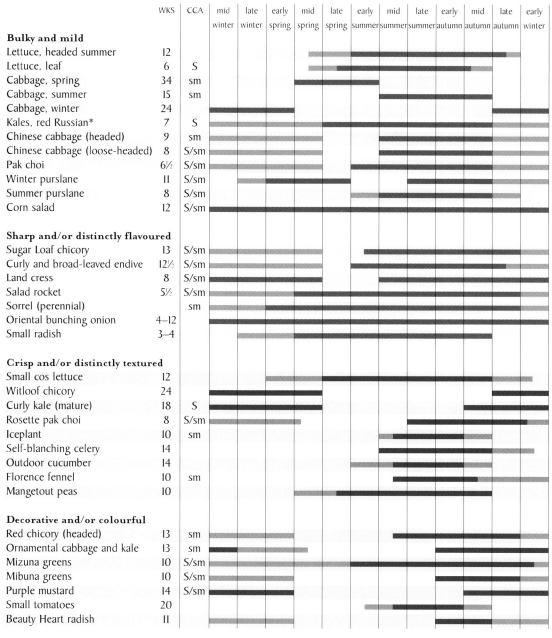

Bulky and mild

	WKS	CCA
Lettuce, headed summer	12	
Lettuce, leaf	6	S
Cabbage, spring	34	sm
Cabbage, summer	15	sm
Cabbage, winter	24	
Kales, red Russian*	7	S
Chinese cabbage (headed)	9	sm
Chinese cabbage (loose-headed)	8	S/sm
Pak choi	6½	S/sm
Winter purslane	11	S/sm
Summer purslane	8	S/sm
Corn salad	12	S/sm

Sharp and/or distinctly flavoured

	WKS	CCA
Sugar Loaf chicory	13	S/sm
Curly and broad-leaved endive	12½	S/sm
Land cress	8	S/sm
Salad rocket	5½	S/sm
Sorrel (perennial)		sm
Oriental bunching onion	4–12	
Small radish	3–4	

Crisp and/or distinctly textured

	WKS	CCA
Small cos lettuce	12	
Witloof chicory	24	
Curly kale (mature)	18	S
Rosette pak choi	8	S/sm
Iceplant	10	sm
Self-blanching celery	14	
Outdoor cucumber	14	
Florence fennel	10	sm
Mangetout peas	10	

Decorative and/or colourful

	WKS	CCA
Red chicory (headed)	13	sm
Ornamental cabbage and kale	13	sm
Mizuna greens	10	S/sm
Mibuna greens	10	S/sm
Purple mustard	14	S/sm
Small tomatoes	20	
Beauty Heart radish	11	

ADDITIONAL PLANTS

Bulky and mild
All year round (S) Texel greens, (S) komatsuna

Sharp and/or distinctly flavoured
All year round (S) mizuna, spinach and cress: shallots, bulb onions, leaf radish
Spring dandelion, spring onions
Summer dandelion, spring onions, mooli radish
Autumn mibuna, dandelion, spring onions, mooli radish
Winter mibuna, hardy winter radish

Crisp and/or distinctly textured
All year round (S) Tuscan and curly kale, (S) alfalfa
Spring (S) mibuna, winter purslane, seakale, radish and radish seed pods
Summer summer purslane, radish and radish seed pods
Autumn mizuna, mibuna, winter purslane, radish and radish seed pods, Jerusalem artichokes
Winter winter purslane, trench celery, winter radish, Chinese and Jerusalem artichokes

Decorative and/or coloured
All year round red lettuce, (S) red Russian, Tuscan kale and curly kales, (S) 'Bright Lights' Swiss chard; 'Bull's Blood' beet leaves; buck's horn plantain
Spring Treviso chicory, (S) purple mustard, winter purslane; flowers: chive, calendula, pansy, bellis and oriental greens
Summer red cabbage, (S) red orache, (S) 'Magentaspreen', iceplant, gold-leaved purslane, flowers: chive, calendula, nasturtium, pansy, tagetes and rose
Autumn red cabbage, purple-stemmed pak choi, (S) red orache, (S) 'Magentaspreen', flowers: chive, calendula, pansy and tagetes
Winter Treviso chicory, red cabbage, purple-stemmed pak choi, winter purslane, flowers: winter pansy

KEY
CCA = cut and come again
S = cut-and-come-again seedlings
sm = cut-and-come-again when semi-mature/mature

* = also other thin-leaved kales, see § on p. 159
wks = average weeks to maturity

▬ season of availability
▬ season extended under cover

Special situations

Awkward spots

Most gardens have shaded, dry or wet areas that are unsuitable for some crops. Here are some salad plants that tolerate less favourable conditions.

Light shade These plants can tolerate lightly shaded situations, provided they have adequate moisture.

Angelica, chickweed, chicory (grumolo, red and Sugar Loaf), chives, chrysanthemum greens, endive, garlic mustard, lemon balm, lovage, mizuna greens, Hamburg parsley, Jerusalem artichoke, land cress, marjoram (golden-leaved forms), mint, mitsuba, sweet bergamot, salad rocket, sorrel, sweet cicely, wood sorrel, Alpine strawberries, comfrey and Good King Henry, although not strictly salad plants, are also shade tolerant.

Light shade in summer only Chinese cabbage, chervil, coriander, lettuce, pak choi, parsley, peas, radish, spinach, Swiss chard.

Dry conditions These plants grow reasonably in fairly dry conditions, provided there is enough moisture initially to get the plants established. They may need occasional watering.

Alfalfa (lucerne), basil, buckler-leaved sorrel, *Calendula officinalis*, clary sage, winter purslane, iceplant (*Mesembryanthemum crystallinum*), kohl rabi, lavender, leaf amaranthus, marjoram, New Zealand spinach, red valerian (*Centranthus ruber*), reflexed stonecrop (*Sedum reflexum*), rosemary, summer purslane, sage, salad burnet, thymes.

Moist conditions The following tolerate moist conditions, provided they are not waterlogged.

Golden saxifrage (*Chrysoplenium oppositifolium*), lady's smock (*Cardamine pratensis*), lemon balm, chicory (Grumolo, red and Spadona), Chinese cabbage, corn salad, Florence fennel, Jerusalem artichoke, land cress, leeks, mint, mitsuba, sweet bergamot, watercress.

Containers

While almost any salad plant can be grown in a container, provided the container is large enough, the following give the best returns, mainly because they are compact or mature rapidly.

Salad plants All cut-and-come-again seedlings (see chart on p. 159), carrots (early types), dwarf French beans, chrysanthemum greens, endive, lettuce (especially small and Salad Bowl types), mizuna greens, mibuna greens, pak choi (ordinary and rosette), sweet and chilli peppers, radish, spinach, Swiss chard, tomatoes.

Annual and perennial herbs Basil, leaf celery, chives, Chinese chives, dill, marjoram, parsley, summer and winter savory, thyme.

Edible flowers Bellis perennis daisies, *Calendula officinalis*, nasturtiums, pansies, signet marigold (*Tagetes tenuifolia*), society garlic (*Tulbaghia violacea*).

Further reading

Other books by Joy Larkcom

Creative Vegetable Gardening, Mitchell Beazley, revised paperback 2000, ISBN 1 84000 292 1

Oriental Vegetables: the Complete Guide for the Gardening Cook, John Murray, revised paperback 1997, ISBN 0 7195 5597 3

Salads for Small Gardens, Hamlyn, revised paperback 1995, ISBN 0 600 58509 3 (available from Ecologic Books)

The Vegetable Garden Displayed, Royal Horticultural Society, completely revised edition 1992, ISBN 0 906603 87 0 (out of print)

Vegetables for Small Gardens, Hamlyn paperback, revised edition 1995, ISBN 0 600 58510 7 (out of print; Frances Lincoln revision due 2002)

Books on vegetables

Bleasdale, J.K.A., and others (eds), *The Complete Know and Grow Vegetables*, Oxford University Press, revised edition 1991, ISBN 0 19 286114 X (the scientific basis of vegetable growing)

Caplan, Basil (ed.), *The Complete Manual of Organic Gardening*, Headline Book Publishing, 1992, ISBN 0 7472 0515 9, paperback 1994, ISBN 07472 7830 X (organic techniques, including greenhouse crops)

Dobbs, Liz, *The Gardening Which? Guide to Growing Your Own Vegetables*, Which? Books, 2001, ISBN 0 85202 834 2 (general)

Evelyn, John, *Acetaria: a Discourse of Sallets*, 1699, facsimile Prospect Books, 1982, ISBN 0 9073 2512 2 (original inspiration for salad lovers)

Kitchen Garden Magazine, 12 Orchard Lane, Woodnewton, Peterborough, PE8 5EE, UK (monthly magazine on all aspects of vegetable growing)

Marshall, Terry, *Organic Tomatoes: the Inside Story*, Harris Associates, 1999

McFadden, Christine, and Michaud, Michael, *Cool Green Leaves and Red Hot Peppers*, Frances Lincoln, 1998, ISBN 0 7112 1223 6 (inspirational on growing and cooking for flavour)

Salt, Bernard, *Vegetables*, B.T. Batsford, revised edition 2000, ISBN 0 7134 8621 X (general vegetable growing)

Schwartz, Oded, *Preserving*, Dorling Kindersley, 1996, ISBN 0 7513 03453

Vilmorin-Andrieux, MM, English edition edited by William Robinson, *The Vegetable Garden*, 1885, Ten Speed Press facsimile 1993 (out of print), 089 815 0418 (superb classic)

Other aspects of gardening

Buczacki, Stefan, and Harris, Keith, *Collins Guide to the Pest, Diseases and Disorders of Garden Plants*, Collins, revised 2000, ISBN 000220063 5

McVicar, Jekka, *Jekka's Complete Herb Book*, Kyle Cathie Ltd, 1994, ISBN 1 85626 161 1 (very practical)

Rose, Francis, *The Wild Flower Key* (British Isles–NW Europe), Frederick

Warne, 1981, ISBN 0 7232 2419 6

Stickland, Sue, *Back Garden Seed Saving*, Ecologic Books, 2001 (heritage varieties and seed saving)

Wilkinson Barash, Cathy, *Edible Flowers*, Fulcrum Publishing, 1993, ISBN 1 55591 164 1

Other sources

Eco-logic Books, 19 Maple Grove, Bath, BA2 3AF, UK (book suppliers)

Henry Doubleday Research Association (HDRA), Ryton Organic Gardens, Coventry, CV8 3LG UK. Organic gardening association, and Heritage Seed Library. Step-by-step leaflets include: *Worm Composting*, *Pest Control*, *Comfrey for Gardeners*, *Gardening with Green Manures*.

Seed suppliers

The mail-order companies below are among those that currently offer a wide or unusual range of salad seed. For other sources, consult the gardening press. Addresses change frequently, so check before ordering.

Cook's Garden Seeds, PO Box 535, Londonderry, VT 05148, USA

Diggers Garden Company, PO Box 300, Dromana, Vic 3936, Australia

Dobies Seeds, Long Rd, Paignton, Devon TQ4 7SX, UK

Ferme de Saine Marthe, Export Service Harry Kramer, BP 77, F-78490, Montfort L'Amaury, France and PO Box 358, Walton, Surrey, KT12 4YX, UK

Frøposen, Postbox 35 2980, Kokkedal, Denmark

Graines Baumaux, BP 100, 54062, Nancy Cedex, France

Halycon Seeds, 10 Hampden Close, Chalgrove, Oxford OX44 7SB, UK

Johnny's Seeds, Foss Hill Rd, Albion, RR no. 1, Box 2580, ME 04910, USA

King's Seeds (NZ) Ltd., PO Box 283, Katikati, Bay of Plenty, New Zealand

Marshalls Seeds, Wisbech, Cambs PE13 2RF, UK

Mr Fothergill's Seeds, Kentford, Newmarket, Suffolk, CB8 7QB, UK

Nichol's Garden Nursery, 1190 N. Pacific Hwy, Albany, Oregon 97321, USA

Organic Gardening Catalogue, Riverdene Business Park, Molesey Road, Hersham, Surrey KT12 4RG, UK

Simpson's Seeds (tomato specialists), 27 Meadowbrook, Old Oxted, Surrey RH8 9LT, UK

Shepherd's Garden Seeds, 30 Irene St, Torrington, CT 06790-6658, USA

Totally Tomatoes, PO Box 202, Newton Abbott, Devon TQ12 67H, UK

Suffolk Herbs, Pantlings Lane, Coggeshall Road, Kelvedon, Essex CO5 9PG, UK

Terre de Semences, BP2. 03210 Saint-Menoux, France; (UK) Chris Baur, Ripple Farm, Crundale, Canterbury, Kent CT4 7EB, UK

Thompson & Morgan, London Rd, Ipswich, IP2 OBA, UK

Tucker's Seeds, Brewery Meadow, Stonepark, Ashburton, Newton Abbot, Devon TQ13 7DG, UK

Xotus Delft, Middelweg 1, 2616 LV Delft, The Netherlands

Index

Page numbers in *italics* refer to illustrations; page numbers underlined refer to main entries